Queen for a Day

Perverse Modernities   A series edited by Jack Halberstam and Lisa Lowe

Queen for a Day

Transformistas, Beauty Queens, and the
Performance of Femininity in Venezuela

Marcia Ochoa

Duke University Press · Durham and London · 2014

Printed in the United States of America on acid-free paper ∞
Designed by Courtney Leigh Baker and typeset in Arno Pro
by Tseng Information Systems, Inc.

Library of Congress Cataloging-in-Publication Data
Ochoa, Marcia, 1970–
Queen for a day : transformistas, beauty queens, and the
performance of femininity in Venezuela / Marcia Ochoa.
pages cm — (Perverse modernities / a series edited by
Jack Halberstam and Lisa Lowe)
Includes bibliographical references and index.
ISBN 978-0-8223-5611-0 (cloth : alk. paper)
ISBN 978-0-8223-5626-4 (pbk. : alk. paper)
1. Transsexuals — Venezuela.
2. Beauty contestants — Venezuela.
3. Femininity — Venezuela.
I. Title. II. Series: Perverse modernities.
HQ77.95.V4O24 2014
306.76′8 — dc23   2014000755

You gonna be beautiful, girl.
Like revolution
in the flesh.
Like hope.
—ADELA VASQUEZ, quoted in
Jaime Cortez, *Sexile*

Contents

Acknowledgments

One autumn a long time ago, I had to rake the leaves at my father's house. It was a crisp Saturday morning as I set out to rake his manicured yard. My father, true to his linear nature, quickly started on the opposite end of the yard and efficiently raked neat rows into a pile. I began working on my area, raking along the contours of the yard, the decorative boulders, the flower beds, working in from the periphery and slowly massing leaves into various centers. I started to despair after a while, worried that I was not progressing efficiently. My father finished his part of the yard and left for an errand, and I spent the rest of the day raking and wondering, massing up little piles here and there, moving the little piles into bigger piles, and eventually all the leaves were raked. That's how this project has felt — lots of little pieces here and there, massing into something much greater in scale than the sum of its parts. In this arduous, euphoric, and heart-wrenching process, I have had the great pleasure to be accompanied and helped along by some wonderful people. I would like to thank:

My mother, Marlene Camacho Ochoa, for teaching me what it is to be a scientist, and to ask questions of the world. My father, Ricardo Ochoa, for giving me space to study my own kind of *patología*. Thanks also to my siblings, Ariana and Ricardo, and their families.

My teachers have blessed my life and work in so many ways: Catherine von Moltke, Mary Haab and Ron Quick, Ruth Behar, *la* Sandra Cisneros, Alicia Ríos, Greg Niemeyer, Ann Stoler, Cherríe Moraga, and Barbara Voss. My advisors and committee members Yvonne Yarbro-Bejarano, Charles Briggs, Lawrence Cohen, Purnima Mankekar, and Renato Rosaldo provided unflagging support, engagement, and debate on this work. It has been my privilege to work with each of you. Charles Briggs and Clara Mantini-Briggs have supported this work since its inception, and provided vital advice in the field.

I thank the many brave transgender and *transformista* activists who live and struggle in Venezuela: Rummie Quintero, Estrella Cerezo, Guillermo Galindo, Yahaira, and Desiree. The organizations TransVenus de Venezuela and Divas de Venezuela, and the dedicated support of Argelia Bravo Melet are deeply necessary and appreciated. I also thank Tamara Adrián, the accomplished law professor and litigator, who declared to the entire nation of Venezuela her status as a transsexual woman and her candidacy to the National Assembly and who continues to struggle for gender recognition and transgender rights in her country. My colleagues in Venezuela were instrumental to the development of this project, and I hope I have honored them with it: Daniel Mato, the late and very much missed Yolanda Salas, Carmen Hernández, and Abdel Güerere.

Many thanks to the people who loved and supported me during my time in Caracas: *La gente de Contranatura*—Argelia Bravo, Carlos Rodríguez, Rodrigo Navarrete, Cesar Martínez, Marianella Tovar, and everyone else. My dear friends and companions, who brightened my days and sparkled at night with mischief: Jesús Ravelo, Richard Martinez, Gisela Kozak Rovero, Edgar Carrasco and Renate Koch, Gaston Torres Márquez, Alberto Nieves, and the ACCSI staff. Andreína Fuentes provided crucial support both to my work and to trans art and activism. Thanks also to Lambda de Venezuela and ASES de Venezuela. I am very grateful to all the people who assisted me in my research activities in Venezuela: Rummie Quintero, Antonio Borges, Gaston Torres Márquez, Argelia Bravo, and Estrella Cerezo. Gustavo Marcano, Gilles Rigoulet, Andrés Manner, and María Gabriela Ponce generously gave permission for the use of their images.

The Organization Miss Venezuela, particularly its president, Mr. Osmel Sousa, and its press chief, Mr. Igor Molina, for allowing me to observe its castings and pageant production in 2002–2003. The many pageant contestants who gave their permission for me to observe their hard work in preparing for and participating in the pageant, and who engaged me in very interesting and challenging dialogue during the course of these observations. Adriana Meneses of the Museo Jacobo Borges also provided some important reflections on the beauty pageant.

My queer and trans Latin@ communities in San Francisco and throughout the Américas have inspired and conspired with this work on many levels. Starting with Proyecto ContraSIDA Por Vida in San Francisco and the Village that grew out of it: Jaime Cortez, Tisa Bryant, Veronica Majano, Teresita la Campesina, Adela Vázquez, Gigi Otalvaro-Hormillosa,

Nao Bustamante and the rest of Las Cucas, Diane Félix, Ricardo Bracho, Horacio Roque-Ramírez, Pato Hebert, and Laurence Angeleo Padua. The work I've been privileged to do with El/La Para Translatinas has accompanied the writing of this book, and for their dedication and commitment I am always grateful to Alexandra Byerly, Isaías Noyola, Jovana Luna, Adrián Maya, and Susana Cáceres, as well as all the *chicas de El/La*.

Friends, homegirls, and colleagues have provided the support and love that saw me through this process: Jessamyn Neuhaus and Douglas Butdorf, Sarah Patterson, Andreana Clay and Joan Benôit, Rachael Joo, Vida Mía García, Kyla Wazana Tompkins, Sharon Holland, Juana María Rodríguez, Nancy Mirabal, Elisa Diana Huerta, and Mónica Enríquez. My UCSC *familia* B. Ruby Rich, Cindy Cruz, Wanda Alarcon, Felicity Amaya Schafer, Neda Atanasoski, Lourdes Martínez-Echazábal, and Irene Gustafson. Though she never got to see it, tatiana de la tierra's fearless and scandalous work shaped and inspired my own weaving of perversity in *tierra firme*, and I miss her dearly.

Many thanks also to colleagues near and far who have shaped and buttressed this work through their readings, questions, and encouragement throughout the years: Jen Brody, Maylei Blackwell, Jack Halberstam, Beth Freeman, Karen Tongson, Micaela Díaz Sánchez, Scott Morgensen, Gayatri Gopinath, Mary Gray, Diane Nelson, Salvador Vidal-Ortiz, Susan Stryker, Carlos Decena, Larissa Pelucio, and Richard Miskolci. Many thanks to Ken Wissoker and Jade Brooks of Duke University Press for their patient and persistent belief in this project. I owe a special debt to Fernando Coronil, who was taken too soon. His insightful critique of the early versions of this manuscript profoundly shaped the book you hold in your hands.

None of this would have been possible without the financial support of many people and institutions, including my parents, Sarah, Bob, and Kathy Patterson, and fellowship funding from the Department of Cultural and Social Anthropology at Stanford University. A Dissertation Fieldwork Grant from Wenner-Gren Foundation for Anthropological Research made it possible for me to live, work, study, and imagine this project in Venezuela. The Institute for Research on Women and Gender and the Center for Latin American Studies at Stanford as well as the Social Sciences Division and the Committee on Research of the University of California, Santa Cruz generously provided funding for the completion of this project. I am eternally grateful for all of this support.

Introducing . . . the Queen

It is 1998 and I find myself on a crowded airplane in San Antonio del Táchira, on the border between Colombia and Venezuela. Through a complicated series of events that involves a canceled bus trip and a cousin without the proper papers, I'm flying through the Juan Vicente Gómez International Airport to visit family living on Isla Margarita, a tourist resort in
the Venezuelan Caribbean. It is my firm belief that as a queer child of a
diasporic Colombian family with branches in the United States, Colombia, and Venezuela, I am uniquely positioned to witness the spectacle that
unfolds before me.

A new flight crew comes aboard in San Antonio. A young woman, tall,
gaunt, and arduously stylized, takes command of the cabin. Her close-
fitting polyester uniform is crisp and gleaming, hat cocked precariously
atop a mound of hair immaculately pulled back into a *moño*, with two precise spit curls gelled down along her mandible, tapering off into whisper-
thin points. Her eyebrows are cleanly plucked and delineated in black pen-
cil, a bemused arch against the moderately applied foundation the color
of café con leche that coats the skin of her face. Her lips, dripping with a
mocha-tinged red, pout as she proceeds to give a performance of the air-
line safety procedures such as I have never seen before.

Every gesture is studied and designed, it seems, to cast an aura of glamour over the rows of weary travelers. And yet our flight attendant seems
not the least bit interested in her charges' reactions. She makes no eye contact, staring intently at the exit signs at the rear of the plane as the baubles
on her wrist jangle with the motion of the instructions. It seems that the
aisle of the airplane, in her mind, has become a runway.

As our plane sits on the San Antonio airstrip, the flight attendant seems
to be referencing the runway walk and poise of the beauty queens who
have been a national obsession in Venezuela. From my place among the
travelers, I watch the flight attendant and marvel at her behavior, a form

of femininity completely alien to my own gender presentation. At this moment, the thread of the inquiry that this book represents begins to show itself. How might we make sense of beauty and glamour in Venezuela? How might these discourses lead a young woman to act the way she did on this flight? How might we make sense of her performance in front of a planeload of people, we who were her audience, but not quite? Was she alone in this kind of comportment? What does a person stand to gain by invoking an air of glamour the way the flight attendant did? The distinction of the supermodel–beauty queen? Recognition?

The flight attendant's everyday performance struck me in particular because it recalled how the divas in my own queer Latina/o community invoke glamour — by reordering time and space to center on a silent gestural language that might be as direct and powerful as an arched eyebrow. Not *everyone* acts this way, and certainly not all of those who try are successful at invoking glamour. Although the flight attendant's performance may seem trivial, perhaps even frivolous, it reflects an important facet of the project of self-making: the ways we style ourselves (and our bodies) in dialogue with mass-media spectacle. Though the flight attendant was not on a screen, nor in front of a live studio audience, she styled her performance of femininity using the conventions of modeling and what I call *spectacular femininity*. The flight-safety routine is an everyday instance of the connections among gender, media, nation, and bodies. Though the flight attendant was cisgender and not a transgender woman, her performance reminded me of the glamour with which many transgender Latinas, gay men, and femme lesbians in my own community carry themselves.[1] This is not because any of these people were miming the other but rather because all were using similar symbolic resources to produce and perform femininity. For example, many of these different people would use similar kinds of hand or eye gestures, makeup, posture, and other techniques to create the effect of glamour. It is how these symbolic resources become available and the uses to which they are put that have become a central concern for me. This book winds its way through these initial questions surrounding the national beauty pageant in Venezuela and its relationship to the production of femininity in order to explore the cultural logics and embodied practices in which Venezuelan femininity becomes material.

The flight attendant's spectacle, however, is only one part of this scene. The other part is about what I was doing on that plane. It was not completely by chance that I came to be sitting on a plane on the tarmac of the

Juan Vicente Gómez airport at the border of Colombia and Venezuela, nor that I made note of the flight attendant's spectacular performance. It was a kind of observation I was particularly attuned to within my questions about what it meant to be queer—a butch woman—and from this place. I was flying to Venezuela because I wanted to cross the wide gulf that separated me, as a queer, as an immigrant to the United States, from the extended family we had left behind upon our migration. I was trying to make sense of the broad sweep of history that had made me feel so different—in body, in culture, in desire—from the people to whom I was supposed to be the closest. I was exploring what it would mean to refuse the fragmentation of identity that accompanies both migration and some forms of queerness. Actually, I was visiting an uncle and his family who had relocated to Isla Margarita as part of a significant migration of unskilled labor between the two countries that traces its roots back to the mid-twentieth-century petroleum economy. I was on the plane because I was making the first moves to understand how I am a product of this place, with its own perversions and displacements. In this way, I situate this project as a *queer diasporic ethnography*.

The Queen of Transformation

While visiting my uncle and his family in Venezuela, I came across a sign of queer life on a crowded beach. At the time, I had surrounded myself with fabulous queer *latinidad* in San Francisco and Oakland, California.[2] I had little notion of the possibility of queer life in Latin America—my own shortcoming, to be sure. But there she was, cavorting on the beach with her band of gay boys. She is now a dim memory, but I remember that she wore a hot-pink bikini and extensions in her hair. "Un travestista," said my uncle.[3] I later learned that in Venezuela she would be called *una transformista*.

Transformista is a term used in many parts of Latin America. In Brazil, it is used to refer to cross-dressers or transvestites, a quite different set of people from the *travestís*, who have been the focus of so much ethnographic attention. In Argentina and Spain, the word *transformista* is used to refer to female impersonators on stage. In Venezuela a *transformista* is a person who is assigned male sex at birth, but who from an early age begins to transform her body and make herself a woman. She does this by plucking her eyebrows, using makeup, wearing clothes designed for women, and doing women's work, as well as taking hormones and getting breast implants. The word has associations with the sex work performed by many *transformistas* and is considered an insult by some, although it is also used for self-definition. *Transformistas* transform their bodies from man to woman. And these changes are often made silently. There is no "coming out" moment as we often see in a North American lesbian- and gay-identity formation; instead there is a series of actions that leads to an inevitable result: the transformation of a male body into a *transformista* body.

Transformistas in Venezuela are subject to the policing of gender in practically every site: in the home, on the street, in shopping malls and other privatized public spaces, and at school and other institutional settings. Though my first encounter with a *transformista* was a joyful one on the beach, I quickly learned that life for many *transformistas* in Venezuela is defined by social exclusion and violence. Amnesty International's 1998 report on LGBT human rights, published in booklet form in 2001, specifically names the case of a *transformista* named Dayana who was brutally killed by police in the city of Valencia. She was one of many *transformistas* who experienced incredible violence from police, private security, family, and other individuals over the course of my work in Venezuela.[4] In a report I compiled with Edgar Carrasco of the Latin American and Caribbean Council of AIDS Service Organizations, we found that the overwhelming majority of transgender and transsexual people we surveyed (including *transformistas*) had experienced some form of physical or structural violence. Exclusion from mainstream educational and economic opportunities leads *transformistas* to carve out the economic niches they can find, which is often either in sex work or beauty, but can also include food preparation, nursing, and spiritual work.

Transformistas fit within the wider concept of transgender, although this concept is fairly new to Venezuela, and I have seen people use the term *transgender*, a Spanish appropriation of the term in English, as a way to differentiate themselves from *transformistas*.[5] I define *transgender* as a general category that refers to people who take identitarian, physical, and social measures to express a gender that society says does not belong to the sex assigned to them at birth. *Transformistas* fit within this definition, but not all transgender people are *transformistas*.

Transformistas, like other Venezuelan women, assemble their notions of femininity from their bodies, their environments, the expectations placed on them by their communities, their own ideas about the currency of specific forms of femininity, mass media, and the material forms of production available for the project of accomplishing femininity. This study presumes Simone de Beauvoir's well-known claim that "one is not born, but rather becomes, a woman" and asks: How is femininity accomplished? Through what practices, technologies, and ideologies does a feminine subject become intelligible? How are transgender and cisgender femininities produced in the same discursive frame?

Resisting the impulse to treat transgender femininities as somehow exceptional, I found it productive to employ a parallel structure to understand my analytic field: cisgender and transgender women are producing femininities with similar symbolic resources, in dialogue with shared discourses, and employing similar kinds of techniques and technologies. This is what I call, after Harold Garfinkel, "the accomplishment of femininity."[6] *Queen for a Day* examines the accomplishment of femininity among *transformistas* and *misses*, the term used to describe participants in Miss Venezuela, the national beauty pageant produced by the Organización Miss Venezuela. In this way, I unite the two key figures I encountered on that long-ago trip to reconnect with my family: the cisgender flight attendant and the beach *transformista* share a kind of Venezuelan feminine performativity that caught my attention and sparked this entire line of inquiry. This book considers the production of the mass-mediated beauty pageant in the same analytic frame as the everyday accomplishment of femininity. Consequently, the book attends to transnational, regional, national, scenic, and corporeal levels of the negotiation of power. There is no linear connection between *transformistas* and *misses*, but both produce their femininities in the discursive context of national femininity in Venezuela. For the flight attendant and many other, though certainly not all, Venezuelan women, Miss Venezuela as a mass-media product provides fuel for the *fashioning* of femininity.

I use cultural studies, media studies, and the ethnography of media to analyze the relationship between the Miss Venezuela pageant and the everyday accomplishment of femininity. I do this quite conscientiously in terms of working with *transformistas*. While much of the literature on transgender women in Latin America focuses on small community studies, the transgression of gender ideologies, or the risk of transmission of HIV, *Queen for a Day* embeds *transformistas* within the logics of power and gender at play in local, national, and transnational contexts. By looking at the role of the mass-media spectacle in the self-making projects of differently situated actors in Venezuelan society, this book speaks not just to the conditions of existence for transgender women but also to the ways in which these women are *produced* by the same society that treats them with so much violence and rejection—the same ways that nations produce all their subjects: through processes of gendering, racialization, labor, and mediation.

In many ways, Venezuela is a *transformista*. Let me explain. *Transformistas* and the nation of Venezuela have something in common: they both use beauty and glamour to negotiate power and marginality.[7] Of course, beauty and glamour are not the only tools available for this negotiation, but they are useful tools for *transformistas*, *misses*, and for Venezuela as a nation. Venezuela changed its image as an out-of-the-way place in the twentieth century through the beauty pageant industry. Individually, *transformistas* and *misses* create possibilities for themselves through beauty and glamour. The ways *transformistas* and *misses* employ these tools have taught me about the power of dreams and glamour in the micropolitics of gender.

The Miss Venezuela Beauty Pageant

Not all Venezuelan women accomplish the same femininity—far from it—but women in Venezuela accomplish their various femininities within a discursive context.[8] This discursive context, along with the practices, technologies, and ideologies of femininity, is produced at the level of the nation and within transnationally mass-mediated circuits of exchange. What it means to become a Venezuelan woman is shaped as much by women's own negotiations of their bodies as by the discursive context of femininity in Venezuela. One key element in this discursive context is Venezuela's place as producer of global beauty queens. There are various genders attendant to the production process of the Miss Venezuela beauty pageant, but its primary product is the *miss*.[9] I discuss this production process in more detail in chapter 3. *Misses* are participants in the Miss Venezuela pageant, its castings, or any of the numerous local pageants that occur at all age ranges in Venezuela. A *miss* might also be someone who does not participate in beauty pageants but who looks like s/he could. For example, to a person who looks like the flight attendant, you might say, "Eres toda una miss" (You are such a *miss*).

The Miss Venezuela beauty pageant is produced by Venevisión, a leading national broadcaster in Venezuela since 1960. Venevisión, known during the time of my fieldwork in 2002–3 as "El Canal de la Belleza" (The Beauty Channel), produces Miss Venezuela through a national casting system and sends delegates to prestigious international beauty competitions such as Miss Universe and Miss World.[10] The international competitions bestow a license upon one organization in every nation to send a delegate; so essentially the Organización Miss Venezuela, owned by Venevisión, has the monopoly on preparing women to represent Venezuela in international beauty contests. There are also countless local beauty pageants that are organized throughout Venezuela. This book focuses on the production of Miss Venezuela as a primary site for the discursive construction of national femininity.

Beauty contests have been very important in the twentieth-century history of Venezuela. Beauty queens are often mentioned, after petroleum, as a top export of the country. A 1994 study sponsored by Venezuela's Instituto de Estudios Superiores de Administración (Institute of Advanced Management Studies) listed media productions, including the Miss Venezuela beauty pageant, as one of the top ten products that would make Venezuela competitive on the global market (Güerere 1994). The pageant, in addition to providing competitive advantages to the nation, is seen by many as a source of social mobility. Stories of nubile, innocent young women suddenly finding wealth and fame after being picked off the streets of Caracas by the producers surround the pageant. Many Miss Venezuela contestants go on to become politicians, actresses, runway models, and television stars, and they live very public lives in the eyes of their nation.

The Organización Miss Venezuela has produced eleven title winners in the Miss Universe and Miss World beauty pageants alone and winning entrants in a score of other international beauty pageants.[11] The Organización Miss Venezuela's success at producing international beauty pageant titleholders throughout the twentieth century has put Venezuela on the map. Indeed, until the Bolivarian Revolution, beginning with the election of President Hugo Rafael Chávez Frías in 1998, Venezuela was not well known to outsiders for much else besides beauty queens and petroleum. As the political scientist Terry Karl summarizes, the trope of isolation and marginality has defined Venezuela throughout its history and shaped its processes of state building (Karl 1997, 74). Given this history, how do beauty pageants make sense in Venezuela? How do we account for the record-breaking success of Venezuelan beauty queens on the global stage? What possibilities does the *miss* privilege or occlude for Venezuelan women? While the beauty pageant may be considered a national pastime in Venezuela and a way to produce international fame for the country, as a transnational mass-media spectacle, the pageant also has specific implications for daily practice and self-fashioning for some Venezuelan women.

The title of this book refers to the transitory nature of this form of recognition and self-fashioning. *Queen for a Day* is not a reference to the 1950s television show in which beleaguered housewives were granted domestic appliances to ease their burdens, but rather to the momentary authority granted an individual who is able to access beauty, glamour, and femininity. The momentary possibility of recognition and reward when one fits the form required by the beauty pageant fuels an entire industry in Venezuela, and many more dreams not specifically tied to that industry. Even those who don't fit the form can employ it for their own purposes. Rather than seeing this possibility as a fleeting moment, I think of it as a kind of micropolitics.

To be a queen for a day in the context of the beauty pageant requires a great deal of investment in a particular form of hyperfeminine corporeality and implies a reward that is highly contingent on patriarchal power and recognition. Nevertheless, it is a form of power that serves *transformistas* and other women in Venezuela on a daily basis to provide legibility, affirmation, income, and other elements necessary for survival. I expand the metaphor of *queen for a day* to the nation of Venezuela itself, in its own negotiation of peripherality and power on the global stage. My central argument in this work is that imaginary projection and participation in transnationally mass-mediated spectacle has place-making power for the Venezuelan nation and figures as a survival strategy for *transformistas*. It is this aspect of the relationship between media and everyday life that often remains unexamined in how we consider the dynamics of power in transnational mass media.

Media and Everyday Life

The ways that media impact our daily lives have been the subject of much inquiry in many fields. It is not the intention of this book to outline these approaches, but rather to expand on ideas that have developed in cultural studies, media studies, and the ethnography of media. These three fields have approached the relationship between media and everyday life by prioritizing ethnographic and discursive analyses of media practices and representations, and by focusing on the production of meaning in various contexts and circuits in the production and consumption of media. In particular, my approach to media in Latin America has developed in dialogue with the idea of mediation proposed by the Spanish Colombian communications theorist Jesús Martín-Barbero in his study on Colombian telenovelas (1993).[12] Martín-Barbero responds to the deterministic hypothesis of media reception—sometimes called *the hypodermic needle theory* or *false consciousness*—that presumes that media inculcate empty minds with meaningless distraction and fantasy. Mediation is his way of complicating that model by embedding the pleasure of watching in a wider cultural logic. In this ethnography, I came to understand mediation not as caught up in a binary between fantasy and reality but as an approach to ideology and discourse that pays attention to the how these become materialized. Rather than focusing on media texts themselves, Martín-Barbero suggests that we examine what media practices themselves produce—everything from the temporality of watching television to the moral and ethical universes of melodrama.[13] Mediation, for Martín-Barbero, thus encompasses not only the narratives communicated by media but also the ways these forms of communication materialize ideological processes through forms, behaviors, and temporalities. Through mediations, I locate media reception outside the moment of spectatorship and attend to the ways in which *transformistas* and *misses* fashion their femininity as a form of participation in a larger discourse. Further, I locate the accomplishment of femininity in the broader discourse of modernity in Venezuela, encompassing not only beauty and bodily practice but also hygiene, public health, and urban planning. I consider the beauty pageant industry one among various mediations of modernity that take specific form in the Venezuelan context.

My use of the concept of mediations harmonizes the multiple senses of *medium* and *media*. I think of mediations as rooted in these words in all their senses: something in-between; an artistic medium, or the material in which art is elaborated; someone who mediates between opposing parties in a dispute; a spirit medium, a person who becomes the vessel for a spirit, who channels the spirit world. In this sense, *medium* and *media* have many applications, but their basic function remains: the communication between the materialization of intangible things like spirit and ideology.

The bodies of *misses* and *transformistas* are mediations of national gender ideology—physical manifestations of what Martín-Barbero calls the "long process of enculturation" of modernity in Latin America (1993, 88). This process shapes media production and consumption practices, as well as *miss* and *transformista* bodies. I extend Martín-Barbero's argument into the realm of the body, showing how media inform everyday practice, including the production of gender. In the case of *misses* and *transformistas*, this involves using mass-mediated representations to create spaces of possibility and distinction, momentarily centering the body that invokes the representation. I explore this idea of *spectacular femininity* further in chapter 6. The same questions about mediation could be asked of all of our bodies. I ask them of *miss* and *transformista* bodies because of their unique emergence as gendered bodies in Venezuela. The task, then, is to attend to the specific cultural processes that have produced the particular mediations I explore. These processes include the production of modernity and periphery in the region (and their attendant spatializations, racializations, and genders), transnational mass mediation, and technologies of gender.

Louisa Schein's idea of "imagined cosmopolitanism" (1997, 477) has helped me track the mediations of gender, race, and nation in Venezuela. In attending to the social conditions that surround the consumption of images of whiteness and ethnicity in China, Schein deflates the agency of "the media," and instead opens a ground on which to understand what people do with representations. What is important about Schein's approach is that it makes the question of false consciousness irrelevant—an important intervention in considering the politics of the beauty pageant—and focuses its analytical lens on how imaginative practices produce local forms of meaning. Mirroring the relationship among consumption, citizenship, and development articulated both by Martín-Barbero and Nestor García Canclini (1995a, 1995b), through imagined cosmopolitanism, Schein connects consumption to a sense of mobility in globalization.[14] The imagination as a social practice is a key component in the sense of movement within globalization and mass mediation. Even while they are standing still, people do things to feel as if they're not. These uses of the imaginary are the central questions I explore in Venezuela through a queer diasporic lens.

Queer Diasporas

I began this introduction by invoking the moment when I first became conscious of Venezuelan femininity. The moment, not exactly an arrival story, was part of a transit that I was making. A transfer, really, of planes, of flight crews, on my way to visit a branch of my family that lives in Venezuela. I locate this transit within diaspora. More specifically, I locate it within queer diaspora. Over the past ten years, work on queer sexualities in processes of transnationalism, globalization, and U.S. racialization (queer-of-color critique) has employed the concept of queer diasporas to describe various forms of connectivities and mobilities employed by queer subjects in these contexts.[15]

The term *queer* in this literature signals multiple, nonheteronormative categories of gender and sexuality in various contexts. Authors employ the fluidity of this term as a shorthand and catchall for multiple and relational forms of difference.[16] My articulation of this book as a queer diasporic ethnography is informed by the growing body of work on queer diasporas, which has created a productive intersection of transnationalism, postcoloniality, and diaspora with sexuality studies and queer theory. Much of this work, however, focuses on the "fully formed" subject in transit—the tracks of queer migrants in "sexile" and their interactions or cultural production with or within U.S.-based queer communities of color.[17] While this focus is important, it is also important to recognize the multiple and shifting identities and processes *within* diaspora and migration.[18]

The underpinnings of this work were formed in the community where Juana María Rodríguez described "queer Latinidad" (2003). The transgender Latinas I met as I worked at Proyecto Contra SIDA por Vida in San Francisco in the mid-1990s first set off this inquiry. It was Proyecto's multi-gendered world making—through aesthetics and cultural production—that informed my own research into the ethnography of media and queer Latin American self-making and world-making practices. This book does not describe such a diasporic community. Rather, this book is a *product* of a diasporic process. As a "1.5" generation immigrant, I had not grown up with a strong sense of Colombian identity, community, or nation, but I did know that the histories and displacements of the region had produced my own migration. I had acquired, however, a very U.S.-centric notion of the impossibility of modern or queer life in Latin America. This manifested itself in the question: "would I still be queer if we had stayed?" Much of my early work sought the conditions of possibility for queer life in Colombia and among U.S. Latinos and Latinas. But the nation of Colombia was not a sufficient formulation to answer this question. Meeting and talking to Colombian lesbians and gay men did not produce the sense of home I had initially thought it might. Instead, I settled in San Francisco to, as Cherríe Moraga said, "make *familia* from scratch" (1986).

I made sense of the kinds of racialization I experienced growing up in Bogotá and the U.S. Deep South and Midwest through the work of Chicana feminists such as Moraga, Gloria Anzaldúa, and Sandra Cisneros. In the San Francisco Bay Area, I sought out queer Latina/o and lesbian-of-color communities. The work of Anzaldúa and Cisneros informed my own interest in the particularities of the histories and genealogies that shaped my existence. This in turn shaped my scholarly inquiry. I began to imagine this project with an interest in the region of Colombia and Venezuela, but with no real sense of the processes involved in producing the region. What I had was a false sense of home—a certain familiarity and fluency that was not quite reliable. This is what led me, awkwardly, to be on a plane on the runway of the Juan Vicente Gómez airport in San Antonio del Táchira. Not "at home," an idea I had long since dispensed with, but uncannily, perversely, in diaspora, somewhere in the middle of La Gran Colombia, following the not-so-straight lines of history and genealogy.

Of course, many scholars of diaspora have called the concept of origin or home into question.[19] Avtar Brah identifies, notwithstanding, a kind of "homing desire" (2003, 615)—one that marked my transit through San Antonio del Táchira, and that placed me in a front-row seat to the flight attendant's spectacle. Perhaps this is one possible example of what Brah calls "diaspora space." For Gayatri Gopinath (2005), diaspora space provides an opportunity for the emergence of nonheteronormative desires, a way to "belong," but not to the nation. Diaspora space extends the social map of the imagined community of the nation to contested spaces and creates room for queer cultural producers to renegotiate and contest the terms of their belonging.[20]

For this project, a queer diasporic approach has taken me across vertiginous social disparities that coexist in uneasy and perverse intimacy. The days I spent shuttling across Caracas from the studios of Venevisión and the Quinta Miss Venezuela, the headquarters of the pageant, to the warm night air of Avenida Libertador as the *transformistas* who worked there started settling in for the evening most vibrantly illustrate this journey. Coming down from the *colina* (hill) in my starched business shirt and slacks, I would marvel at the shift in landscape and perspective. How easy it was for me to pass through the social barriers that separated these worlds, and how impossible it seemed for either of the two fields to ever meet. How my own queerness and gender nonconformity read on the way back to my apartment, couched as they were in a first-world embodiment that shifted the terms of recognition and mobility in society for me. These worlds do meet on occasion, of course, a stylist here, a nightclub there, but not in ways that fundamentally change the conditions of life for *trans-formistas*. The stories I was able to hear of the ways *transformistas* navigated these exclusions, the ways they created and pursued their dreams, gave me hope at the same time as they often terrified me. I hear the echo of La Contessa, one of the *transformistas* of Avenida Libertador whose experience most showed me what it meant to live this life, reminding me of her travel to Milan—a place where she could exist "in beauty." "Allá estás en lo bello," she would say, and teach me of the power of dreams and hallucinations. So I wended my way through the landscape of dreams—for *misses* and *transformistas* in Venezuela—and began to understand something about how modernity shapes us all.

I locate the start of my inquiry in my transit across the border between Colombia and Venezuela precisely because of how this crossing decenters the nation as a primary site of identification. The multiple displacements and exiles of this place have both shaped my own family's genealogy and compelled me to undertake a *regional* approach, perhaps best exemplified by the visionary yet short-lived nation of La Gran Colombia (circa 1819–30), which encompassed most of what we now know as Venezuela, Colombia, Panama, and Ecuador. This approach recognizes the violent and fragmenting processes that produce the nations and the continuities of their colonial legacies. At the same time, it allows me to attend to the lived experiences of nonheteronormative subjects and the ways they are disciplined by the state and the nation.

In order to define queer diasporic ethnography, I submit the following characteristics: queer diasporic ethnography is grounded in the questions, literacies, and transits of queer diasporic subjects. It questions the boundedness of the "native informant" as a point of entry for ethnographic projects. Based in these questions, transits, and literacies, queer diasporic ethnography follows the not-so-straight lines of histories and genealogies that produce the intelligibility of queer diasporic subjectivities. It attends to performances of gender and sexuality with respect to the nation, and to genealogy and intimacy in the production of power. It is also attentive to the perverse and uneven transits that create unexpected opportunities to witness such processes. Queer diasporic ethnography is not necessarily *about* queer diasporic subjects. It prioritizes the perverse paths that make queer existence tenable, perhaps even legible.

This project traces the discourse of femininity in Venezuela as one form of power, which is available (unevenly) within local contexts that are already crosscut with the transits of their own inhabitants. The book signals a politics of scale available through transnational processes and discourses, including migration and media.[21] As an "unhomely" kind of diasporic move, *Queen for a Day* seeks the conditions of possibility for queer existence—for gender-variant life—in Venezuela, but even more so it seeks to embed these existences in the contemporary logic of the nation and the processes that have shaped it.[22] The book does this ethnographically, in a queer diasporic way, engaging subjects for whom the notion of queer is irrelevant.[23] What is queer and diasporic about this ethnography is the focus on modernity, and the production of femininity and nation within the marginalizing processes that produce those who are deemed impossible to the nation. This ethnography describes the fraught and uneven terrain of power in one aspect of Venezuelan life and connects this aspect of life to long historical and cultural processes in the negotiation of power and production of marginality in Venezuela.

Perversion and Modernity

The idea of perversion came up many times during my fieldwork in Venezuela, but not the sort of celebratory perversion that I live and embrace. The idea of perversion that pervaded was more like an unintended or undesired effect. A perversion of democracy. Corruption and police abuse as perverse. Perversion—like diversion, subversion, inversion—as a directional metaphor, the place reached by a trajectory intended for somewhere else. Throughout my time there, I began to see Venezuela as a profoundly and perversely modern place. I came to understand the project of being modern as inherently productive of perversions of all sorts, including my own fabulous and charming perversions. I went to Venezuela to find a point of reconciliation within the idea that the lives we make are embedded in a cultural logic that seeks to destroy us. To honor the fact that sometimes riding the razor's edge between our perverse existences and the perversions of modern institutions—like the police state, democracy, or science—is part of the fun.

There is a fundamental contradiction at work here: the process of modernity extinguishes humanity yet creates other possibilities for existence. This contradiction frames the long project of modernity in Latin America, and it is part of the conditions of contemporary Latin American existence. The contradiction is the same mechanism that allows us to understand nature as a legitimizing force, but at the same time it becomes the thing upon which order and civilization must be imposed, and violently. I felt this contradiction most during a conference I organized in Caracas—TRANSforo—which brought together physicians, psychiatrists, legal scholars, and transgender people to open a dialogue and exchange information. One of the presentations was by two transgender women (who do not identify as *transformistas*), Rummie Quintero and Estrella Cerezo, who brought their mothers. Rummie's mother, Gisela, talked about her experience of her now-daughter in the womb, how she always "knew" that she was different. Someone asked her what it was like, watching her son transition into a daughter, and she said: "Si se opone la naturaleza lucharemos contra ella y haremos que nos obedezca" (If nature opposes us, we will fight against her and we will make her obey us) (see figure intro.1).

These words were first delivered by the Liberator, Simón Bolívar, on March 26, 1812, in Caracas. A massive earthquake had decimated an already struggling and war-torn Caracas. Bolívar's followers began to fear that this earthquake was God's retribution for rising up against their king. Bolívar reassured his compatriots that their struggle to impose a new order in the land that would become the nation of La Gran Colombia, and later Venezuela, that their struggle was righteous, and not in a godly way. That righteousness could come from imposing order, from shaping nature and making her obey. The project of citizenship in nineteenth-century Venezuela became, for people such as Bolívar, the shaping of the nature of *el pueblo* (the people) to conform to the functioning of a modern nation-state. That Rummie's mother could employ this foundational bit of national ideology to describe her daughter's need to discipline a "male" body with unruly hairs and testosterone into a "female" body through whatever means she had available to her struck me as profoundly perverse. And again, the contradictory notions of nature as that which is worked by modernity and that which legitimates discourse emerged as Gisela Quintero explained to us that when she was pregnant with her daughter, she be-

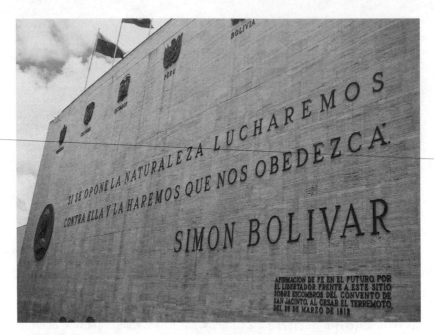

FIGURE INTRO.1 · Mural commemorating Simón Bolívar's 1812 speech on the ruins of the San Jacinto monastery after an earthquake. Plaza San Jacinto, Caracas. Photo by author, 2003.

lieved she was pregnant with a girl because of how her body felt — softer, she said, and calmer. Certainly, what it means to accomplish femininity in Venezuela is marked by this history of nature, modernity, and marginality. I know my own sense of queerness is richer and deeper for having considered it.

Closing Down the Analytical F-Stop

How to tell this twisting and perverse story of modernity and femininity in Venezuela? The organization of this book eluded me for several years, until I realized the dramatic shifts in scale that characterized my approach. In one moment I would consider the way an eyebrow was perfectly arched, and in another I charted the sweeping path of history, just to see how an acrylic stiletto wound up on a particular piece of asphalt. But it is this kind of vertiginous change in scale that makes it possible to hold contradictory and complex social relations in the same frame. While my descriptive writing tries to honor these details, my analytical frame seeks to embed them in

Martín-Barbero's "long processes of enculturation." Thus, this story must be told on various registers. From descriptive voice to images to detailed technical discussion, I try to account for and describe the social processes attendant to the accomplishment of femininity in Venezuela. I do this by focusing on the production of the Miss Venezuela beauty pageant and on the lives of *transformistas*. This book is organized along orders of magnitude that describe various points on a politics of scale. The three parts of this book describe these orders of magnitude: "On the (Trans)National," "On the Runway, on the Street," and "On the Body."

The first order of magnitude, "On the (Trans)National," describes both the context of transnational circuits in which the beauty pageant produces meaning and the ways in which this study seeks to embed transgender subjects centrally in the logic of the nation. Chapter 1, "*Belleza Venezolana*," situates the beauty pageant in the production of media, race, modernity, and nation in Venezuela. *Belleza venezolana* is an often-cited concept of national beauty that describes not only the beauty pageant industry but also the racial admixture that is believed to be the secret to Venezuela's success on the global stage. This chapter explores the history of the modern beauty pageant in Venezuela. In chapter 2, "*La Moda Nace en Paris y Muere en Caracas*," I use a catchphrase invented by a group of gay men as a point of entry into the fictitious circuit that might produce Caracas as a place where Parisian fashion goes to die. I examine the first Miss Venezuela beauty pageant, through magazines, postcards, and cinema newsreels from 1929 to 1930, and the 1955 European tour of Venezuela's first international beauty queen, Susana Duijm.

The second order of magnitude, "On the Runway, on the Street," describes a *scenic* scale in which women are staged to various ends. Chapter 3, "*La Reina de la Noche*" (queen for a day), examines gender performance, sexual subjectivity, and the form of the beauty pageant in Venezuela. I detail the production process of the Miss Venezuela casting system of regional beauty pageants as I encountered it. The chapter explores the form of the modern beauty pageant in Venezuela and considers this form in the context of two pageants: a Miss Venezuela casting and a beauty pageant for *transformistas* and gay men that is held during Carnaval in Carúpano, a town on the Caribbean shore of eastern Venezuela. This chapter also considers how that cosmopolitan Venezuelans in "el Interior" negotiate *caraqueño* (the word used to describe inhabitants of Caracas) centrality and being in an out-of-the-way place in their staging of beauty pageants.[24]

Chapter 4, "*Pasarelas y Perolones*," describes the scene where *transformistas* do sex work on a well-traveled avenue in Caracas. Based on participant observation and condom-distribution work on Avenida Libertador, this chapter is a social geography of the zone. *Transformistas* use the space of Avenida Libertador for both tactical and symbolic advantage in their sex work and in the imaginary projection of their identity. I focus on two aspects of this site: *pasarelas*, or pedestrian walkways that double as fashion runways, and *perolones*, the trucks the Metropolitan Police use to round up sex workers on Libertador. *Transformistas* use the medium of a mass-transit thoroughfare to project themselves onto a larger public, which facilitates their sex-work "marketing," makes them legendary, and cultivates an urban fear of *transformistas* that can be used to leverage interpersonal negotiations. I locate Avenida Libertador within the long history of modernizing projects in Venezuela, and with the use of Caracas as a site for staging national modernity. This chapter situates Caracas, the capital city of Venezuela, as my primary field site.

The third order of magnitude, "On the Body," describes the technologies and practices of embodiment in the accomplishment of femininity among *misses* and *transformistas*. In chapter 5, "*Sacar el Cuerpo*," I explore the logics of embodiment in which nature and technology are mutually beneficial projects. Chapter 5 also discusses questions of performativity and embodiment in detail. Chapter 6, "Spectacular Femininities," describes in more detail the forms of femininity produced with respect to spectacle through an analysis of video data garnered from *miss* and *transformista* contexts. I conclude the book by discussing the role of mass mediation in the contemporary political climate of Venezuela. Since the election of Chávez in 1998 and the onset of the Bolivarian Revolution, the beauty pageant has undergone many changes and has certainly become less primary in the ways that Venezuela is recognized throughout the world. The conclusion discusses the role of spectacle in Venezuelan political culture based on my observations of the political conflict ongoing there throughout my fieldwork and to the present day. I explore the relationship between symbolic and political representation, the relationship between media producers and the state, and the question of ideology and reception, and I suggest future work on the nature of melodrama and other narrative genres in political spectacle and struggle in Latin America.

PART I. On the (Trans)National

Belleza Venezolana

MEDIA, RACE, MODERNITY, AND NATION IN THE
TWENTIETH-CENTURY VENEZUELAN BEAUTY CONTEST

La mujer venezolana no tiene prototipo y por eso la Miss Venezuela tampoco. Yo creo que la mujer venezolana, por no estar tan marcada, es muy internacional y eso es lo interesante. Puede ser morena, negra, blanca, catira, pelirroja, de todo. Se destaca en los concursos internacionales por el garbo, la manera de actuar, la forma de moverse, la forma de caminar, de contornearse. Cuando la ven llegar todos dicen: "esta niña tiene que ser venezolana."

The Venezuelan woman has no prototype, and for that reason, neither does Miss Venezuela. I believe that the Venezuelan woman, because she is not so marked, is very international, and that is what is interesting about her. She can be *morena* [dark skinned], Black, white, blonde, redheaded, everything. She stands out in the international competition for her clothing, her way of acting, how she moves, how she walks, how she makes herself appealing. When they see her arrive, they all say: "this girl must be Venezuelan." —OSMEL SOUSA, president of the Organización Miss Venezuela, quoted in Museo Jacobo Borges, *2000 Miss Venezuela*; my translation

The *missólogo* (expert on the beauty pageant and its history in Venezuela) Diego Montaldo Pérez notes in his introduction to the commemorative series *Un siglo de misses*, "Rivers of ink have been written about beauty contests in this country."[1] Missólogos, journalists, and cultural commentators alike have acknowledged the distinction and success of Venezuelan beauty queens on the global stage throughout the twentieth century and into the present. National and international beauty contests have been seen as sites for the production of a distinctive kind of Venezuelan femininity, one that, generation after generation, garners success for the Organización Miss Venezuela (OMV) and recognition for Venezuelan beauty. It is this kind of

Venezuelan femininity, this femininity informed by the beauty pageant industry, that I first encountered when I witnessed the spectacle of that flight attendant in San Antonio del Táchira. And though beauty pageants were probably the last thing I ever thought I would study, I became interested in them because of how immediately recognizable this kind of gender performance is, how intrinsically connected to national ideology.

Belleza venezolana (Venezuelan beauty) is a catchphrase used to refer to this particular kind of beauty.[2] The ideology of Venezuelan beauty and the processes that produce it reveal important elements in the production of nation through racialization, markets, and media. These four elements — nation, race, markets, and media — are sutured together on the bodies of *misses* and in the national imaginary throughout the history of the beauty contest in Venezuela, as they are in Osmel Sousa's declaration in the epigraph of the enigmatic allure of Venezuelan beauty. I first became interested in the beauty pageant precisely because of the ways these elements are sutured by and through the gender formation of the *miss*. Lauren Berlant has called this kind of suturing part of the production of the "National Symbolic" (1991, 22). Using Berlant's framework as developed in her "national sentimentality" trilogy (1991, 1997, 2008), I trace the development of the modern beauty pageant in Venezuela and its attendant discourses of nation, race, and production. These discourses are, of course, integral parts of the gender that *misses* inhabit and produce. While chapters 3, 4, and 6 focus on the implications of these formations to gender in Venezuela, here I will explore more centrally the suturing of nation, race, markets, and media as they pertain to the national beauty pageant in Venezuela.

Berlant proposes the National Symbolic as a space in which national subjects are bound together, not only through historical, political, or juridical mechanisms but also through "a set of forms and the affect that makes these forms meaningful" (1991, 4). These forms, which Berlant proposes are reflected in cultural production, become a site for "national fantasy." In her notion of national fantasy, Berlant suggests a way to understand "how national culture becomes local" (5), an idea that I have extended here beyond the national into the transnational frame. In the context of Venezuela, the beauty pageant certainly reflects national fantasy, but the character of this fantasy is simultaneously transnational; it is about participating on the global stage, and the *miss* is one key form and fantasy through which this participation takes place.[3] This form is profoundly shaped by Venezuelan racial and national ideology.

The simultaneous production of both national and transnational fantasy foregrounds how these two senses of scale mutually constitute each other—to speak of the nation without its geopolitical context in a global division of labor is to ignore the audience of other nations and societies in which national projects are formed. The nation is thus a legible form of political existence, eclipsing other forms of solidarity and political deliberation, and it is always formed in the context of other nations. The structure of the two chapters in this part reflects the simultaneous production of national and transnational fantasy. This chapter focuses on the national fantasy of *belleza venezolana*. The chapter that follows further elaborates the idea of the (trans)national—embedding the production of nation in transnational and international processes, and at the same time understanding the trans and queer subject as a product of the nation rather than treating trans- and queer-subject formations as exceptional. The national fantasy of *belleza venezolana* has shaped the form of the beauty contest in Venezuela. Specifically, this form has become a site of social contention, of embodied notions of racial democracy, an articulation of Venezuela's place in the global market, and at the same time the form has become a way for the nation to imagine itself through various media. An abbreviated history of the national beauty contest in Venezuela demonstrates a shift from local beauty contests to international competitions in the media, beginning in the first years of the twentieth century. I also examine the discourse of race as it is employed in the production of *misses* and elaborate how the nation is defined through geography, media, and national industry in the context of the national beauty contest. Finally, the figure of the *miss* becomes what Berlant calls a "national brand" (2008, 107), a way to mediate national racial ideology through iconography, employing the body of the *miss* to accomplish what I call *miss-ing race*.

The Modern Beauty Contest in Venezuela

To consider the beauty contest as a form, it is important to note a difference between a narrative sense of the term *form* and a ritual sense. In *Beauty Queens on the Global Stage*, Colleen Ballerino Cohen, Richard Wilk, and Beverly Stoeltje (1996) consider the "ritual form" of the beauty pageant's performative structure. They analyze the sequence of events, conventions of performance, and players or characters of beauty pageants as they are conducted in diverse contexts. For example, in Robert Lavenda's discussion of the conflict between, and the ultimate hybridity of, the debutante cotillion and the beauty pageant models in small-town Minnesota "community queen" pageants, the pageant form is important but vacillates between two distinct genealogies to produce both local and regional meaning (Lavenda 1996, 40–42). But the history of the Miss Venezuela beauty contest includes a series of shifts more related to the narrative form of the contest over time than to the ritual structure of specific contests. The elements of the narrative sense of the form, or its mediation, include differences in the media employed to carry out the beauty contest, the kinds of rules employed in deciding the contest, the structure of the contest narrative itself, and the technologies assumed to bind the nation together in order to arrive at a decision. Thus, my examination of the modern beauty contest in Venezuela pays close attention to its mediations: the media, rules, structure, and technologies through which the beauty contest is produced and consumed.

Contests where women are judged for their physical beauty have been observed at many different points in time and in many places. Here I do not attempt to establish a universal chronology of beauty contests in Venezuela or anywhere else. Rather, I illustrate the beginnings of a modern beauty contest in Venezuela and examine the characteristics that distinguish it from its predecessors. This brief history of the beauty contest provides some context for understanding the Miss Venezuela beauty pageant's role in Venezuelan society. In particular, I focus on incidents in the life of beauty contests in Venezuela that reveal these as sites of contestation for conflicts over race, class, and social power.

Following the history of Miss Venezuela, we find changes in the way the contest is structured—the media through which it is contested and the kinds of performances that are included in its staging. A national beauty queen is only conceivable as the nation coheres and begins to see itself as needing a representative. This shift requires a form that selects the queen of the nation through a deliberative process. I trace the history of the modern beauty contest in Venezuela, meaning the first beauty contests held under the rubric of the nation—Señorita Venezuela or Miss Venezuela, rather than local or event-specific contests such as La Reina del Carnaval (Carnival Queen).

It is important to distinguish between beauty *contests* and beauty *pageants*. A beauty contest is an event in which the beauty of individuals is judged. A beauty pageant is a form of a beauty contest that involves pageantry. In the early days of modern Venezuelan beauty contests, the pageant form had not yet emerged. The first national beauty contest in Venezuela was carried out not as a pageant but as a contest held through various media and in several forms of publication and circulation. The beauty pageant form more clearly emerged when the national beauty contest entered the television era in the early 1950s. In the early twentieth century, Venezuelan national beauty contests were deliberated in the media of the nation—magazines, newspapers, and cinema.

The existence of national beauty contests in Venezuela has been dated back to 1905, when the tobacco producer La Hidalguía held a contest based on photo postcards (*carte de visite*) distributed where its cigars were sold throughout Venezuela. Customers collected these postcards and mailed the one representing their choice for Señorita Venezuela to the company.[4] The 1905 Señorita Venezuela contest departed from other beauty contests of the time—primarily observed to crown local carnival queens—in its national character. This contest clearly established links between a national market (the cigars and their distribution method), national infrastructure (the post, a relatively new service at the time), existing media (the postcard), and the idea of national beauty. Although the nation-building project had existed for more than a century (and the nation of Venezuela for seventy-five years) by the time this contest was held, national markets were a recent development. What is significant about modern beauty contests is the primary role of commercial sponsorship and their national scale. Is a queen of Venezuela necessary or even imaginable before this point? La Hidalguía's Señorita Venezuela contest reflects the nation seeing itself through the circuits and technologies through which it can be imagined.

At this time, beauty pageants—that is, beauty contests that involved the physical presentation of all candidates on a stage rather than through photographic means—were held at the local, not national, level. The local pageant form became a somewhat safe place to express dissent because of the perception that beauty pageants were apolitical events. Elections of local beauty queens, such as the Reinas del Carnaval, become sites for the assertion or contestation of authoritarian rule. For example, Montaldo Pérez (1999) reported that the 1915 title of Reina del Carnaval in Maracay went to the representative from the entourage of then-president Juan Vicente Gómez, insinuating that Gómez's presence predetermined the outcome of the event. The most famous case of a politicized beauty pageant in Venezuela is the 1928 crowning of the Queen of the Students. That year, during Carnaval in Caracas, "Beatríz I" became the symbol for the emerging student movement against Gómez the dictator. The future Venezuelan president Raúl Leoni, a member of what is known as La Generación del 28, crowned Beatríz Pérez La Reina de los Estudiantes (Queen of the Students). Her coronation was heralded on the front page of the Caracas newspaper *El Universal*. A seemingly apolitical event, the coronation provided an opportunity for the student movement to make its presence known in the heavily censored national newspapers. The coronation took place in the Teatro Municipal (Municipal Theater) of Caracas and the poet Pio Tamayo read a homage to Beatríz I, a foundational poem for Venezuelan democracy in the twentieth century. In "Homenaje y demanda del Indio: A su Majestad Beatríz I, Reina de los Estudiantes" (Indigenous demand and tribute: Her Majesty Beatríz I, Queen of the Students), Tamayo speaks to Pérez as an *indio* (indigenous person) — one who humbly submits homage and demand for liberty to his *majestad* (majesty). The poem was judged to be subversive by the Gómez administration and resulted in Tamayo's incarceration. The student movement's use of the Carnaval pageant form as a vehicle for its critique of the Gómez dictatorship set the stage for later uses of the beauty pageant as a site for the negotiation of power in Venezuela. Both local and national beauty contests are also an important site for the articulation of a raced and classed Venezuelan national public, as can be seen clearly in the early days of *Élite* magazine.

In the late 1920s, the then-aristocratic *caraqueño* magazine *Élite* ran photographs of many young, unmarried society women who were featured each issue as *muchachas bonitas* (pretty girls) (see figure 1.1). *Élite*, which later in its publishing life became a true tabloid for the Venezuelan masses, at this time served as a kind of high-society newsletter, documenting the parties and social life of Caracas-based elites. In addition to the young muchachas bonitas, married women were also sometimes featured in a series titled Damas honorables (Honorable ladies). Another monthly feature, Las reinas del Volante (The queens of Volante), exhibited young women showing off their family automobiles — among the first cars in Venezuela, which *Élite* proudly advertised from its inception.[5] *Élite* also ran photographs of local Reinas del Carnaval from all over Venezuela. These pictorials were intended to demonstrate the beauty of aristocratic women in the most far-flung regions of the nation, as well as to center the wealthy and beautiful in Caracas — as if to its readers that aristocratic

Muchachas Bonitas

FIGURE 1.1 · "Muchachas bonitas" (Pretty girls). Source: *Élite*, November 19, 1927.

glamour could travel to all corners of the nation, and that Caracas, itself considered a far-flung corner of the world, could be just as glamorous as New York or Paris. This was accomplished by importing commodities and technologies (such as automobiles, cigarettes, and lip and nose shapers), and by reproducing European and North American fashion and glamour on the bodies of Venezuelan women. Photography was an important representational device in these efforts—it bore witness to the ability of the Venezuelan elite to produce glamour in Caracas and throughout the nation. An example of this is a feature titled Rincones de la república (Corners of the republic), in which photographs of aristocrats along with their families and cars holding picnics in all corners of the Republic were printed on special plates in the magazine.[6]

In June 1929, *El Universal* (considered the national newspaper of record at the time) received a letter from the Buenos Aires periodical *El Hogar*, requesting that the newspaper elect a Señorita Venezuela to represent the country in the Concurso de Bellezas Interamericanas (Inter-American Beauty Contest).[7] The contest ran concurrently in *Élite* and *El Universal* from June 1929 to the beginning of 1930 but was never finalized. No record of Señorita Venezuela's participation in the *El Hogar* contest, or of the contest itself, was apparent. Despite the lack of culmination in a crowning of a beauty queen of the Americas, the local and national contest received a great deal of mention in the press at the time. A Miss Universo (Miss Universe) pageant, held in Galveston, Texas, was also reported on in the pages of *El Universal* during this time, but there was no apparent connection between the *El Hogar* contest and Miss Universo, nor did Venezuela have a representative in this competition, which was known as the International Pageant of Pulchritude.[8] The proceedings of the Señorita Venezuela contest suggest specific conditions for representing the nation and for constituting a national consensus. Although this ideal plan was never fully executed, it too reflects the ways the nation can be made manifest through media-consumption practices.

The announcement of the contest in *Élite* laid out an elaborate mechanism for electing the Venezuelan representative:

> The different States of the Republic will elect a beauty queen that will bear the name of her State. On a date yet to be determined, every State will send its respective delegate to the General Contest that will be held in Caracas, to elect "Señorita Venezuela." The procedure to be used in the State elections will be adapted to the practices and customs of each one.
>
> The election in the Distrito Federal will be held in the following way:
>
> Once the applications turned in by the appointed date are received by the Editorial department of *El Universal* or the Editorial department of our colleague, *Élite*, there will be a meeting of all candidates to film a movie in which each one appears as well as the group. This movie will be exhibited in the theaters of Caracas . . . along with their theater entry each patron will receive a coupon, which will be filled out with the name of the señorita of their choice, represented within said movie.
>
> Once the queen of the Distrito Federal, who will be called "Señorita Caracas," is elected, and the delegation of the States to the General Contest is complete, the "Señorita Venezuela" contest will be held in an analogous form to "Señorita Caracas," that is, through the production of another movie-competition of the Señoritas of the States and Distrito Federal. This movie will first be exhibited in the Capital to garner votes, and then throughout each and every

capital of the States. Once this has been verified, a group will be charged with general oversight. . . .

Once "Señorita Venezuela" has been proclaimed, a party of a social and artistic nature will be held, in order to bestow upon her prizes to be determined and to provide everything relative to her trip to Mar de Plata.[9]

This contest description holds an important set of assumptions about what constitutes a fair and representative contest, as well as what media — cinema, photography, magazines, and newspapers — suffice for presenting candidates and registering the will of voters. The directions also inscribed who would be a voter. Interestingly, the contest organizers assumed that localities would have different ways of determining their representatives. Caracas does not impose an electoral model on the "provinces," rather the directions suggest that "the procedure to be used in the States' elections will be adapted by them to their own practices and customs." This would hold true until the states elected their candidates, and then the national selection would take place. At that point, it was decreed that, as in Caracas, the cinemas would become polling places, with each moviegoer purchasing the right to cast a ballot along with a movie ticket. It is significant that the pageant aspect of beauty pageants was not at all important here — what was at stake was representation at the local, national, and regional levels. In the end, coupons were printed on the front page of *El Nacional* on a weekly basis throughout May 1929. These coupons did not appear in the pages of *Élite*, which proposed its own candidates through a more informal write-in process.

The practice and ritual of pageantry was not yet important to this process of representation: note that a party was to be held only once Señorita Venezuela had been named. Pageantry entered the national competition in later years, as the form of the beauty pageant in the 1950s became more emblematic of contemporary beauty contests.[10] What was important at the time of the Señorita Venezuela contest was the circulation of images throughout the capital city first, and then the nation. The organizers proposed to accomplish this through the production of, essentially, newsreels. I do not have evidence that these newsreels were ever produced, but I have observed a stream of contestants' portraits published in *Élite* in 1929 and 1930, which culminated in the naming of Señorita Caracas, Angelina Arvelo Crespo. Montaldo Pérez (1999) reported that Arvelo Crespo went on to win the title of Señorita Venezuela, although I could not find evidence of this in the pages of *Élite*. In all, thirteen states were represented in the *Élite* plates, and Montaldo Pérez reported two additional candidates. *Élite*'s account of the selection of Señorita Caracas did not reference the newsreels or any sort of voting process. Instead, the account described a panel of judges meeting in the newsroom of *El Universal*. The judges deliberated over photographs and brief interviews of the different candidates, as well as the expressions of support garnered from the readership—ten candidates came from *El Universal*, one from *Élite*, and nine more were added by the judges themselves. They decided on one of the *El Universal* candidates, Arvelo Crespo. However there are no sour grapes from *Élite*, which lauds her as "the most gentile lady in whom beauty, grace, elegance, distinction and high social status are united harmoniously; qualities and conditions that predispose her to represent with dignity and justification the noble city of Santiago de Leon de Caracas in the National Beauty Contest. Let the fervent and sincere homages of sympathy and admiration of this Magazine fall at the feet of this triumphant woman."[11]

Élite's flowery prose echoes the rhapsodic tone of national fantasy in this time period. The form of the pageant—which was used in Carnaval Queen elections of the time—was not the form of choice when it came to electing Señorita Venezuela in 1929. Instead, photographic portraits printed in magazines and newspapers, and perhaps some cinematic representations, were the media in which this contest took place. This decision on the part of the contest organizers suggests that an articulation of will on a national scale required a different medium, one in which the national public (figured at the time as elite, literate, movie-going, magazine-and-newspaper-reading citizens) could participate in a common practice as a nation. Following Benedict Anderson (1983), I argue that these practices of spectatorship and participation in the popular media of the time produced nationhood as much as other, more sober practices, such as reading the newspaper with breakfast.

But the Señorita Venezuela competition of 1929–30 is a rather out-of-the-way example of how beauty competitions have produced nation in Venezuela. Throughout the history of beauty competitions in Venezuela, the form of these competitions shifted from the print media of the early twentieth century to a pageant and social-event form in which attendees and judges deliberated over the candidates and selected the queens. These shifts indicate a broader place-making project for both Caracas and the nation.

The form of these competitions turned to pageantry later in the 1930s, when the national competition became a social event held in Caracas. The notion of Señorita Venezuela was dropped. In 1936 a competition was held to elect Miss Caracas—the first indication of the Anglo form of address that has now been incorporated into Venezuelan Spanish.[12] Miss Caracas of 1936 went on to represent Venezuela in the Miss Caribe (Miss Caribbean) and Miss Atlántida (Miss Atlantis) competitions, indicating her participation in a Caribbean cultural circuit that very much included Caracas at the time.

Pan American World Airways organized the first Miss Venezuela competition in 1952 to select a delegate to represent Venezuela at the first competition organized by the current Miss Universe beauty pageant, held in Long Beach, California, on June 28 of the same year. The Miss Universe competition was sponsored by the Catalina Swimwear Company, which had recently lost a dispute over the bathing suit portion of the Miss America competition and had created its own alternative pageant. It is unclear from the histories that have been written what Pan Am's motivation was for sponsoring the Miss Venezuela competition, but it may have been related to the company's role in developing U.S. economic and cultural expansion into Latin America and the Caribbean. Certainly having beautiful women travel to Long Beach to represent countries unknown to U.S. travelers might have been thought to increase tourism to the region. In 1954 Pan Am withdrew its sponsorship of the Miss Venezuela competition, ostensibly because Miss Venezuela of 1953 abdicated her throne so she could get married. The journalist Reinaldo Espinoza took over the organization of the national pageant but did not hold another competition until 1955. This competition, held in the brand new Hotel Tamanaco (where the OMV still sometimes holds its presentation of the misses to the press), ushered in the era of the internationally oriented beauty pageant in Venezuela. While previous pageants had sent Venezuelan representatives to international competitions, it was the success of the 1955 pageant that demonstrated the place-making possibilities of international competition. This pageant began Venezuela's reputation as a producer of world beauty pageant title-holders. But before Venezuela received this kind of international recognition, the discourse of *belleza venezolana* had already emerged. As Pepe Alemán remarked on the front page of *El Universal* in discussing the *El Hogar* pageant: "Venezuela, by the grace of God, is a flowering blush of beautiful women."[13] This allegedly God-given beauty has a specific history, and it is an important site for understanding Venezuelan racial ideology.

Beauty, Race, and Mixture

Missólogos point to the 1944 selection of the queen of the seventh Amateur Baseball World Series as a moment when conflict over social class and race played out in the pageant. This is rare in the chronology of Miss Venezuela—a moment when a contestant characterized as Afro-descendant won acclaim despite the overwhelming Eurocentric aesthetic of *belleza venezolana*. Described as "una morenota grandota, muy elegante" (a big, very dark skinned woman, very elegant) by Montaldo Pérez, Yolanda Leal competed against Oly Clemente, the daughter of a high government official, who was represented as a *criolla* (Creole; white Venezuelan woman).[14] The phrase "Oly Clemente para la gente decente y Yolanda Leal para la gente vulgar" (Oly Clemente for the decent people and Yolanda Leal for the vulgar people) emerged from this contest. As in the case of Beatriz I in 1928, the struggle over the winner of this pageant is thought to have reflected the populist political sentiment against elites (Museo Jacobo Borges 2000, 20). However, as a site for the articulation of race and nation, the Miss Venezuela pageant is far more complex than the binary logic that dominates this kind of appearance of "race"—coded as Blackness—in the pageant's discourse.

Winthrop Wright's (1990) work on race and nation in Venezuela describes some of the methodological difficulties in approaching Venezuelan racial ideologies with a U.S. frame, an important limitation being the distinctly explicit segregation of "Black" and "white" as racial categories in the United States. Wright focuses on the "myth of racial democracy" (5) as the defining character of race and racism in Venezuela. The myth of racial democracy elides racializations by employing the national category of "criollo" as a site of elision for the actual racialized distribution of power and capital in Venezuelan society. While "criollo" itself is a colonial racial category that refers initially to the descendants of Spaniards born in the Americas, in contemporary Venezuela this is a category of national belonging and racial hybridity.

Venezuela's success in world beauty pageants is sometimes explained by how racial formations have taken shape there, particularly through the notion of racial admixture. In the example of Susana Duijm, the first Venezuelan beauty queen to receive international recognition through her coronation as Miss World in 1955, racial categories are floating signifiers, called in when needed to locate Duijm in a racial and class hierarchy, and discarded when they are no longer of use in this positioning. The bodies of *misses* throughout the history of the beauty pageant become sites of contention and elision for racial categories. The *miss* becomes a mediation of Venezuelan racial ideology, allowing the nation to enjoy a kind of racialized exoticism, but also to reinforce the value of a Eurocentric aesthetic. Thus, Duijm can simultaneously be india, *negra* (Black), or criolla, or none of these, or all of these.[15] It is this elision and simultaneous reinscription of Venezuelan racial hierarchies in the body of the *miss* that I call *miss-ing race.*

The appearance of fluid racial categories and the ethnic and cultural diversity of the nation are often cited as contributing factors to Venezuela's success in global beauty contests.[16] In the epigraph, Osmel Sousa invokes hybridity and fluidity when he discusses the enigmatic success of Venezuelan *misses*. This hybridity is seen as providing a competitive advantage for Venezuela in the beauty pageant industry, and in fact has been credited in several economic studies as a key factor in Venezuela's success. Anna Ahlbäck and Pia Engholm, two international business graduate students from the Stockholm School of Economics who wrote a competitive analysis of Miss Venezuela and Miss Sweden, also note this as a factor in Venezuela's competitive edge. They see this hybridity as a kind of "raw material": "The demanders for beauty pageants in Venezuela strongly influence the contest and the access to raw materials (semi-elaborated inputs). This is another reason for the segment being relatively larger than the global one" (1997, 8.2.1.1).

They are trying to explain how a "small" place like Venezuela can be competitive in a global economy, a finding that flouts the theory of economic competition and success they are evaluating: "[Jacques] Dréze [in *Les fondements logiques de l'utilité cardinale et de la probabilité subjective*] (1961) . . . argues that small countries with ethnic and cultural diversity are unable to attain the scale to be competitive in style- and design-sensitive goods. This is not in accordance with our findings from Venezuela. On the contrary, in the case of Miss Venezuela, we believe that the ethnic and cultural diversity of Venezuela as a country has strongly contributed to its success. The reason for this is that no matter what the global definition of 'a beautiful woman' is, such a woman can always be found in Venezuela" (1997, 8.2.1.1). Ahlbäck and Engholm, sincere economics students, echo the commonsense understanding of *belleza venezolana*—the *miss* is a kind of racial "raw material" that can be formed for the global market, whatever its tastes happen to be at any particular moment. The flip side of this kind of ultimate racial flexibility is the inflexibility of the Eurocentric aesthetics that dictate beauty in Venezuela, in particular the explicit rejection of what are considered "African" features.[17]

Examining race in the context of the Miss Venezuela pageant proved to be a difficult methodological challenge, and I cannot say that I succeeded in analyzing it completely. Because race is often an unspoken discourse operating in Venezuelan beauty standards, it was difficult for me to target expressions of racial identity and affiliation. The closest I came to these articulations in the pageant were discussions over participants' features, which recognized physicality but did not reveal identities constructed on the basis of race. I was also ill equipped to make determinations as to what "race" the different contestants may have been. My North American optic on race was not appropriate to judge markers that would signify race in a Venezuelan context, and I resisted imposing my own understanding of race and ethnicity on Venezuelans. But there were moments when the discourse of race in Venezuela became extremely apparent in the *casting* for the beauty pageant, particularly around judgments on women's bodies.[18]

In one *casting* I attended, I encountered a woman who had participated in the pageants for approximately three years. She had traveled to various *casting*, both in Caracas and in the rest of Venezuela, in a fierce attempt to make it into the national pageant. She had secured the sponsorship of a plastic surgery practice in exchange for being their spokesmodel. This contestant had moderate success and had placed in another beauty pageant in 2000. She didn't make it into the Miss Venezuela pageant in 2003. Early in the morning on the day of the *casting*, she told my research assistant and me that she had done everything she could to minimize her hips, legs, and nose—including having liposuction performed on the tiny amount of fat between her thigh muscles. She told us that she was having a hard time breaking into the pageant because her legs, as she was advised, "looked like baseball bats"—the implication of this comment was that her legs and backside were too thick, a feature associated with Blackness in Venezuela. Back home I showed her picture to a Cuban American friend of mine, who remarked, "She doesn't even look all that African!" Whether or not I—or any other observer—would have classified this contestant as Afro-Venezuelan is immaterial; according to her, her body, her legs in particular, was marked as Black by the pageant organizers or *casting* agents, and that was enough to block her progress.

Jun Ishibashi's 2003 study of racism in Venezuelan communications media documents this practice of stereotyping and excluding Black people. This form of racism is openly practiced in the media industry.[19] Ishibashi provides excerpts from interviews with advertising, photography, and Miss Venezuela producers. He argues that these aesthetic determinations evidence a Venezuelan racial ideology that disparages Blackness and overvalues whiteness, particularly in the production of representations for mass consumption. Ishibashi's study consisted of a content analysis of five kinds of materials, including promotional materials for the 2000 and 2001 Miss Venezuela beauty pageants. Panels of Afro-Venezuelans in seven communities were asked to determine whether or not contestants in the photographs were *negras*. In the two years, Ishibashi's informants identified only two out of fifty-three contestants as Black. Ishibashi does not provide information about how these determinations were made, but he does note that neither of these contestants played a "protagonist" role, that is, won the pageant. In fact, the only Afro-Venezuelan to ever win a Miss Venezuela pageant (as identified in the OMV's own publicity materials), Carolina Indriago, was crowned in 1998. Ishibashi documents very clear examples of what he calls the "Eurocentric beauty canon" (2003, 43) in his interviews with a photographer and director of OMV. First, Ishibashi presents the photographer, D.A., who tries to explain the enigmatic aesthetics of the Venezuelan woman: "[She's a] white girl, but not overly white, white but tanned, preferably with very straight hair, with eyes a little bit 'Asian' brown or light-colored without being blue or green. It's like a medium tone: she's neither the blond nor the brown woman of the barrio" (43n8; my translation).[20]

Homi Bhabha would be pleased: almost, but not quite, anything! For a clearer idea of the aesthetics of Venezuelan racial ideology, we need look no further than the Venezuelan media industry. Another one of Ishibashi's informants suggests that Afro-Venezuelan women are not as "strong" looking as a Nigerian model he is presented for an assessment: "They have a thin nose and fine lips. They are more mixed, and look more like the white women" (Ishibashi 2003, 50; my translation).[21] Ishibashi more directly addressed questions of race (specifically in terms of Blackness) in his interviews with producers of the beauty pageant, many of the same people I interviewed during my fieldwork. Ishibashi's approach drew out far more explicit rejections of "African" aesthetics than I was able to accomplish. O.S., the director of the OMV as quoted in Ishibashi's study, was a bit more direct about his assessment of Afro-Venezuelan women. When asked why Afro-descendant women are not represented among the contestants, he declared: "In Venezuela there are no good-looking Black women, because their noses are broad and their lips are too thick" (50; my translation).[22]

These ideas are, of course, quite consistent with the devaluation of non-European features that were operating in Duijm's time, whether or not Duijm actually possessed them. Duijm, in fact, could certainly be the woman "D.A." described. What is interesting to note here is that what Ishibashi marks as racist aesthetics are in fact aesthetics that value whiteness against Blackness—the indigenous does not figure, nor does nearly any other sort of racial marker.[23] So the beauty pageant produces a Venezuelan national aesthetics that privileges *mixture* over any clear markers of race, and the pageant favors whiteness—meaning, in this case, profiled noses, thin lips, straight hair, and small hips. As long as a *miss* has these markers, her skin tone is not an issue. Indriago, the first (and only) Afro-descendant woman to be crowned Miss Venezuela, is a perfect example of this.

Through the physical manifestation of these racial ideologies, the body of the *miss* mediates race in Venezuela. This mediation is more complex than the simple appearance or disappearance of Blackness. This is *miss*-ing race. O. Hugo Benavides describes in the case of Ecuador: "National identity takes on complex forms that not only efface oppressed racial identities but that actually insert them in a dual image of representation in which the national identity distances itself from and becomes the other at the same time" (2006, 131). By *miss*-ing race, the Miss Venezuela beauty pageant assimilates all contestants into the same profiled form—one that claims an exotic allure while at the same time remaining within the confines of the Eurocentric beauty canon.

The Miss America beauty pageant, as Sarah Banet-Weiser (1999) argues, reflects an assimilationist narrative of "sisterhood" by employing Black contestants as evidence of the remediation of an exclusionary and racist past. However, Latin American pageants such as Miss Ecuador and Miss Venezuela reflect a different sort of narrative with respect to their Afro-descendant contestants. The simultaneous denial of and desire for

Otherness mark this narrative, what Stuart Hall calls "fetishism and dis-avowal" (1997). This is done primarily by promoting the exotic and hybrid kind of difference that is ascribed to Latin America (particularly to South American countries such as Brazil, Colombia, and Venezuela), and at the same time using a Eurocentric standard of beauty to exclude contestants who exhibit so-called non-European features. This process is forged in the long history of colonial aesthetics, from the imposition of European systems of knowledge and aesthetics as part of the colonization of the Americas through the definition of *criollo* as a national and racial category and the positivism of the late nineteenth century and its recruitment of southern Europeans to Venezuela in an effort to "whiten" the population. The hybridity that is the hallmark of the Venezuelan *miss* is produced through this long process, and so is its psychic residue. The Venezuelan social psychologist Maritza Montero describes this conflicted relationship to colonial aesthetics through her concept of *altercentrismo*. Altercentrismo, according to Montero, is "the negative social identity that defines itself by putting down the in-group and overvaluing the out-group, without actually leading to a motivational direction to change the negative sign of one's own group, or to abandon or revoke it" (1998, 110; my translation).

Though Montero does not directly engage race or racism in her study of Venezuelan beauty pageants, the valuation of Eurocentric aesthetics invokes the discourse of race. Montero suggests that instead of possessing a positive national identity, Venezuelans put themselves down and look to Eurocentric ideals. Montero diagnoses the nation of Venezuela with a "negative social identity" (1998) in which the national culture of beauty and beauty pageants plays a part. Certainly, a racist colonial legacy could produce such a negative social identity among Black, indigenous, white, or not-quite-so-white people. Montero doesn't account for the dual process Benavides describes, that of at once distancing oneself from and becoming the other.

Even though it is embedded within a racial logic of domination, and even though it is a symbol of a kind of Venezuelan opulence and elitism that has quickly become *pasado de moda* (old-fashioned) in the twenty-first century, the pageant has done some important work for the nation of Venezuela within the global order. The *misses*, particularly since Sousa took over the pageant from Ignacio Font in 1981, have made Venezuela a *place* on the global stage in a way that had eluded the country for centuries. The pageant is successful as a media product, and is, indeed, an opening for certain Venezuelan women to enter the national entertainment media. Montero recognizes this while critiquing the psychological structure of the pageant with its Eurocentric aesthetics.

Members of the OMV defend their aesthetic decisions by pointing out that they are not the ones who produce the aesthetics; they are simply responding to market forces and producing beauty queens who will have global success. Angelina Pollak-Etz invokes this argument in her defense of the idea of racial democracy in Venezuela, suggesting that "the fact that the beauty queens are almost always white girls has to do with the ideal of beauty perpetuated in foreign films and in television. . . . These facts have nothing to do with racial discrimination; they are the consequence of immigration and the historical development of the country" (1991, 102).

Pollak-Etz's argument seems surprising from one of the prominent scholars of Afro-descendant populations in Venezuela, but it is the kind of pessimistic functionalism that fuels the racialized regime of representation in Venezuela.[24] The rubric of success on the global stage allows the OMV directors to enforce a Eurocentric aesthetic without having to be responsible for it. Ultimately, the responsibility for such an aesthetic is placed on the audience. In such a circuit, there is no site of intervention. The question of agency is precluded because individual actors cannot be held responsible for larger social phenomena. This feedback loop, which continues to abstract the mass-mediated feminine form as it reinforces existing racial hierarchies, appears to have no end. It clearly reproduces a social order that values European bodies over those of Others.

As Ishibashi's interview with O.S. reveals, so-called African features are not desirable in a *miss*. In this overt way, Venezuelan women with African features, women who are too short (under 1.70 meters), and women who do not conform to the 90–60–90 (the so-called ideal measurements of 5 feet, 6 inches and 36–24–36 inches in metric units) measurements are simply not considered legitimate contestants. This explains the relative absence of such women in the pageant and, to a lesser degree, at the *casting*. But it begs the question of how such an aesthetic predominates in a country where the large majority of people do not fit these criteria — the question of media imperialism. How does the beauty pageant, with its exclusionary aesthetics and elitism, become a popular form in Venezuela? What discourses legitimate the pageant's exclusionary practices? Is it that the OMV and Venevisión have managed to enthrall millions of Venezuelans into accepting an aesthetic that excludes them from the notion of beauty and the possibility of representing Venezuela on the global stage?

The pageant mobilizes a great deal of energy and interest, and at the very least, recognition that its place in Venezuela is unique. Thus, participation in and consumption of this national media spectacle fulfills a specific function in the production of the Venezuelan nation. The body of the *miss*, as she is produced and brokered in the international projection of Venezuela, becomes a site where Venezuelan racial ideologies are materialized. This is accomplished through the association of the *miss* body with modernity in Venezuela. The *miss* is modern throughout her history not only in her reflection of Eurocentric aesthetics but also in the ways her body—as a site of discipline—reflects the project of modernity in Venezuela.

The *miss* represents a mediation of race, nation, and modernity in Venezuela.[25] Of course, the *miss* is not the only national body on which race, nation, and modernity are mediated in Venezuela. In *The Festive State*, David Guss (2000) describes the ways that national folklore and performance produce and reinscribe Venezuelan national, regional, and racial identities as well as the negotiation between what is seen as modern and what is seen as traditional. The bodies of indigenous people are also a site for the mediation of race, nation, and modernity in Venezuela: Charles Briggs and Clara Mantini-Briggs (2003) reveal the genocidal workings of these practices of discipline through their analysis of the cholera epidemic that led to the deaths of five hundred Warao people in the Delta Amacuro region of Venezuela. *Stories in the Time of Cholera* shows the systems of medical administration, representation, and racism that led to this genocide. Though it may at first seem a very different social world than the one the *misses* inhabit, the Venezuela that allowed the mass death of Warao people in 1992 is indeed the same Venezuela that has produced world-renowned beauty queens for more than half a century. The mechanism that Briggs and Mantini-Briggs develop to explain the genocide is a "sanitary citizenship" predicated on the disproportionate distribution of life chances for those members of Venezuelan society who embody modernity and those who are perceived to be a threat to that modernity. As Briggs and Mantini-Briggs define it: "*Sanitary citizenship* is one of the key mechanisms for deciding who is accorded substantive access to the civil and social rights of citizenship. Public health officials, physicians, politicians, and the press depict some individuals and communities as possessing modern medical understandings of the body, health, and illness, practicing hygiene, and depending on doctors and nurses when they are sick. These people become *sanitary citizens*. People who are judged to be incapable of adopting this modern medical relationship to the body, hygiene, illness, and healing—or who refuse to do so—become *unsanitary subjects*" (10).

While Briggs and Mantini-Briggs focus on the ways the Venezuelan state produced the Warao people as unsanitary subjects, I employ the concept to understand the *miss* body at the other end of the spectrum. The sanitary citizen is a medicalized body—one that employs medical universalism to transcend Blackness and indigeneity and become a modern body. This is, of course, a racialized process, even though it is also represented as a question of class. The *miss* body, shaped and disciplined into conformity with hegemonic beauty standards, exemplifies the sanitary citizen, taking the project of making a modern body into the realm of aesthetics and pleasure. *Misses* and pageant producers employ technologies of diet, surgery, and cosmetics to create the *miss* body. Their willingness to subject the body (and be subject to) these technologies is an example of sanitary citizenship and contrasts with those racialized bodies that are imagined as completely outside the logic of beauty. The early twentieth-century history of the pageant shows the *miss* as a site of contestation between elite and popular aesthetics, a locus of projection and place making on the global stage. She is a figure that mediates modernity, race, and the nation, as an icon, as a kind of geography of the nation.

Making *Misses*, Making Nation

Early national beauty contests in Venezuela produced a photographic portrait of elite beauty throughout the nation, represented by delegates from each state. The contemporary pageant places even greater emphasis on Caracas than did Señorita Venezuela of 1929–30. The narrative structure of the pageant demands representatives from each state in Venezuela, although often the states and the delegates don't match up, or states that don't actually exist are just made up when there are more than twenty-six delegates.[26] Some *misses* are assigned to the state from where they originated, but many are assigned a state over the course of the preparations for the national pageant. Clearly, this is the case for the multiple contestants selected at a *casting* for one state. In some ways, this naming is an after-thought, not much to consider, but it also produces a kind of geography for the nation: the provinces (*el interior*) are represented only selectively, when and how it suits Caracas. The *misses* are sometimes racialized by the state that they are given. This became apparent as I watched *casting* after *casting* for the national pageant, as well as the gay beauty pageants that imi-tated Miss Venezuela. For example, for Miss Delta Amacuro, a Venezuelan state that borders Guyana, a contestant with what were perceived to be more African features was often chosen. I'm not sure when this practice began, but it bears mentioning that Indriago, Miss Venezuela of 1998 and the only Afro-Venezuelan to ever win the competition, competed as Miss Delta Amacuro, although she and her parents are from Valencia in Cara-bobo state.[27]

The place of the pageant in Venezuelan national culture—that is, the forms of cultural production and performance that are thought to be rep-resentative of the unique national character of Venezuelans—is contested terrain. While its extreme popularity is widely recognized, and the success of the Venezuelan *misses* is a point of national pride, the pageant itself is not considered an authentic expression of Venezuelan folklore, as are the *joropo* (a traditional music form), the *diablos danzantes* (dancing devils) of Barlovento, and the lives of founding fathers such as Simón Bolívar and Antonio Jose de Sucre. These, and not the *misses*, have been representative of the national identity of Venezuela in the vast amounts of work on cul-ture supported by various Venezuelan government administrations and private foundations, most prominently the Fundación Bigott.[28]

In 2002 the Museo Jacobo Borges, an art and cultural institution in the working-class west-side neighborhood of Catia in Caracas, presented an exhibition titled *90-60-90* in which the ephemera of the Miss Venezuela pageant was presented alongside critical artworks on the topic of beauty. Adriana Meneses, the director of the museum, explained to me her deci-sion to move forward with an exhibit: "One of the museum's objectives is to bring the everyday, the things that are important to the Venezuelan, to the art gallery. Precisely that 'everydayness,' seen through the eyes of an artist, acquires a different connotation and helps you see things in a differ-ent way. One of the themes that we consider *fundamental* in this country's history is the Miss Venezuela [pageant]. We consider the Miss Venezuela [pageant] to be a cultural phenomenon that has transcended the simple fact of being a beauty pageant, and has become an important part of what goes on in Venezuela" (author interview with Adriana Meneses, Caracas, October 21, 2002; my translation).

According to Meneses, Miss Venezuela has taken on a "fundamental" place in Venezuelan history and constitutes part of a Venezuelan "everyday," which allows her to break down the division between high museum culture and low popular culture and create lots of interest in the museum. She explains the reaction to the opening of the exhibition: "The first day many of the *misses* came with Osmel Sousa and the Miss Venezuela people and well, here it was . . . [indicates the museum was packed]! We had to get the *misses* out with the police because they [the public] went crazy. But those are the phenomena of the media; they're as popular as if we had brought performers, or a singer. It's exactly the same, so, well, in truth there was no other way, people were going crazy and we had to get them out with a police escort." The crowds overran the museum to see the Miss Venezuela hall, often bypassing the critical artwork to look at the gowns and crowns worn by different *misses* when they won world beauty titles. What does the pageant signify for its national audience? It is telling that Meneses has noticed a decline in interest in the pageant:

> Due to the political climate of the country, the pageant has lost
> some of its importance to the people. Because there are so many
> other things, let's say, that worry them at this moment, that, for
> example, the last pageant, the one that just happened [in September
> of 2002], I think it was much more "under the radar" when com-
> pared with others. Both on the level of the print media and on the
> amount of time dedicated to it in [broadcast media], as well as at
> the level of the person on the street. Usually people talked about
> the pageant. This year, I noticed — and this is simply my own per-
> ception — that audience interest in the pageant had fallen a bit. And
> I feel that it's because at this moment, people are not in the mood
> for frivolity. Not even as escapism.

The OMV was in fact considering not having a pageant in 2003, the year I was observing it. The *casting* schedule was delayed by a few months, not because Venevisión would not have been able to produce the pageant but because the political changes in Venezuela over the previous years had begun to change the semantic field in which the pageant happens. Mene- ses notes, from her vantage point, a change in aesthetics: "In the past few years there have been . . . important aesthetic changes that I believe . . . it's not yet time to analyze them. But you see the changes, in the way people dress, in haircuts[,] . . . showing off is not well looked upon. Being ostentatious with one's wealth is not well looked upon, totally the opposite of the Venezuela of Carlos Andres, when it was important to show off what you had.[29] Now it's important to show off that you *don't* have."

The pageant is perhaps starting to mean something else to Venezuelans, at least in Meneses's observations. In the OMV there was some concern that a spectacle of the sort normally produced for the pageant would be inappropriate in the midst of political turmoil, particularly with the narrative of economic ruin used by the Opposition against Chávez during this time. However, the pageant was indeed produced in a modest spectacle held in the Venevisión studios before a very small live audience.[30] The shifts in national political culture initiated by Chávez did not favor the aesthetics of the beauty pageant. Chávez was the first president in the history of the pageant not to invite Miss Venezuela to Casa Miraflores after her election.

The concept of national industry is another place where this relationship between the pageant and national identity is apparent. In this case, the identity of the nation is produced with respect to Venezuela's competitiveness in the global economy. The pageant has been the subject of two economic analyses, done during the era of neoliberal reforms in the wake of structural adjustment in 1990s Venezuela. These analyses are difficult to carry out on an industry such as beauty pageants because sales and ratings figures are somewhat inaccessible. In addition, the industry encompasses more than the production of the television broadcast of the pageant, and its reach in terms of both cultural impact and direct revenue generation (from the recruitment and development of new soap opera actresses and emcees to the training of makeup artists for television, modeling classes, photography, sales of beauty products, and so on) is very difficult to quantify. Nevertheless, in 1994 the Venezuelan economist Abdel Güerere published his analysis of the Venezuelan beauty pageant and telenovela sector as part of a multisectorial analysis of Venezuelan economic potential. In this study, Güerere suggests that Venezuela's distinction as producer of *misses* provides a strategic advantage in the global economy. Based in Güerere's work, Michael J. Enright, Antonio Francés, and Edith Scott Saavedra (1994, 79–85) use the Miss Venezuela phenomenon as an example of the factors that make Miss Venezuela a successful national product. The scholars employ the economist Michael E. Porter's diamond framework for competitive analysis (1990). Porter's framework follows a neoliberal logic that considers several determining factors as functioning in producing competitive advantage. First, "factor conditions" are considered homegrown advantages. Early involvement in pageant culture for Venezuelan girls and an unexplained pool of experts in beauty pageant preparation are cited as important factor conditions. The second aspect of the Porter framework results from "demand conditions." Enright, Francés, and Saavedra cite the "national passion" for the pageant, the prestige involved in participating in pageants, and the "instant celebrity" conferred by winning the pageant as strong advantages in this aspect, as well as the high consumption of personal-hygiene products among Venezuelan women. Strong national demand results in a better product for export. "Supporting and related industries," such as the television and personal-care industries, are considered the third aspect of the Porter diamond, and a high rate of television viewership is considered to create demand for models and spokespeople. Industry "strategy, structure and rivalry" make up the fourth aspect, which in the case of the pageant is favorable due to the virtual monopoly that Venevisión holds on the pageant in Venezuela. Competition between private television stations is also heralded as creating a "better" product (although anyone who has ever watched Venezuelan television might dispute this claim). Finally, Porter's model considers the "role of government." For these authors, a complete lack of intervention from the state in the development of the beauty pageants has been seen as a great boon due to the lack of attention and regulation. While Porter's model seems to allow for state support of the development of industries, the Venezuelan team seems to value a complete lack of involvement on the part of the state in fostering the competitiveness of the beauty pageant industry. The Venezuelans' conclusion: Miss Venezuela is incredibly successful because it has favorable conditions in all of Porter's criteria.

The Stockholm School of Economics thesis by Ahlbäck and Engholm, "Miss Venezuela vs. Miss Sweden, or Diamonds Are a Girl's Best Friend" (1997), used a comparison of the two beauty pageants to evaluate the Porter diamond. This thesis establishes several important points, so I will use it here to expand on the market rationale for the pageant as emblematic of Venezuela's competitiveness on the global market. First, the thesis establishes that Miss Venezuela and the OMV are taken seriously as an industry; while the pageants themselves may be considered frivolous by some, they are a business, and they are a very successful business in Venezuela. "Miss Venezuela vs. Miss Sweden" also documents the international projection of Venezuela through the pageant and the primary role of Sousa in the production of *misses*. Sousa's genius for satisfying global aesthetic trends is used to explain the success of the pageant internationally. The authors suggest that Venezuela is more successful because it is more geared toward international participation, while Sweden engages with its *miss* as solely a national icon and not an international representative figure. The combination of raw material, talent, a streamlined (authoritarian) production process, and shrewdness at the level of the global market (as opposed to Sweden's nostalgic ties to its nationalism) positions Miss Venezuela to be a successful endeavor. Ahlbäck and Engholm also attribute "hybridity" as a factor in the production of *misses*. As a product, then, Miss Venezuela has a place in the economy and reputation of the country. Meneses summarizes the change in opinion among intellectuals that occurred in the 1990s regarding the pageant:

> In the last few years, the way the Miss Venezuela [pageant] has been regarded has changed a bit. In other words, Miss Venezuela began to be considered a successful product. It was named by IESA [Instituto de Estudios Superiores en Administración]; them and petroleum were one of the most important and successful exports of the country. And people started seeing, well, how this man, maybe he doesn't do what we like, but . . . Osmel Sousa, what he does, he does *well*. He does it, he seeks perfection, and he attains perfection. And our name, the name of our country, is heard outside Venezuela. You go to another place, everyone asks you the same thing. You get in a cab in New York, and they talk to you about Venezuelan women. And all over you hear it, the Venezuelan woman, and the beauty of Venezuelan women, and everything related to the beauty queen. Because the contest is seen outside, it's a product for export and it attains its goals. So now they're not so tacky, not so terrible, not so . . . I don't know, but rather, all that tackiness, everything kitsch about it, it's all appreciated. Like, all right, this makes us sound good, this brings up Venezuela's name, and well . . . it's considered something that positive for the country, successful, something we do *well*, in a country in which the majority of things don't work well.

Miss Venezuela is not just a source of national pride; she is a marker of modernity, of progress and successful production, in a country in which the discourse of failure haunts the national project.

The pageant and its contestants produce a hegemonic geography of the nation. That is, an exclusive and elitist representation of the nation is made through the pageant, where the bodies of the participants stand in for the nation both inside and outside the country. This representation is produced through a process that erases class and race as discourses, and yet embodies the disciplinary project for both discourses. Beauty contests throughout the twentieth century in Venezuela served as sites of contestation for the politics of race, class, and democracy. The silences and erasures that occur in this process of representation reveal tensions in center and periphery, national, and social relations in Venezuela. The *miss* has become, over the course of the history of the pageant, an iconic representative of all that is right or wrong about Venezuela, from its beautiful women to its preoccupation with frivolity, but most important, the *miss* figure becomes an incarnation of modernity. If we see her as an artifact, we can trace some of the ways this icon came to represent the paragon of modernity in a place marked by long and public struggles over modernity—a place that can be both hypermodern and antimodern at the same time. One of her manifestations gives us an opportunity to see this iconicity at work: the Harina PAN mammy.

Miss-ing Race; or, How the Harina PAN Mammy Became a Beauty Queen

Mimicry, as the metonymy of presence, is, indeed, such an erratic, eccentric strategy of authority in colonial discourse. Mimicry does not merely destroy narcissistic authority through the repetitive slippage of difference and desire. It is the process of the fixation of the colonial as a form of cross-classificatory, discriminatory knowledge in the defiles of an interdictory discourse, and therefore necessarily raises the question of the authorization of colonial representations.—HOMI BHABHA, *The Location of Culture*

In his discussion of the representation of Black cultural practice in U.S. white mainstream film of the 1980s, Cameron Bailey suggests that such representations "tend to *drain* the cultural forms, removing them from their social and political contexts, and presenting them as interesting ciphers, fascinating and unknowable" (1988, 40). This is what he calls the "artefacting" of Black culture. The Harina PAN mammy is just such an artifact.

I use the term *artifact* in two senses here: one is informed by material culture and another is informed by digital imaging. The notion of the artifact in material culture is one that I think is familiar to most of us: the artifact in the collection, the example, gathered from the field, which represents a class of objects, the traces of events, and material forms. The second sense of *artifact* is that of digital imaging (and you will unfortunately see lots of these kinds of artifacts in the images I have been able to find). In raster-based video and still-image graphics formats, compression algorithms remove pixel detail from larger image files to produce smaller versions. They do this by grouping similarly colored pixels into larger chunks of color or detail. This produces the characteristic "blockyness" or pixelation and ghosting of low-quality JPEG and video files. A single element is replicated and comes to stand in for the whole, thus obscuring detail. Artifacting is a kind of digital metonymy. Artifacts are those blocky chunks that result from this compression scheme. So an artifact is a thing that obscures detail and comes to stand in for the whole. It is a trace of a racialized regime of representation, crystallized into a single icon. The artifact that I consider here is a common sight in homes and grocery stores among populations of Colombians (who will not always admit they use it) and Venezuelans: Harina PAN *arepa* (corn cake) mix.

Harina PAN is precooked corn flour, packaged in shiny yellow or orange plastic (see figure 1.2). It is available in yellow corn for empanadas and white corn for arepas. Cornmeal in the form of the arepa is a staple of Venezuelan and Colombian diets. It comes in many forms, but it usually accompanies or encloses a meal, similar to the tortilla in Mexican diets. Arepas are traditionally made by soaking and softening corn, peeling and grinding it with a large wooden pounding stick called a *pilón*, and then making it into dough. Suffice it to say that arepas are part of daily food consumption in Colombia and Venezuela, and are part of food practices that are thought to predate the colonial period, and which have persisted and changed from colonialism to the present. The arepa is part of national identity for both Colombia and Venezuela, and arepa mix is now a staple in most Colombian and Venezuelan kitchens on the order of sugar and flour. Arepa mix is so commonplace as to be completely unremarkable. According to the Venezuelan marketing magazine *Producto*, Harina PAN

FIGURE 1.2 · The Harina PAN logo on packaging. Photo by the author, 2007.

occupies a full 70 percent of the market share in precooked corn flour in Venezuela.[31] *Producto* goes as far as to say that Harina PAN has become a symbol of the nation in Venezuela. How does Venezuelan nationalism come to be attached to the commodity of precooked corn flour, particularly Harina PAN? And how should we account for the history and meaning of the "mammy" figure on every Harina PAN package, a logo known to many Venezuelans simply as *la negrita de la Harina PAN*?

In 1956 Empresas Polar, manufacturer of a popular brand of beer and distributor of food products throughout Venezuela, began developing a precooked corn flour for arepas. In 1960 Polar launched the Harina PAN brand in Venezuela. This time period, between the late 1950s and mid-1960s, was an important moment in the production of modernity in Venezuela, as the rise of the beauty queen and the massive public works projects (see chapter 4) became important ways to imagine the nation. Harina PAN was developed in the context of modernization projects involving hygiene, urban planning, technology, and public works. During this time, Venezuela transitioned from dictatorship to democracy. Polar promoted Harina PAN as a mass-market commodity of high and consistent quality that preserved tradition and saved labor. Television and film advertising from the late 1960s and early 1970s equated Harina PAN with tradition, nation, technology, and convenience.[32] Harina PAN represented a clean, modern Venezuela, free of conflict and complications, emblazoned with a mammy figure who loses her Blackness and becomes, somehow, a stylized, spit-curled, criolla beauty queen. This figure, as well as the processes that produced Harina PAN as a commodity, represent the accomplishment of sanitary citizenship in Venezuela. Sanitary citizenship is a kind of racialized citizenship — especially when the bodies of unsanitary subjects are defined as racialized Others.

National Brand

As an example of what Lauren Berlant (2008, 107) has called a "national brand," the Harina PAN mammy functions as an artifact of the racialized and gendered ideologies employed in national fantasy. That is, her iconicity "fills in" the gaps of the national fantasy to create a new, abstracted, mediating form. For Berlant, this "prosthetic body" stands in for actual bodies and the historical processes they experience and with which they are laden. However, reading the Harina PAN mammy as a national brand reveals a very different set of conditions from those of U.S. mammy figures, such as Aunt Jemima. Berlant suggests that the trademark or logo is a prosthetic body that "replace[s] the body of pain with the projected image of safety and satisfaction commodities represent" (112). As a "consensual mechanism," the trademark becomes a "'second skin' that enables the commodity to appear to address, to recognize, and thereby to 'love' the consumer" (120). In the case of the Harina PAN mammy, we see an important shift in iconicity between two national brands. In Berlant's example, Aunt Jemima serves as a "condensation of racial nostalgia, white national memory, and progressive history," as well as an analogy for "the notion of the bourgeois housewife's domestic 'slavery'" (122). The Harina PAN mammy is a hybrid of two iconic figures: the mammy (*negrita*) and the *miss*.[33] This blending provides a friendly reconciliation between tradition and modernity as they are imagined in 1960s Venezuela. The iconicity of the *miss* body, with her profiled nose, high cheekbones, and almond-shaped eyes is a marker of Venezuelan modernity in this logo. She ushers in an age of mass production and grocery-store convenience; she saves women (and in one ad, young girls) from a life of backbreaking toil grinding corn for arepas. Yet she wears the familiar and comforting trappings of the colonial order for the Venezuelan middle class, for the *ama de casa* (housewife) imagined to be her consumer. Her headscarf and earrings place her in the category of mammy figure, but something has happened to her body. The representation of Blackness on which the Aunt Jemima figure in Berlant's argument relies—abstraction, sexual abjection, alterity—has morphed into a complete disappearance of Blackness in the body of the *miss*. In Venezuela the comfort and tradition of the colonial order can easily rest on the modern body of the *miss*.

The early television commercials for Harina PAN further elaborate the way this brand was positioned as a mediator between tradition and modernity for the Venezuelan market. Three commercials, run from the mid-1960s to the 1970s, demonstrate a sense of change that Harina PAN ameliorated by providing ways to preserve tradition. Two of these ads, "P.A.N. Caracas" and "P.A.N. Llanero," were shot in black and white, while a third, "P.A.N. Parque del Este," appears to date from the late 1970s, judging from the use of color film and the style of clothing.[34]

"P.A.N. Caracas" is shot from a vehicle driving through the luscious colonial landscape of Caracas. Light flute music is playing as the deep-voiced announcer recites rhyming couplets celebrating the four-hundred-year anniversary of the founding of the exulted capital city. We enter a tunnel and exit to the modern landscape of Caracas with skyscrapers, and highways, then the music changes:

> Caracas: how you have changed
> from the time of your founding
> But time has left us
> a wealth of tradition
>
> Four centuries have passed
> and although many more will pass
> Arepas are still with us
> thanks to the Harina PAN.[35]

As the guitar music fades in, we go under an overpass and cut to pan down from above the red-tile roofs that characterize the colonial part of Caracas. The camera pans to a rough-hewn wooden table, on which is placed a basket of fresh arepas. The pan ends on a packet of Harina PAN. The proposition is plainly stated: Harina PAN is the solution to maintaining Venezuelan national culture despite the changing landscape of Caracas. As in all of the advertising, actual *misses* have no place in this domestic landscape except in the form of the mammy. Instead, the *miss* is the new feminine form of modernity, desirable but unsuitable for the labor required to uphold tradition.

The second commercial, "P.A.N. Llanero," equates Harina PAN and its production technologies with quality, consistency, and *criollismo*. This ad employs the national folklore movement of the time, specifically joropo music and folkloric *llanero* dance. A dance troupe was filmed in the studio, and this footage of their precise movements is intercut with images of what seems to be the Harina PAN production line—all machines, no workers. The male announcer proclaims the quality and consistency of the product to the plucking of a joropo harp rhythm:

> As the harp sounds
> with its constant vibration, so too Harina PAN
> conserves its constant quality.
>
> . . .
>
> Harina PAN has what you are
> looking for: quality. Constant and criollo
> quality.[36]

The chorus comes in with the Harina PAN jingle encouraging the *señora* to trust in the product. The precision of the machines mirrors the precision of the dancers' movements, and these dancers are themselves elaborated within the national folklore framework of the time. Both the dancers and the machines represent the aesthetics of modernization, and through this fusion of rhythm and sound, both assure access to tradition. Quality and consistency are an important theme in this ad and are linked to the Venezuelan national and racial ideology of criollismo through refined production processes in both the case of national dance tradition and the case of arepa flour.

The third commercial was shot in color and presents an enigmatic version of the Harina PAN mammy, one that I have not found since. "P.A.N. Parque del Este," as the ad is titled, is well known among Venezuelans who grew up in the 1970s and 1980s for its jingle "Vivan las vacaciones" (Long live vacations). Color television broadcasts began in Venezuela in December 1979, which indicates that this commercial was most likely produced after that time, unless the commercials were also shown in cinemas. The ad consists of shots of children playing with a colorful inflated ball in the recently built Parque del Este. Designed by the Brazilian landscape designer Roberto Burle Marx, the park was built from 1956 to 1961 on the upscale east side of Caracas.[37] As a landscape, it represents the modernity of middle- and upper-middle-class caraqueño childhood, providing a fantastical safe place to enjoy abundant leisure time for middle-class and middle-class-aspiring caraqueños. The multicultural group of children sings about the joys of leisure during vacation to jolly organ music:

> During vacation we eat empanadas,
> *hallacas*, and arepas made of corn
> Because we don't have problems shelling or grinding
> We make them with Harina PAN
> Long live vacations
> Long live fun
> Here we are all happy
> and we're all going to sing:
> PAN, PAN, PAN![38]

Harina PAN provides leisure and fun, saving the girls from having to grind corn. As the song describes the liberation from shelling and grinding, an older girl interrupts two younger girls by miming the motion of the *pilón*, the implement used to shell and grind corn into arepa dough. The girls are reincorporated into the playgroup, freed from the drudgery of traditional food preparation. At the end of the commercial, we see the spread of delicious foods you can make with Harina PAN circling a small yellow package emblazoned with a different logo from previous ads.

In the first two ads, the Harina PAN mammy appears on the packaging as light skinned, with thin lips, a small nose, and high cheekbones, similar to the one found on the packages today. In the color clip, the mammy is figured as Black. She has brown skin, thicker lips and cheekbones, and a broader nose. I have as yet been unable to determine the order of release for these figures, but it would appear that the black-and-white ads predate the color ad, and these use the light-skinned mammy figure. It is possible that the introduction of color technologies had something to do with a decision to represent the Harina PAN mammy as a darker-skinned figure. Whatever the status of her skin color, it is significant that she remains a mammy figure. While a figure such as Aunt Jemima in the United

States retains her Blackness but loses the markers of class, the Harina PAN mammy loses her Blackness, maintains the trappings of the colonial order that signify servitude, and comes to embody another key figure in the Venezuelan national imaginary: the beauty queen, or *miss*.

A discussion of the mammy (*negrita*) figure in the Venezuelan context represents the difficulties of engaging in a hemispheric dialogue about race and racism from a North American framework. First, the image exists within a very different racialized regime of representation. The Venezuelan mammy indeed represents the colonial order, but a different colonial order from the North American one. The loss of Blackness in the case of the Harina PAN mammy is more a symptom of the tendency to erase traces of Blackness through mestizaje and hybridity than it is a corrective to a history of racist representation, as in the changes to Aunt Jemima over the history of that logo. The *miss* body is the one chosen to erase the mammy's Blackness, and this is not by chance. The figure is clearly read as a *miss* through her long neck, profiled facial features, and aestheticized hair. The sublimation of Blackness to prioritize a Eurocentric aesthetic is important to the potential success of any contestant. Blackness is what women must "overcome" in order to become successful beauty queens in Venezuela—the thought of any of the features stereotypically associated with Blackness as being beautiful is actively rejected by pageant producers.

Revolutionary Mammy?

It is in this context that we have to evaluate the appearance of the mammy figure in Venezuela. The Harina PAN mammy's seamless transformation into a *miss* signifies very differently from the way Aunt Jemima loses the trappings of servitude over the course of the late twentieth century.[39] By way of example, I offer the new logo for Misión Negra Hipólita (MNH) (see figure 1.3).

The logo of this Bolivarian mission, institutionalized in Venezuela in February 2006, employs the legend of La Negra Hipólita (Black Hippolyta), Simón Bolívar's wet nurse. She and La Negra Matea (Black Matea) are, in popular legend and national history, the women who nurtured Bolívar. Hipólita is sometimes also thought to have been his mother or aunt, providing an alternative genealogy for an Afro-descendant Bolívar.[40] Hipólita and Matea are important figures in the Bolivarian project of asserting

FIGURE 1.3 · Revolutionary mammy: an early logo for Misión Negra Hipólita, one of the missions of the Bolivarian Revolution, 2007. Source: Misión Negra Hipólita website http://www.misionnegrahipolita.gob.ve/.

visibility for the African origins of Venezuelans, and the two women have been named at various points over the course of the revolution to invoke Blackness, femininity, nurturing, or women's labor.

Chávez invoked Hipólita and Matea as a way to assert a Bolivarian aesthetic that embraces Blackness and rejects Eurocentric aesthetics. A particularly clear example of this concerns a struggle over control of several oil tankers during the Opposition general strike of 2002–3. The tankers bore the names of *Maritza Sayalero* and *Pilín León*—two world beauty pageant titleholders from the 1980s heyday of Venezuelan beauty dominance—and *Susana Duijm*, Miss World of 1955, the first Miss Venezuela to win a world beauty title. These tankers were the focus of a political spectacle when the merchant marine refused to enter port, effectively freezing the Venezuelan petroleum economy for a short time. The tankers were recaptured by the Venezuelan Navy, returned to port, and commissioned with new names. The tanker *Susana Duijm* kept her name, but the *Pilín Leon* and *Martiza Sayalero* were renamed. Leon and Sayalero were vocal opponents of the Chávez administration during this time, and Duijm did not comment either way about the incident. The *Pilín Leon* and *Martiza Sayalero* were renamed *Negra Hipólita* and *Negra Matea*, respectively (República Bolivariana de Venezuela 2006).

The mission statement of MNH quotes Chávez's maternal mandate: "Negra Hipólita represents the love and generosity of Venezuelan mothers, equity, solidarity and justice for a population unattended in Venezuela and full of misery." Focused specifically on the "most excluded sectors" of Venezuelan society, MNH attempts to redress the "sloth" of previous governments with respect to this population.[41] MNH works to provide health care, food, and shelter to people on the street, including *transformistas*. I learned about the name and the logo when I visited some of *transformistas* I've worked with who had become involved with the mission. The mission has been an important place for some *transformistas* and other street people to receive much-needed services and begin to get off the street.

Since the first publication of this Negra Hipólita logo on MNH's website, Hipólita's image has changed, her scarf and lace collar are deemphasized, she appears to have lost a little bit of weight, and the sun's rays are behind her.[42] Her eyes have gotten bigger and her lips and nose a bit smaller.[43] Interestingly, this follows the pattern I described with Aunt Jemima, who retains her Blackness but slowly loses the trappings of servitude. The first logo, figure 1.3, emphasizes Hipólita's Blackness as well as the uniform of her occupation. When I first saw it, I understood the difference between a Venezuelan politics of representation and one based in the United States. Hipólita's Blackness, in the Venezuelan representational context, reads as an affirmation, an intervention to create visibility in a visual culture that tends to erase (or *miss*) Blackness. It is in this context that MNH can present this figure without the kinds of ideological baggage the logo would certainly have in the United States. And at the same time that the logo celebrates Hipólita's (and Matea's) nurturing and labor for the liberator, the story elides the slavery on which it is predicated. But this figure might be read, from a U.S. framework, as similar to a representation of the enslaved women who cared for Thomas Jefferson, as a form of recognition of their existence in the story of the nation. Is it possible to imagine such a figure coming from the U.S. government?

Is a revolutionary mammy even possible? It would seem to be the case in Venezuela. But this is worlds apart from what that might mean in the United States. In both the case of MNH and the renaming of the oil tankers from *misses* to *negras*, the Bolivarian Revolution employed existing tropes of social stigma to resignify the state. Renaming the tankers can be seen as a peremptory move that directly assailed the association of beauty queens with opulent Venezuelan society, and this move offered recognition and visibility for excluded populations in its place. Negra Hipólita and Negra Matea were presented as strong, maternal Black women who signified the opposite of the *miss*, in a binary that values Blackness and those affected by social exclusion over Eurocentric beauty and opulence. Whether this is indeed what the *misses* mean any more is a shifting question, one that will not be addressed with a binary representational politics.

Conclusion

This chapter has traced a historical trajectory in the development and representation of the *miss* figure in Venezuelan popular culture. I have argued that *belleza venezolana* is produced through four important elements: nation, race, markets, and media. These elements are mutually constitutive, sutured together on the bodies of *misses* and through the iconicity of the beauty contest. The development of the modern beauty contest in Venezuela reflects the form and scope of the nation through markets and media as much as predominant racial and gender ideologies. Mixture and hybridity are important elements in the ways that experts account for the success of Miss Venezuela on the global stage. As a representation of the nation, *misses* become a site for the production of national racial ideology. The ideology of criollismo plays over the bodies of *misses* to conjure nonwhite racial categories while at the same time subsuming all aesthetics into a Eurocentric beauty canon, at once, to repeat myself, distancing itself from and becoming the other. In the 1990s the pageant began to be seriously considered as a national industry in the neoliberal concerns over the competitiveness of Venezuela in a global market.

Throughout its history the *miss* figure became an incarnation for modernity, one that could be both hypermodern and antimodern at the same time. As the ultimate sanitary citizen, the *miss* figure mediates racial ideology for the national market, and this is part of how she accomplishes modernity. The early advertisements by Polar Industries for its precooked arepa mix, Harina PAN, demonstrate the negotiation of modernity and aesthetics in Venezuela. This mediation of race and modernity is clear in the case of the Harina PAN mammy, who performs an act that I call *miss*-ing race by sublimating Blackness into her iconic form. The Bolivarian Revolution responded to this history with its own binary iconicity, promoting and resignifying the mammy figure into a strong, revolutionary Black woman.

But the question of revolution is also not well served with a binary approach. With all the enthusiasm and strife that surrounds the Bolivarian Revolution it is easy to forget that Venezuelans have found a wide range of strategies to negotiate systems of oppression. I offer the revolutionary mammy as a figure to show a non-Venezuelan audience the complex politics of representation, visibility, and race that are at play in Venezuela, and to ask Venezuelans to question the racialized regime of representation in which they participate. The racialized regime of representation in Venezuela is marked by the sublimation of Blackness and indigeneity in a social anxiety about the threat that Black and indigenous bodies pose to Venezuelan modernity. The hygienic maintenance of these bodies as a threat to the health of a *criollo* nation takes a seemingly benign form in the body of the *miss*. Venezuelans also revel in the possibility of the failure of modernity — a kind of disidentification with modernity that transcends Montero's altercentrismo. We will see this by going to a few parties, visiting with a countess and a queen, and following the circuit in which fashion goes to die in Caracas.

La Moda Nace en Paris y Muere en Caracas

FASHION, BEAUTY, AND CONSUMPTION
ON THE (TRANS)NATIONAL

In his catty memoir and chronicle *Morir de glamour: Crónica de la sociedad de fin de siglo*, Boris Izaguirre, the flamboyant Venezuelan expat turned Spanish pop icon, recalls the days of "Caracas Mortal" (2000, 230). *Caracas Mortal*—which you could translate as "Caracas to die for"—was a set of parties thrown by a group of gay men, some of whom were activists. These parties took place in the mid- to late 1980s, the waning days of the oil-rich illusions of *la Venezuela Saudita* ("Saudi Venezuela"), the boom times of the petroleum industry.[1] The idea behind Caracas Mortal was to create a medium for social "revulsion"—mixing up people from all walks of life in Caracas. Not exactly revolutionary, the goal was to break up some of the monotony and elitism of the Caracas social scene as it appeared to these gay men. Izaguirre describes the mix at one of the clubs where they held Caracas Mortal: "We mingled with Brazilian soccer fans, transvestites, and prostitutes. The photographer Fran Beaufrand, Ángel Sánchez, national fashion designer and I took turns with the transvestites and gave them advice on their outfits. Even they explained to us, super nicely, that we were dressing them like señoras and 'that, my love, is the death [of us]'" (230; my translation).

Eso, mi amor, es la muerte (That, my love, is death). Even the *transformistas* of Avenida Libertador, usually reviled as street people, were put into the mix of Caracas Mortal. Edgar Carrasco, one of the organizers of the party, described it as being inspired by Truman Capote's Black and White

Ball of 1966. Izaguirre describes the organizers as influenced both by Andy Warhol's Factory and the publication *Madrid me mata* (Madrid kills me). They put together lists of invitees, including Venezuelan celebrities, intellectuals, street people, students, *transformistas*, and even Jacqueline Onassis. The organizers would find a place willing to let them to hold the event and plan it within two days. The party would descend, and become legendary.

Caracas Mortal is the kind of campy, too-cool-for-school phrase that this group of gay men would often banter around with each other. It is the kind of humor you come up with as you play within queerness and death. Campy. Sordid. A little morbid. By the time I met Carrasco, Izaguirre was long gone for Spain. Carrasco had become a human rights attorney, who has worked on LGBT issues and HIV/AIDS for more than thirty years in Venezuela. And I was there working with Carrasco's organization, Acción Ciudadana contra el SIDA (Citizen Action against AIDS), to develop my work with *transformistas* in Venezuela.

As a newcomer to Venezuelan society, I attentively made note of everything that I heard that mentioned beauty, fashion, *misses*, or *transformistas*. So when Gaston Torres Márquez, one member of this group of friends (who later assisted with my research) casually said, "La moda nace en Paris y muere en Caracas" (Fashion is born in Paris and dies in Caracas), I was intrigued by this figuration of a cultural circuit that ended in death in Caracas. I heard the phrase repeated among this group of men and mistakenly thought that it was a common saying in Venezuela. It isn't. When I asked about it, Gaston and Edgar said they made it up with their friends in the 1980s. This is a pitfall of the ethnographic method: the meaning you find is particular. Still, this phrase stayed with me, partially because it is one of many, like *Caracas Mortal*, that somewhat joyfully equate Caracas, the capital city of Venezuela, with death, failure, and disorder. This is not an uncommon trope in Latin America, and death means different things to different people. In the case of *la moda* (fashion) and Caracas Mortal, death is invoked by queerness, but they also conjure the idea of pollution, the understood contamination of something pure with something impure or taboo. The cultural logic of death undergirds the production of sanitary citizenship and unsanitary subjects, on Venezuelan bodies and in the production of space in Venezuela.[2] Anxieties about death and pollution manifest themselves in a concern with the inability of Venezuela and

Venezuelans to properly value European aesthetics. This is the case with the production of beauty and racial hybridity in Venezuela.

¡Adiós Corotos!

By what cultural logic does a place such as Caracas consume European fashion through death and pollution? The circuit proposed by the phrase *la moda nace en París y muere en Caracas* appears at other points in time. The founders of La Gran Colombia and the Venezuelan state looked to the French Revolution as an example, through the specter of the Haitian Revolution. Arturo Almandóz discusses the Guzmanian preoccupation with Parisian and other European architecture in the late nineteenth century, and the Guzmanian attempts to transform the physical and social landscape of Caracas through architecture and public hygiene.[3] While this Parisification of the city was not unusual in Latin America at the time, it illustrates the imaginary, rather than actual, character of the cultural circuit between Caracas and Paris. This is not a relation of colony and metropole of which the metropole was necessarily aware, nor did it need to be.

The imaginary nature of this cultural circuit is best exemplified by the apocryphal story of the emergence of the word *coroto* in Venezuelan Spanish. The term *coroto* can be used to refer to a generic "thing," or domestic wares such as plates and bowls. The term can at times mean something of little value, but it can also occasionally mean something akin to "the family jewels," a euphemism for testicles. As Angel Rosenblatt (1987) details in his *Estudios sobre el habla de Venezuela*, the story of the origin of this word invokes nineteenth-century dictatorship in Venezuela, either that of Antonio Guzmán Blanco or José Tadeo Monagas. In either case, ordinary Venezuelans in the form of servants or a looting mob encounter two paintings by the French painter Jean-Baptiste-Camille Corot, favored by the dictator, and transform the painter's name into *coroto*. In the case of Monagas, an observer of the looting mob carrying off the paintings exclaims, "¡Adiós corotos!"—an expression that can refer to being emasculated. In the Guzmán Blanco version of the story, servants in the president's residence remind each other: "Cuidado con los corotos." Rosenblatt dismisses these stories as too good to be true. He suggests that *coroto* is indigenous in origin, although he doesn't specify further. María Josefina Tejera's *Diccionario de venezolanismos* (1983) also documents the word and its various senses in Venezuelan Spanish. The Colombian linguist José Joaquín Montes Giraldo (1979) describes the various uses of the word in Colombia and Venezuela, which include both its mundane and precious senses. He argues that the sense of the word that encompasses both "testicles" and "spherical fruit" derives from the Quechua word *koróta* (190). He suggests that the sense that encompasses "domestic wares" could have derived from an indigenous Caribbean language (191), but is likely not related to the Quechua word. In Colombian and Venezuelan Spanish, these two genealogies produce the word *coroto* in its multiple senses.

"True" origins notwithstanding, the imaginary etymology of the word *coroto* does two things — it centers a Venezuelan folk term on the inability of Venezuelans to properly handle European value, and it elides the indigenous origin of the term. This is the same cultural logic of pollution and the failure to be modern that undergirds the saying *la moda nace en Paris y muere en Caracas*. When I invoke the "failure to be modern" (*el fracaso*, as it's often called) and pollution, I hope it is clear that I approach fracaso and pollution in the same way as I approach the terms *marico* and *transformista*: celebrating their alterity and perversity. Rather than implying *actual* failure or pollution (which may or may not also be going on), I focus on the cultural logics of these ideas and how they are employed in understanding Venezuela. I attempt to reflect back to Venezuela, in the queerest and most faithful way possible, the beauty and tragedy of these cultural logics, and to honor the forms of survival and style that have emerged from them. What could be more perverse than to begin with an act of pollution?

Pollution, Perversion, and Modernity

The metaphor of pollution cropped up again and again as I conducted my fieldwork in Venezuela, and it surfaces repeatedly in this book. I was surprised to find a kind of irreverent celebration of pollution, even as the negative implications of pollution were explicit. This stance with respect to contamination was best exemplified in the ending to Manuel Herrera and Miguel Manaure's 1981 documentary *Las TRANS de Caracas*.[4] In the film a *transformista* who is actually named Venezuela leads a group of *transformistas* into an *Age of Aquarius*–inspired dip into a national monument, the massive and iconic fountain in Plaza Venezuela, just a few blocks from the avenue on which *transformistas* have performed sex work and built

FIGURE 2.1 · *Transformistas* in the fountain at Plaza Venezuela. Still from Manuel Herrera and Miguel Manaure's *Las TRANS de Caracas* (1981).

up their legend in Caracas for more than years (see figure 2.1).[5] I discuss the documentary and the Avenida Libertador further in chapter 4. Here I focus on the *transformistas'* occupation of the fountain at Plaza Venezuela.

The fountain at Plaza Venezuela is a tribute to the engineering of its time. Its previous incarnation, designed by Santos Michelena Carcaño, was inaugurated in 1983.[6] This monument became an icon of la Venezuela Saudita with its colored lights and hydroelectric engineering. An automotive tunnel passes underneath the fountain, making the engineering feat even more impressive. In the documentary, Venezuela, the *transformista*, leads her friends the few blocks from Avenida Libertador to the fountain. Silhouetted against the changing colors of the water in the inky night, Venezuela steps up onto the fountain's pedestal, picks up a small sign, and dashes it to the ground, beckoning her friends. They make their way up the fountain's architecture with the Plaza Venezuela traffic circling around them, oblivious as they climb each level, until finally they reach the top reservoir and stand dramatically on its lip. The soundtrack plays the raucous 1980s Wilfrido Vargas merengue "Abusadora," horns blaring. Venezuela's flyaway reverse apron skirt billows behind her, as her hips seem to hit the rhythm of the merengue perfectly. The girls hold hands and gingerly enter the fountain. The merengue in the background reinforces the transgression: *¿qué hiciste, abusadora?* What did you do, woman you who abused my hospitality? In this act, as well as in her choice of name, Venezuela imposes her belonging in the nation: she and hers *are* the nation of Venezuela, whether anyone likes it or not. But this insistence is not without its price, as La Contessa, who we will meet in chapter 4, reminds me when her haunting voice recalls those times.

LA CONTESSA: Uy! You know what ugly years I lived through? Honeymoon years? Ay, *mi amor*, no honeymoon year. The eighties for me were horrific years. My family didn't know what I was suffering through over here. Ay, *mi amor*! I see th—. Nothing, my love, I had no . . . They would take me to jail and I had no one to take me even a piece of bread.

OCHOA: So you went hungry?

LA CONTESSA: Not even something to wear, nothing. Ay, that was horrible. I had a hard time here in the eighties — ghastly. Those were years that . . . I went hungry, you have no idea. You don't know the hunger I lived through in those years. Hunger and beatings and everything and uy, as if . . . As if I had done something and was paying a terrible crime.

OCHOA: How horrible.

LA CONTESSA: But I say, I was paying for a terrible crime, but if I've never done anything to anyone, why do I have to pay a crime? What have I done to deserve this? What have I done to have to pay, to be . . . suffering this calvary? Because it was ghastly, horrible . . . a torture to end all tortures. Even working indoors I would get it. Almost everyone from my time of the eighties, almost all of them are dead. . . . Look, one of them just died. Tell me my friend's name that just died.

OCHOA: La Candy.

LA CONTESSA: She suffered, like you have no idea. She . . . all of it because she went to El Dorado, she also went to El Dorado.

OCHOA: What's El Dorado?

LA CONTESSA: It was an island that . . . they sent prisoners there. *Transformistas.*

OCHOA: Did you go there?

LA CONTESSA: I went there too.

OCHOA: And what was that like?

LA CONTESSA: Ayyy . . . don't even talk about it.

OCHOA: Under what president was that?

LA CONTESSA: I don't know. I can't remember.

OCHOA: El Dorado.

LA CONTESSA: Like an island, ugly, ugly, ugly, terrible. I would
never wish anyone to go there. I left there destroyed, as if . . .
I left like a *latera* [destitute, a woman who picks up cans in the
street]. Uy! A destruction, I'm telling you. (Interview with "La
Contessa," conducted in San Agustín, Caracas, on September 4,
2003; all quotes from this interview are my translation.)

We will come back to La Contessa a bit later, but for now I want to take
a moment to marvel at how a group of *transformistas* under the regime
of the Policía Metropolitana (Metropolitan Police) of Caracas and the
Ley de Vagos y Maleantes (the "Vagrants and Crooks Law"[7]) in the 1980s
would have dared to mock the rules of Plaza Venezuela in such a public
way—at a time when the price of this mocking included the distinct possibility of being sent to El Dorado. How does Venezuela, the *transformista*,
take on the name of the nation that so actively polices her and subjects her
and many other *transformistas* to the kind of violence that La Contessa has
experienced? How do we account for this way of speaking to power, one
that reinscribes the nation and yet pollutes it? Or in the case of the Caracas
Mortal crowd, how do we account for this way of reinscribing Eurocentrism while polluting it? The act of pollution—the essence of being "where
fashion goes to die," of being the publicly visible *transformista* on Avenida
Libertador—is itself a powerful response to coercive relations of power.
This is not merely unconscious and hopeful copying; it is a purposeful
muddying of relations of power, a kind of pollution through reinscription.

An imaginative and productive response to the kinds of physical, structural, and psychic violence that shape the lives of *transformistas* in Venezuela, the pollution of the fountain at Plaza Venezuela by the *transformista*
named Venezuela and her friends functions by appropriating what Mary
Douglas calls the "inarticulate powers vested in those who are a source of
disorder" (1966, 99). Douglas, in her classic anthropological text on pollution and taboo, *Purity and Danger*, describes the process through which
dirt is stripped of its identity—reincorporated into a sense of order—
eerily reminding me both of Venezuela's sauntering in the fountain and
La Contessa's experience in El Dorado:

In the course of any imposing of order, whether in the mind or in the external world, the attitude to rejected bits and pieces goes through two stages. First they are recognizably out of place, a threat to good order, and so are regarded as objectionable and vigorously brushed away. At this stage, they have some identity: they can be seen to be unwanted bits of whatever it was they came from, hair or food or wrappings. This is the stage at which they are dangerous; their half-identity still clings to them and the clarity of the scene in which they obtrude is impaired by their presence. But a long process of pulverizing, dissolving and rotting awaits any physical things that have been recognized as dirt. In the end, all identity is gone. The origin of the various bits and pieces is lost and they have entered into the mass of common rubbish. It is unpleasant to poke about in the refuse to try to recover anything, for this revives identity. So long as identity is absent, rubbish is not dangerous. . . . Where there is no differentiation there is no defilement. (160)

Venezuela knows what she is doing, teetering on the lip of the fountain. She knows what she risks by doing it—and she does it, just the way she chooses her name, as a kind of insistence on belonging—to the nation, the landscape of Caracas, the society that fetishizes and rejects her, the circuits of glamour that define femininity in la Venezuela Saudita. To the same social order that produced her and yet would render her unidentifiable in the multitude of ways it does to *transformistas*.

Don Kulick and Charles Klein suggest that *travestís* in Brazil are "reterritorializing shame" (2009, 325) as a response to coercive forms of power in their examination of scandal as an interpersonal and political tactic. According to Kulick and Klein, *travestís* use scandal as both an interpersonal and a political tactic. A *travestí* succeeds in demanding more money from a client by creating a scandal, implicating her client in his own socially devalued desires, embodied in her relations with him. To quiet the scandal, he hands over the money. As such, the *travestí* employs her power from the margins of social order and her knowledge of her client's sexual desire to her advantage. In this she creates an equivalency that, as I see it, "pollutes" the presumed heterosexuality of her client with his undeclared (unidentified or unidentifiable) object of desire—her. Kulick and Klein propose that this ability to negotiate power serves *travestí* social movements as well: rather than appealing for social acceptance, these movements employ political shame to mobilize transformation. These are survival strategies in a world that actively marginalizes and debases transgender women. These strategies suggest that resistance and opposition are only two possibilities in a universe of ways to respond to oppression, and that for *transformistas* and other transgender women in Latin America, survival requires creativity and resourcefulness. The fountain frolic performed by Venezuela celebrates her contamination of a national symbol and inspires the beginning of an answer to one of the central questions that motivates my inquiry: how do perverse people and places negotiate their continued existence in hostile circuits of power?[8]

I ask this question not just on the scale of the individual or interpersonal but also on the scale of the nation in its own negotiations of power. Indeed, scale has a lot to do with this negotiation of power. In equating Caracas with the death of Parisian fashion, Venezuelans with the destruction of democracy and fine art, and *transformistas* with the nation of Venezuela, these subjects embody an equivalence that appropriates, negotiates, and transforms Eurocentric ideals of beauty, value, and modernity. So I formulate the question, ultimately, at the level of the (trans)national — that is, embedding transgender people in existing logics of the nation rather than seeing them as exceptional, and understanding the nation as producing itself in transnational economies, both symbolic and material.

Licia Fiol-Matta's engaging study of the Chilean pedagogue Gabriela Mistral, *Queer Mother for the Nation* (2002), proposes a similar approach to the status of the queer subject in the project of nation building. An enigmatic, secretive, and decidedly masculine figure, Mistral was a founding figure of Chilean national identity in the early twentieth century through her work as a schoolteacher. Fiol-Matta argues that Mistral's queerness — both in terms of her gender presentation and the rumors surrounding her sexuality — is central to her deployment as an icon of state, national, and racial ideologies: "Mistral 'queered' the nation, to be sure, yet this queering advanced not only heteronormativity but also the unspoken Latin Americanist racial project. . . . Not only Mistral as a queer but also Mistral's nationally projected queerness helped articulate the state discourse about the reproduction of the nation, an example of Foucault's 'right to life' within biopower" (36).

In proposing the scale of the (trans)national, I am arguing not only for the centrality of *transformista* existence to the project of defining the nation but also for the role of transnational processes such as mass mediation in the consolidation of national identities and ideologies. Caracas Mortal and the examples I have given so far hint at the cultural logics — logics deeply embedded in the process of modernity in Venezuela — that make these circuits possible. While the subjects of this book don't have the social power that Mistral held, they participated in the production of national and racial ideologies that are produced in the process of modernity. These are forged in what Michael Taussig has called "the space of death" (1987, 374). So how is it possible to equate queerness and death with the nation of Venezuela? How do these logics of queerness, pollution, and death *produce* nation in Venezuela? How does Venezuela come to be seen as a space of death, failure, and pollution — a perverse place? Let us think of Venezuela in the same frame as Venezuela. Venezuela the *transformista*, Venezuela the nation.

The Space of Death

Taussig has famously identified, through his work on terror in the Colombian Putumayo, the space of death as the psychic residue of the excess signification of violence in the colonial project. Because of the excessive forms of violence to which *transformistas* and gay men are regularly subject in Venezuela, they occupy a space of death in Venezuelan society. Even though they may be attending some fabulous parties or sauntering into fountains dripping with glamour, let us not forget that they are also engaging in these acts amid daily violence, poverty, disease, emotional blackmail, and social marginalization. While I am hesitant to dwell too much on this reality (as La Contessa says, "ni hablar" — don't even talk about it), sometimes the fabulousness of Venezuela's and La Contessa's strategies of survival misleads those who are not familiar with the contexts of violence and social marginality from which these strategies emerge.

Let me reiterate in no uncertain terms that *transformistas* occupy a space of death in Venezuelan society: the process of social cleansing and pulverizing identity is visited on their bodies and in their lives in both daily and spectacular manifestations.[9] They occupy a liminal space, defined by social, physical, economic, and educational exclusion; state and private suppression; and multiple forms of violence. Though the Bolivarian Revolution has in more recent years begun to offer some hope of social inclusion, this slight aperture has not yet transformed the social condition of *transformistas*.[10] And it has certainly not transformed the kinds of exclusions that many *transformistas* continue to live. But we were talking about the space of death.

For Taussig, the space of death is the product of the ineffable and overly charged process of signification that emerges from the terror of conquest and the violation of the bodies of colonized people and places — a dialectic between fetishism and disavowal with deadly consequences. He describes how the system of colonial production relied on both the torture and reification of indigenous bodies in the nineteenth-century rubber industry of the Putumayo in Colombia and the residue of this process in contemporary life, what he calls "Putumayo terror":

> Going to the Indians for their healing power and killing them for their wildness are not so far apart. Indeed, these actions are not only intertwined but are codependent — and it is this codependence that looms in so startling a fashion when we consider how fine the line is that separates the use of Indians as laborers, on the one hand, and their use as mythic objects of torture on the other.
>
> Putumayo terror was the terror of the fineness of that line as international capitalism converted the "excesses" of torture into rituals of production no less important than the rubber gathering itself. Torture and terror were not simply utilitarian means of production; they were a form of life, a mode of production, and in many ways, for many people, not least of whom were the Indians themselves, its main and consuming product. (Taussig 1987, 100)

According to Taussig, the forms of alterity encountered in the colonial project populate the Western social imaginary of the space of death: "With European conquest and colonization, these spaces of death blend into a common pool of key signifiers binding the transforming culture of the conquerer [*sic*] with that of the conquered" (5).

Sharon Holland has used Taussig to locate queerness, the queerness of U.S. people of color, in this space of colonial death. While Taussig develops this concept in the perversions of the Putumayo, it is Holland who deploys the space of death as a way to imagine the bankrupt possibilities of Black subjectivity in the U.S. national imaginary.[11] In this project, she issues the call that I attempt to answer in Venezuela:

> If we are to expand the definition of *queer* to encompass other bodies, then we will need to do some hard work here. We will need

to focus on what we really mean when we equate the queer body/ subject with liminal spaces. That these liminal spaces might be so dangerous as to *become* death itself is more than frightening. It represents an apocalyptic moment for queer studies and a challenge to read "race" into the equation of its origins. Bill's and Tupac's bodies are emblematic of the queer—refusing to go away, Still/ Here, coming at you soft and hard, embracing the contradiction as if it were a religion. The space of death is marked by blackness and is therefore always already queer. (Holland 2000, 180)

As Holland invokes the bodies of Black gay dancer Bill T. Jones and gangsta rapper Tupac Shakur—both emblems of the queer, she argues—she performs a radical equivalency that inspires me to bring together Venezuela the *transformista* and Venezuela the nation. Holland's contribution lays the groundwork for understanding the sexual and racial alterity that constitute the production of modernity in the Americas. Cannibalism and sodomy. The twin tropes of Spanish colonization. The bodily acts that rendered Amerindians so outside of Western cultural logics as to make them a threat to the social order. These forms of sexual and racial alterity continue to work on the policing of modernity in Latin America. Whether violence, poverty, AIDS, colonialism, slavery, or genocide is the mechanism, these are the bodies that remain, and this is the world in which we produce the conditions for our survival.

The conflation of queerness, death, and nation is not accidental, nor is the conflation of queered and racialized bodies with the terror of the failure to be modern. In these overlapping liminalities, bodies and lifeworlds that are Othered, queered, and otherwise pushed aside in the normative project of nation building keep reappearing, like so many flies in the national ointment. These inconvenient bodies emerge in spaces of abjection and prestige, never allowing the nation to be quite as it would like to imagine itself, as a part of modernity. This is why *transformistas* and other visible reminders of marginality are subject to so much violence, why they are seen as polluting society. As with all symbolic systems of pollution, *transformistas'* role as a threat to the social order reinforces the perceived boundaries of that order. The power that Venezuela and her friends have as they saunter into the fountain at Plaza Venezuela is the power to reterritorialize shame through the nation. *Transformistas* have the power to inhabit the space of death and exploit the fetishism that is the flip side to social disavowal. These are the kinds of tactics that queer and transgender subjects invent as we negotiate the violence of normalizing power.

While *transformistas* and other queer and transgender subjects in Venezuela use the Caracas Mortal logic, and things like it, to contest and reinvent the space of death they occupy, the nation of Venezuela also employs similar techniques to produce authority for itself in a transnational division of labor that makes it into what Anna Tsing calls an "out-of-the-way" place (1993, 9). Marginality, then, is something *maricos, transformistas, and* the nation of Venezuela have in common—they must all make a place for themselves in systems that decenter them. This has required me to grapple with the metaphor of center and periphery in describing power relations. While I share the critique of totalizing notions of both centers and peripheries, I also encountered spaces in which the absolute power of the state broke across nonconforming bodies, in which these bodies were rendered absolutely peripheral to any normalized or legitimated economic or social activity.[12] I encountered the imposition of Eurocentric and *caraqueño* ideas of beauty on bodies throughout Venezuela, but most particularly in what is called *el interior* (the provinces) from a caraqueño perspective that considers itself the center.

Center, Periphery, Variegation, and . . .

Though often produced as a peripheral space in the logic of modernity, the nation of Venezuela has contested and reshaped this status throughout its history. In the conclusion to *The Magical State*, Fernando Coronil provides a way to recognize the ways power is spatialized through a center-periphery model and at the same time contest these hegemonies: "The West's self-constitution through the domination both of other societies and of nature continues to draw legitimacy from a map of the world polarized into centers of modernity and backward areas waiting to be 'enlightened'—now through 'internal adjustments' of reform rather than through the civilizing mission of direct external control" (1997, 394). Understanding center and periphery as part of a "relational process involving the contrapuntal constitution of subaltern and Occidentalist modernities," Coronil refuses a "sharp separation between the West and its periphery" (388). While Tsing might describe this process as the production of "out-of-the-way" places, the proximity that Coronil suggests between Occidental modernity and its foils implies that we should consider the spatialization of power through multiple metaphors. This is a kind of politics of scale, in which actors have or can leverage power at various levels. The (trans) national is one order of magnitude on this scale.

Indeed, violence and terror are key sites for the imprinting of these social relations, and in these sites, while neither pure nor coherent, the boundaries of the body and the state can become eminently clear. Coronil and Julie Skurski suggest that this is a form of communication:

> The corporeality of people has served as a privileged medium for the political imagination in Latin America, as states that have but partial control over populations and territories have inscribed on the bodies of their subjects assertions of power directed to collective audiences. These inscriptions encode not only the reasons of state but the unquestioned foundations of these reasons, the bedrock of common sense that makes a social landscape seem natural. In this respect, physical violence, not unlike printing, is a vehicle for making and encoding history whose specific form and significance cannot be understood outside that history. (1991, 330)

And, following Taussig, Charles Briggs, Coronil, and Skurski, I examine the communicative dimensions of these carnal processes. One thing is clear: histories and encoded forms of power imprint themselves both on the flesh and the landscape. This clear communication of boundaries, porosities, and sovereignties reiterates and reinscribes social order. I have found the concept of variegation useful in understanding the encoding and decoding of power and politics in Venezuela. Variegation involves the striation of zones of power and subalternity rather than any sense of the purity or coherence of these. Venezuela is a variegated place, like a leaf striated with pigments. The colonial violence that formed Venezuela has also produced it as a variegated space of death and terror.

Aiwha Ong develops the idea of "variegated sovereignty" in her book *Flexible Citizenship* (1999) to describe zones of complicity between the state and capital, which facilitate the exploitation of labor and the mobility of privileged subjects. In Venezuela, and in Caracas in particular, this variegation is a topography of uneven striations of marginalization, accumulation, poverty, and privilege. It is in this variegated landscape that an aesthetic of deep contrast develops: poverty and luxury, side by side and always a sideward glance away. The sociologist María Gabriela Ponce's

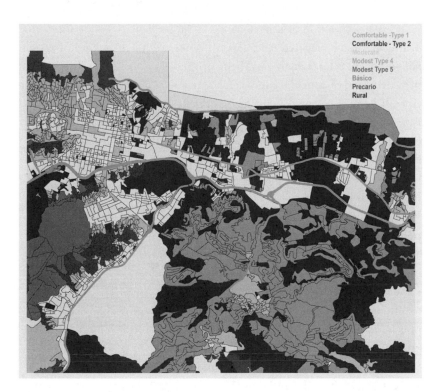

FIGURE 2.2 · Variegated zones of poverty and *confort*; detail of area of Avenida Libertador, Caracas. Source: María Gabriela Ponce, Universidad Católica Andres Bello, Caracas (see Ponce 2005). Image used with permission of Ponce.

(2005) maps of economic stratification in Caracas provide a graphic example of what I mean by variegation. These maps assign colors and shading to different socioeconomic levels of poverty and *confort* (comfort) throughout the city. Figure 2.2 identifies the variegated pattern of wealth distribution in Caracas. According to Ponce, these patterns of poverty and wealth are more dependent on the price of petroleum at the time than on what administration is in power in Venezuela.

While variegation helps visualize the heterogeneous patterns of power and poverty, the examples I bring together in this chapter show that multiple responses to marginalization, colonialism, and exploitation have emerged from these systems of domination. The consumption and production of beauty and femininity have provided opportunities for individual Venezuelans as well as the nation of Venezuela to capitalize on asymmetries of value and center themselves as a response to marginality.

Cannibalist Cosmopolitanism?

Transiting this variegated landscape of power produces a kind of *cosmopolitanism*, another term that has been proposed and celebrated as a way to provide a kind of ethics in an uneven landscape of power. Kwame Anthony Appiah defines cosmopolitanism as a type of universalist humanitarianism: "It underwrote some of the great moral achievements of the Enlightenment" (2006, xiv). He tries to recuperate the term from its jet-setting associations with wealthy, stylish, mobile people. Instead, he argues, "the well-traveled polyglot is as likely to be among the worst off as among the best off—as likely to be found in a shantytown as at the Sorbonne" (xviii). Yet there is something disquieting about Appiah's formulation of cosmopolitanism, that ecumenical ethics to which we might all apparently have access. Bruce Robbins points it out, quite simply: "Celebrations of cosmopolitan diversity have largely been uninterrupted by the issues of economic equality or geopolitical justice" (2007, 51).

This is the flight of fancy that is difficult to swallow about cosmopolitanism as ethics. However, we might think of cosmopolitanism not as ethics but rather as a form of consumption. This is what Louisa Schein (1997) calls "imagined cosmopolitanism," which she defines in the context of post-Mao China as "an imagining of mobility through the consumption of foreign objects and media and through the potential for global access implied by the 'opening' policy" (483n9). Ulf Hannerz (1990) is very clear about the connection between cosmopolitanism and consumption: cosmopolitans are *connoisseurs, aficionados*. This clearly excludes those who travel (in his example, Nigerian market women who jet between Lagos and London) and "only" consume that which is familiar to them. The true cosmopolitan "surrender[s] to the alien culture" in order to possess and master it—a "conditional" surrender (240). Through imagined cosmopolitanism, people in out-of-the-way places participate in forms of mobility that are possibly just outside their reach. These imaginaries provide powerful ways to negotiate power in a local context.

I take Schein's idea a bit further to suggest that what Venezuela and her friends are doing, what connects the Caracas Mortal crowd with La Contessa and (as we'll see) Susana Duijm, is a kind of *cannibalist* cosmopolitanism: imaginary and actual travel that devours the West, and in so doing, transforms it. Forged in the space of terror and death, the cannibalist cosmopolitan looks sidelong at Eurocentric, first-world aesthetics, gives over to the alien culture just enough to get close, then consumes and transforms it. As the Brazilian artist Oswald de Andrade proposed in the 1924 *Cannibalist Manifesto*, cannibalism is the stance that Latin American art must have toward Europe, recognizing the role of the Americas in the constitution of European identity: "We want the Caraíba [cannibalist] revolution. Greater than the French Revolution. The unification of all man's efficient uprisings. Without us Europe would not have had even its sorry declaration of the rights of man" (Andrade 1999, 92).

The Cannibalist movement in Brazilian art has certainly not addressed issues of economic inequality or geopolitical justice, particularly for the Tupí it constantly invokes in its catchphrase, "Tupí or not Tupí." Despite its exclusions the *Cannibalist Manifesto* is an early example of the kinds of irony with which some Venezuelans approach Eurocentric aesthetics. A cannibalist cosmopolitan consumes Eurocentric aesthetics in a way that radically misunderstands Western value, and transforms it through the act of consumption.

We are riding along the thin line of a fundamental contradiction: the perversions of modernity that seek to normalize, or perhaps extinguish, our messy bodies are also those in which we produce our own perverse, colored, and queer existences. There are many names to describe the ways we negotiate this contradiction—disidentification, *chusmería*, *rasquachismo*, queer Latinidad, postcolonialism, cannibalism. Recall again the flight attendant in San Antonio del Táchira whose performance set me on this perverse path. She, with her jangling baubles, what is she doing? She is casting an aura of glamour over her captive audience; she is engaging in imaginary travel, transporting herself to another runway, somewhere else. This is a tool for negotiating a landscape of contradiction. In Venezuela cannibalist cosmopolitanism takes the form of glamour—both in the ways the nation of Venezuela and queer and trans Venezuelans make space for themselves in the world.

I want to bring Holland's optic back to the colonial space of death that is (still) Venezuela—a dangerous move, which risks flattening transgender, queer, *negro* (Black), *indio* (indigenous), and *criollo* (Creole) existences in a place layered with complexity. I do this to honor the cannibalistic logic that makes it possible for Caracas to become the place where Parisian fashion goes to die. I have followed this imaginary circuit through several trajectories (beginning with Caracas Mortal and corotos). We will return to La Contessa, a contemporary of Venezuela the *transformista*, and I will explain her transit between Caracas and Milan. Mary Louise Pratt's (1992) idea of "Creole self-fashioning" is another imaginary circuit between Caracas and Europe. We will also follow the very brief European tour of "Carmen la Sauvage," Susana Duijm, Miss World of 1955, and her reception in Paris. We will arrive at glamour as a technology of intimacy that gives some insight into how these kinds of imagined and actual cosmopolitanisms leverage extralocal authority for a highly contingent semblance of local power. In a variegated landscape, glamour refracts power in useful and unpredictable ways.

A Visit with a Countess

La Contessa haunts Avenida Libertador in broad daylight. Always in long black garments, she glides down the street and hovers at the curb, tentatively working her next client with one eye always on the horizon, scanning for police. In a sense, the police haunt La Contessa as much as she haunts the Avenida. When we begin our interview, she is telling me: ". . . and so I told him, 'You are corrupt, you are this, you are that.'" She repeats the police officer's exclamation in response: "What do you mean I'm corrupt?" In her imaginary conversation, she replies, "Here is the proof . . . *cháss!*" Fantasmatic papers land conclusively on an imaginary bureaucrat's desk.

A little violin plays old boleros on the radio in the background. We're in her rented room in San Agustín. No gas, no water, but a bed and a closet. And cheap. Pungent ammonia soaks the hallways after someone swabs an aging gray mop over the checkerboard tiles, porous and calm since their glaze wore away years ago. We are sitting on her bed. The ceiling is low and the heat of the afternoon slows time as we talk to the drone of the radio. "Uuyy," I respond.

She elaborates: "Uuyy, they have it [the proof] there. [In Europe] the police are like this . . ." She curls into herself, opens her eyes wide, and speaks with a hushed voice. The Countess, she is called. I offer her reassuring comments; I have heard a lot about her experiences with police because we talk regularly on the street during condom distribution. She's history on the Avenida: walking, gliding, hovering history. She's been through it all, the fantasy life of many *transformistas* on the Avenida: making enough to pay for some plastic surgery, emigrating to Europe to do sex work, making enough there to pay for your sex-change operation, falling in love with a handsome man who wants to marry you. Now she's back where she started again: "It's another world over there, it's another world. There, exactly, there is not like here, it's different there. There . . ." She trails off. I fidget with the recorder, announce the interview. She comes back: "I lasted ten and a half years."

La Contessa is telling me about the difference between police in Caracas and police in Milan. She finds herself again in Venezuela because of problems with her papers. She's going back though, soon. Once she gets the papers sorted out. She wants to go back to her life there, to her man, an Arab, she says, with a house in his home country and a wife and kids in Paris. And her in Milan, if she can get back. Milan is another world, she is saying. Worlds apart from Caracas.

> LA CONTESSA: Yes because there, they're all . . . it's another world over there. Models everywhere. Over there everything is beautiful. Understand me?
> OCHOA: Yes.
> LA CONTESSA: Everything is gorgeous. Everything is pretty, it's all . . . it's all another world, you understand? It's not like here. Here, here people see things differently, they always see things . . .

Then La Contessa tells me something that still haunts me: "There, although you may go hungry, you are always in beauty."

Benedict Anderson wonders how people die for a flag; I wonder how people die for fashion and glamour. La Contessa says the cold kills a lot of girls in Europe. Cold beauty is much easier to tolerate than what you leave behind in Venezuela. I ask her about the scars on her arm, spidery beige welts long ago healed over:

> LA CONTESSA: The scars?
> OCHOA: Aha. What happened?
> LA CONTESSA: Here, these, that was, *ay mi amor*, long story.
> OCHOA: Yes.
> LA CONTESSA: It's a story that, the years I worked on the street, that . . . that was horrible.
> OCHOA: Here on Libertador?
> LA CONTESSA: Uuuuyyy. Here that was, before, that, they applied it to you.

I've heard this before — to apply something (*aplicar*); it's what they call it when the police use a specific method to punish you. Usually a very painful or humiliating method.

> LA CONTESSA: *Ay, mi amor.* That, these girls [on the Avenida Libertador] now are, ah . . . how would you say it? They're [treated like] queens. The years I lived through in the eighties were the most horrifying for me. Oh, how they would apply it to me.
>
> OCHOA: The police? Those were hard years.
>
> LA CONTESSA: From the eighties to the nineties, that was ten years that I, it was like I was paying for having done a crime. I don't know what crime I was paying for that. . . . My love, they [the police] came up to me, they gave me beatings, left me broken from head to toe, every day. *Every day* I came home with my head broken, my legs broken, my face fractured, without . . . totally destroyed. Every single day! They would hit me, and they would do this or that and I would have to cut myself — so they would let me go.
>
> OCHOA: You would cut yourself to get out of custody?
>
> LA CONTESSA: All the girls in that time cut themselves. I also cut myself.

This is not the first time I've heard of this way of getting out of custody. La Contessa talks about the beatings she suffered, the hunger. She changes the subject, in a sense. She remembers suddenly about another cut, one that changed her forever into someone who can't put up with that level of violence anymore: her sex-change operation.

> LA CONTESSA: Those were some times. . . . Now I have nothing else to cut, because I cut the primary. . . . But in those times I was happy because then I could go with a man and vent my frustrations [*desahogarme*]. And everything would pass, all the anger and all those things, do you understand? The struggle, all that. Now I can't.
>
> OCHOA: No?
>
> LA CONTESSA: Now I have no way to vent. How can I? When you get your sex change you . . . well, you're not the same as before.
>
> OCHOA: You can't orgasm?
>
> LA CONTESSA: It's not that you can't; it's just that before I would

go with a man and vent my frustrations, "*Ay*," I would say, "I'm with a man, now everything has passed, now all the anger will go away, everything the police have done to me, now it doesn't." None of that. That's why the operated girls don't come back to Venezuela. The postop girls stay in Europe for the rest of their lives. A postop girl is already European. She doesn't want to, she *can't* live here. Because she would go crazy. Understand?

Colony versus metropole and center versus periphery don't even begin to hint at the complexity of La Contessa's imaginary and actual transits, at her way of making her life through glamour, sex work, and travel. As she is narrating the impossibility of being a postop transsexual in Venezuela, she is also living that impossibility. This is the root of La Contessa's cosmopolitanism, her flight from daily, terrible violence and hunger to a cold world of possibility. One that will never accept her, of course. One that has deported her. And as impossible as it is to stay, La Contessa has few options at this point. She is still in Caracas every time I go back to visit, still planning her return.

Creole Self-Fashioning

But the nation of Venezuela, the Bolivarian Republic of Venezuela, is not an out-of-the-way place. While parts of Venezuela certainly could be seen this way now, and the region has been seen as peripheral, marginal, or out of the way in various iterations of global economy throughout the history of colonization, Venezuela as a nation has fashioned itself since the early nineteenth century as a *criollo* landscape, very much engaged in transnational circuits of ideas, goods, and people. Pratt (2002, 169) describes the project of "Creole self-fashioning" in her book *Imperial Eyes*, and refers to a number Latin American intellectuals of the time, but she notably begins with Andres Bello, a founding statesman of the Venezuelan nation. Bello's *Repertorio Americano* magazine was published in Europe but circulated among the Euro-American, or Creole, elite residing in Europe and the Americas. The magazine became a place for these revolutionaries to develop their imaginary of landscape, economy, political philosophy, and nation for the postindependence era.

On first glance, it might seem that Creole aspirations for *liberté, egalité, fraternité* (liberty, equality, fraternity) are a simple imitation of French social thought and political action (as well as political aesthetics) on American soil, but Pratt warns us against this way of seeing things: "One would seriously misinterpret creole relations to the European metropolis (even in their neocolonial dimensions) if one thought of creole aesthetics as simply imitating or mechanically reproducing European discourses" (1992, 187–88). Pratt suggests, rather, that another process is going on, one of "transculturation," a process described by the Cuban anthropologist Fernando Ortíz (1995) in his ethnography of the Cuban sugar and tobacco industries originally published in 1940. As Alicia Ríos summarizes, transculturation is Ortíz's answer to the dominant anthropological concept of "acculturation" to describe the cultural process by which non-Western people adopt Western ways of living. Ríos explains: "Acculturation implies a one-way process in which the 'barbarian' is always being 'civilized,' while the new term, transculturation, demonstrates the manner in which coexisting cultures and cultures in conflict simultaneously both gain and lose through contact" (Ríos 2004, 24).

Ortíz's concept of transculturation understands the process of culture change as being embedded in economic and historical processes, but at the same time as being uniquely marked by existing cultural logics and practices. Ortíz describes the transculturation of sugar and tobacco in different contexts. This accounts for differential forms of adoption, as well as the similarities that might emerge within these processes. Pratt's use of *transculturation* is also resonant with Angel Rama's reformulation of the concept (1996, 13), which acknowledges more centrally the mutually constitutive transformations that result. As Pratt recognizes that Creole elites do not reflect the interests of the large majority of Latin Americans, she also defends a more complex analysis of Creole elite positionality with respect to European ideas of the time: "One can more accurately think of Creole representations as *transculturating* European materials, selecting and deploying them in ways that do not simply reproduce the hegemonic visions of Europe or simply legitimate the designs of European capital" (Pratt 1992, 188; emphasis in original).

Creole elites, according to Pratt, "projected moral and civic dramas onto the landscape" in order to legitimate their mediating role between colonial powers and the greater populace, and, of course, to maintain their hold over Latin American property and labor (1992, 188). This positionality provides a two-headed kind of consumption for Creole elites: the ability to consume European culture and customs abroad while consuming indigenous, Black, and mestizo labor and land at home. Indeed, it is precisely this kind of actual and imagined cosmopolitanism that marks a Venezuelan relationship to European aesthetics, and to the production of power at home. The specter of pollution returns as well in the binary formulation of cultural contamination and corruption proposed by acculturation theory. Transculturation proposes an interesting set of possibilities, though Pratt's description of how Creole elites employ the term rests on a kind of conscious consumption and deployment of European value. The possibility also exists that consumption itself—conscious or not—might corrupt or pollute that which it consumes, and thus transform it. Further, in addition to the Creole elite, all manner of colonial subjects might (gleefully, perhaps?) participate in this kind of corruption.

To understand the logic of domination in Venezuela, we have to develop ways of thinking about power that account for its perversions, distortions, and, most important, the places from which such power can be interrupted or transformed.[13] My approach to the questions of beauty and fashion in the production of nation suggests that these contemporary phenomena are rooted in what the Spanish Colombian communications theorist Jesús Martín-Barbero calls a "long process of enculturation" (1993, 88). While it may at first be confusing to think of what beauty pageant contestants and *transformistas* in Venezuela have to do with Simón Bolívar in Napoleon drag (figure 2.3), I seek continuities across these figures.[14] In the end, this is not a story of liberation from colonialist norms. It is a way to understand the intimate negotiations of modernity, center, and periphery that take place on the bodies of Venezuelans. The example of Susana Duijm, who was crowned Miss World in 1955 and ushered in the era of Venezuelan prominence in the international beauty pageant, gives a good sense of how Venezuelans have capitalized on these cultural logics to make names for themselves.

The Brief European Tour of Carmen la Sauvage

Venezuela in 1955 was a country in the midst of dictatorship. Marcos Pérez Jiménez had ascended to power four years after a military coup had deposed Rómulo Gallegos and the democratic coalition that had formed out of the *generación del 28* (generation of 1928) student movement against the other great dictator of the twentieth century in Venezuela, Juan Vicente Gómez. Pérez Jiménez leveraged his power by providing "modernity,"

FIGURE 2.3 · Equestrian portrait of Simón Bolívar by José Hilarión Ibarra, ca. 1826. Source: Wikimedia Commons.

most notably in the form of public works, to the citizenry of Venezuela. As Coronil argues, the Venezuelan state in the twentieth century had to magically produce ("prestidigitate") modernity to legitimate its power (1997, 68). The development of beauty as a form of international presence in Venezuela traces its roots to this moment in history, when the Venezuelan public had little autonomy in overtly political sites. The "apolitical" world of the *misses* becomes one place where feminine glamour decenters masculine authoritarianism. This drama played itself out in the coronation of Carmen Susana Duijm Zubillaga as Miss Venezuela in 1955.

Duijm is the prototypical exotic Venezuelan beauty queen. The reputation of Venezuelan beauty queens on the global stage begins with her. A tall, dark-haired, unpretentious, and unrepentant criolla, Duijm still carries herself with an easy confidence. The use of the word *criolla*, which is often used to signify belonging in the white ruling class, is complex in the context of Venezuelan national identity. While I am not arguing that the term is not racialized (it is rooted in the distinction between European-descended landowners who were born in the Americas and Spaniards), it is also taken to signify Venezuelan nationality (not coincidentally figured as descended from the *criollo* elite), and thus can be applied to people of any race or racial mixture who are considered part of the Venezuelan nation.[15] Here *criollo* produces African and indigenous Others who are outside the imagined community of the nation, subsumed, to the extent that they can be masked through cultural performance, in the catch-all category of "criollo." Duijm is figured as a *criolla* in her unapologetic taste for Venezuelan aesthetics, customs, and foods. The construction of her *criollismo* becomes clear in her public demeanor toward all things European, as we shall see in her brief tour of London and Paris following her coronation as Miss World.

According to popular accounts, at nineteen, Duijm was approached by a contest organizer who saw her on a Caracas sidewalk on the way to her job as an office worker. This organizer reportedly begged her to enter the contest. In keeping with what appears to be a pattern in narratives of Venezuelan beauty queens, Duijm did not enter the pageant initially; rather she was "discovered" while waiting for a bus on a Caracas sidewalk, and the pageant organizer convinced her to enter at the last minute. The story of Duijm's appearance in the pageant, her surreptitious entry and triumph, is based on the idea that her beauty is *unrefined*, that it is natural, not labored. And this is an interesting element of the narrative of beauty in Venezuela—beauty is at the same time natural, intrinsic, *and* laborious, artificial. The labor of beauty is glossed over in the story about why Venezuelan beauty queens are so successful, but indeed it is an important factor: they work very hard at it. Osmel Sousa, the president of the Organización Miss Venezuela himself asserts this, explaining the success of Miss Venezuela on the global stage to the curator of a 2000 exhibition about the *misses*, titled *90-60-90*: "Because Miss Venezuela goes very well prepared, she knows what she has to do in every situation. All of the details are taken care of, the aesthetic part as well as her manners and behavior, the clothes she'll wear on every occasion. . . . In the field of beauty pageants, the Venezuelan *misses* are the most professional, well to be Miss Venezuela *is* a profession" (Museo Jacobo Borges 2000, 15; my translation).

In many ways, the story of beauty in Venezuela is like the story of petroleum—by geographic coincidence, it appears in the land that Venezuela occupies, a gift given to Venezuela. But beauty must be refined, and the process by which it is refined and exported is hidden from view. What is important is what it does for Venezuela in the end. Beauty's origins are magical; its production is mystified; its presence (once processed and ready for export) is celebrated. Given this parallel, it makes complete sense that Venezuelan oil tankers were named, among other things, after Venezuelan world beauty titleholders, such as Duijm.[16]

While Duijm by no means represented the large majority of Venezuelans who are poor or working class, she nevertheless hailed from the middle class. She was an office girl in a contest for debutantes. Duijm, representing the state of Miranda, made it to the finals alongside the representative of Bolívar state and Mireya Casas Robles, who represented Caracas (and therefore the elite). Wolfgang Larrazábal, but three years away from his coup d'état and short-lived presidency of Venezuela, rose up as one of the judges and is reported to have proclaimed: "As the only military officer on the jury, I decide that the winner is Mireya Casas Robles." Another jurist, Carola Reverón, also stood and countered: "As the only woman on the jury, I propose that we let the public decide by applause." The public, apparently, preferred the more *morena* (brunette) Duijm. Montaldo Pérez, who documented this account in his newspaper insert series *Un Siglo de Misses* (1999), reported that Duijm was called *india, negra, fea* (ugly), and *pata en el suelo* (barefoot).[17] Let us remember, however, that this "public" was the very elite public in attendance at the Hotel Tamanaco for the

Miss Venezuela contest—the conflict over the pageant would be decided against the elite candidate by a public of elites themselves.

Duijm's tenure as Miss Venezuela began with a trip to Long Beach, California, for the Miss Universe pageant, where she made the semifinals. There she was approached by British telecommunications magnate Eric Morley. Morley had recently founded the Miss World competition in response to what might be identified as a more commercial tendency in the Catalina Swimwear Company's sponsorship of the Miss Universe pageant. Duijm was crowned Miss World that October, and she was celebrated in London, Paris, and Caracas. She was featured on the cover of *Paris Match*—the only Venezuelan to ever appear there (see figure 2.4).

Duijm embodied the contradiction between *criollo* and European value systems. Highly prized for her beauty, she enchanted Europeans but reportedly disparaged their customs, their attention, and their food. She modeled in Paris for a short time after winning the Miss World title, was nicknamed "Carmen la Sauvage" (Carmen the Savage) by *Paris Match* for undoing a very expensive hairdo, and ten days later she returned to Caracas (see figure 2.5). Montaldo Pérez says that this was because she was fed up with the "refined world" of London and Paris, and she missed her *caraotas* (beans) and loved ones. London and Paris notwithstanding, she returned to a lifetime of adoration as a national icon and entertainment figure.

In her positioning as "savage" with respect to Europe and as a *criolla* incarnate, Duijm personifies a kind of Venezuelan relationship to modernity that criticizes European norms while at once embracing and embodying them. Duijm was able to capitalize on the European imaginary of South America to appear exotic and savage. At the same time, she was safe and recognizable enough to play well in Europe, and in Venezuela. She was "uncivilized" enough to ignore the value of fine coiffure, yet she was not so outside the logics and aesthetics of Western modernity that she was actually rendered unintelligible. The categories into which she was hailed at different times ("negra," "india," "fea") would have put her outside of the Venezuelan logic of beauty if she had actually embodied them—this is still the case in the beauty pageant industry. For however much Duijm was maligned in Venezuelan elite society or the press after her coronation, she is not *india, negra,* or *pata en el suelo,* but rather a consummate *criolla*. By skirting this line of inclusion and exclusion, Duijm found ways to leverage European fascination with the Other to garner recognition.

FIGURE 2.4 · Miss World of 1955 on the cover of *Paris Match*, November 5, 1955.

PREMIER SOUCI DE CARMEN LA SAUVAGE : CHOISIR SES ROBES DE REINE. ARRIVÉE A PARIS AU LENDEMAIN DE L'ÉLECTION ELLE A FAIT LE TOUR DE TOUS LES GRANDS COUTURIERS

UNE MISS MONDE PAS COMME LES AUTRES

VINGT ET UNE « miss » nationales briguaient à Londres, le 21 octobre, le titre de Miss Monde. Miss Venezuela fut élue (ci-dessus et notre couverture). Son nom : Carmen Sabillaga. Son âge : 19 ans. Hauteur : 1 m 74. Poids : 60 kilos. Poitrine : 86 cm.

Tour de taille : 54 cm. De hanches : 86 cm. Cheveux : bruns et longs. Signe particulier : sauvage. Son prix lui rapporte un million et demi tout de suite et des contrats au Venezuela où, toutes les fois qu'elle apparaîtra en public, elle gagnera 500.000 francs.

REPORTAGE FRANÇOIS PAGES

69

FIGURE 2.5 · "Une Miss Monde pas comme les autres: *Carmen la Sauvage*" (A Miss World Unlike the Others: Carmen the Savage"). Source: *Paris Match*.

So how do we, like Duijm, like La Contessa, like death, get from Paris or Milan to Caracas? What do Duijm and La Contessa tell us about the (queer) art of death? Unlike Bill T. Jones and Tupac Shakur as invoked by Sharon Holland, Duijm does not necessarily locate herself in the space of death. But as Carmen la Sauvage, she speaks back to Eurocentric norms and capitalizes on the excess signification produced by the colonial imaginary, working the fetishism of exotic bodies to her advantage. She embodies, if somewhat uncritically, the cannibalism called for by Oswald de Andrade in the *Cannibalist Manifesto*. La Contessa also consumes and leverages European aesthetics (and fetishism) to create possibilities for her life. So too do Venezuela and the Caracas Mortal crowd. They do this through what I call the *intimate technology of glamour*.[18]

Glamour

Yes, glamour as a way of reordering space and time—if temporarily—around one's self for the purposes of enchanting. Izaguirre has much to say on the subject in his memoir *Morir de glamour* (2000), flitting between a narration of the Eurocentric jet set in the twentieth century and his own negotiations of fabulousness in daily life. How else can the *sudaco* (a derogatory term for "South American" used in Spain; it is a racialized category of geographical corruption) son of a cinema archivist infiltrate Spanish society so thoroughly as to become a pop icon? Etymologically related to illusion or magic, glamour runs the risk of being revealed as empty. It is still, however, useful as a way to make space for one's self—to make an entrance as it were. It is glamour that is operating in the transportation of airplane runway to fashion runway as the flight attendant who started all this performs her safety routine. I became interested in glamour as a technology of intimacy in Venezuela after reading Izaguirre's memoir and observing the ways *transformistas* and participants and producers in the Miss Venezuela beauty pageant invoked glamour in everyday practice.

Stephen Gundle's (2008) cultural history of glamour understands the phenomenon to be one of modernity.[19] He connects glamour with consumption but sees it as a bourgeois, not aristocratic, phenomenon. His Habermasian approach dates the appearance of glamour to the emergence of the bourgeoisie in the late eighteenth century: "Glamour was about the way in which the most visually striking manifestations of aristocratic privilege were taken over and reinvented by newly emergent people, groups, and institutions" (19). Although Gundle does not recognize the cultural transformations that occurred in Europe as a result of the colonization of many distant parts of the world, these were of course important in the formation of a bourgeoisie that became accustomed to consuming goods and lore from faraway places.[20] Indeed, the colonial project was where the "second sons" of the aristocracy could make a name for themselves.[21] This process begins in the seventeenth century, and ultimately produces the Creole elite to which Pratt refers. I would propose that Gundle's model of the emergence of capitalism needs to be embedded in the rise of European colonialism and the creation of the colony-metropole relationship in order to fully account for these cultural shifts, as well as for the malleable character of glamour. While the term *glamour* itself was not in use during this time, the cultural foundations of what we now know as glamour were already in process.

Gundle does recognize that "distance is a necessary factor in the maintenance of glamour" (2008, 14). He is referring to the distance between performer and audience, which "serves to conceal or disguise the aspects of a person's being that are not glamorous." But in addition to the distance of staging, another kind of distance is necessary for glamour—that of distant rule: the distance created by having a locus of power outside one's own context. This is what I call *extralocal authority*. Rather than focusing on a cultural history of glamour in Venezuela, I believe it is important to consider glamour ethnographically, as a set of practices that can and do produce specific effects in the negotiation of power.

Glamour is a slippery, shiny thing, invoked in many ways, necessarily mystified and rarely theorized in a sustained way. Glamour, beauty, and femininity are technologies with specific practices that result in social legibility, intimate power, and, potentially, physical survival in a hostile environment. Thus, the production of glamour, beauty, and femininity functions within transnational economies of desire and consumption. Within these economies, glamour allows its practitioners to draw down extralocal authority, to conjure a contingent space of being and belonging. However, glamour is not redemptive; it will not save you—and here is where it becomes difficult to make a case for glamour as a politic. As a technology of intimacy, glamour can function to create space out of hegemonic discourse, but just as easily, this space can be crushed by the power of the state, patriarchy, normativity, or colonialism. Glamour is a form of power that serves *transformistas* and other women in Venezuela on a daily basis

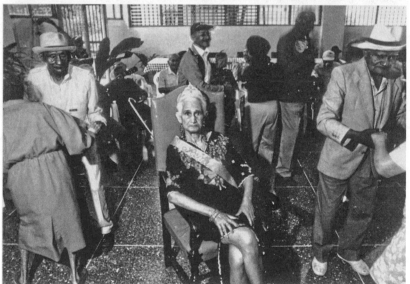

FIGURES 2.6–2.9 · (above and opposite) From the series Misses de Venezuela by Gilles Rigoulet. Exhibition catalogue for *90-60-90*, Museo Jacobo Borges, Caracas.

to provide legibility, affirmation, income, and other elements necessary for survival. Glamour is what makes someone into *la reina de la noche* (queen for a day).

In a series of photos titled *Misses de Venezuela*, published in the *90-60-90* exhibition catalog, Gilles Rigoulet, a photographer for Venezuela's Turner and Turner advertising agency, documents the presence of the *miss* in what appears to be all walks of daily life (see figures 2.6–2.9). From the Mini-Miss Venezuela contest where six-year-olds display perfect beauty queen poses with hands on hips and smiles strained for the judges (figure 2.6) to the octogenarian *miss* of the elder-care facility, regal on her throne and surveying her subjects as they dance (figure 2.7), these photographs hint at the power of the *miss* gaze and the complex set of negotiations surrounding these girls' and women's lives. The photographs were commissioned by the curators of the *90-60-90* exhibition in 2000 to demonstrate the depths to which the pageant permeates everyday life. The images also reveal the kinds of marginalities and variegated paths that beauty and glamour transit as Venezuelans make use of these technologies to make places for themselves in the world.

Another photo shows the light-skinned *miss* of the Venezuelan Navy in front of a tank, holding her tilting crown atop her peroxided locks and supporting herself on the shoulders of two very serious soldiers (figure 2.8). Her thick blue sash spells *Armada* in glittering gold letters. This *miss* is most like the *misses* of the national pageant, charming the camera with her smile and playing off the contrast of the darker-skinned soldiers who surround her, an island of shiny whiteness amid the olive drab. But the image that most strikes me is one with a different backdrop: a rambling *cerro* (shantytown), one of many that circle the Caracas Valley. In front of this cerro, the commanding presence and steady gaze of a young girl, somewhere in her early adolescence, holding a staff or perhaps a section of pipe in white lace gloves and her Sunday finest (figure 2.9). An electrical cable runs behind her head. This girl, the queen of her barrio, shows me the power that the *miss* has in Venezuela—the power to transport one, if only momentarily, from a *rancho* (improvised working-class and poor housing built without permits) to the throne. The girl seems to have no illusions about this moment: she has won her barrio's beauty pageant, and she is proud of where she's from and what she's accomplished. Though the camera fames her from the point of view of someone taller than she is, she returns its gaze calmly yet powerfully. She is not the kind of girl who would ever be crowned Miss Venezuela—she has darker skin and curly hair, and her clothing masks her body rather than revealing it. And yet here she is: queen for a day. I expand the metaphor of *queen for a day* to the nation of Venezuela itself, in its own negotiation of peripherality and power on the global stage.

As a figure that mediates marginality in Venezuela, the *miss* provides numerous possibilities for response in the negotiation of national, transnational, and local power. We have seen how different actors use glamour in Venezuela to negotiate a variegated and often deadly landscape of power, and how the nation of Venezuela has employed this technology to make a name for itself in the world through the beauty pageant. In the next part, we will move to another order of magnitude in this politics of scale: from the (trans)national to the runway and the street, a scenic level, on which femininity and women are staged to strategic ends. In the next chapter, we begin an examination of how staging the *miss* through pageantry produces specific forms of sexual subjectivity.

PART II. On the Runway, on the Street

La Reina de la Noche

PERFORMANCE, SEXUAL SUBJECTIVITY, AND THE
FORM OF THE BEAUTY PAGEANT IN VENEZUELA

La luciérnaga es un bicho que alumbra la noche por el culo.

The firefly is a bug that lights up the night with its ass.
—SANDY JURAXIS AND ARIKLER, 2004; my translation

Miss Venezuela *casting* and pageants since 1974 always begin with the
trademark Miss Venezuela hymn: "En una noche tan linda como ésta,
cualquiera de nosotras pudiera ganar" (On a beautiful night like this one,
any one of us could win). Contestants march out rank and file, in a pha-
lanx toward the stage, then spread out, poised in the classic beauty queen
pose: hands on hips, fingers splayed across waist, hips angled back, chest
out, shoulders back, legs one in front of the other in a *T* formation. "Ser
coronada Miss Venezuela! En una noche . . . tan linda . . . como ésta" (To
be crowned Miss Venezuela! On a beautiful night like this one.) Head up,
smile with teeth, hold, hold, hold . . . .

In pageant after pageant, *misses* parade before the judges in formation. From the darkness, judges drink scotch and sodas, write on note-
pads, and scrutinize the contestants as they pass by. Musical acts book-
end the different acts of the pageant: the introduction of the contestants,
the *traje típico* (regional or national costume), the bathing suit competition, the interviews, and the evening gowns. Finally, after much deliberation, there is the coronation. The form of the beauty pageant, that is,
the structure of the proceedings and types of presentation, is imminently
recognizable. Though the form may be adapted to local conventions or in-

terpreted differently, it remains recognizable as a beauty pageant: beauty pageants have a certain order; how much you know about it depends on how close you are to the production of the pageant or how much it matters to you. And when the event culminates in the coronation, the contestant becomes "queen for a day" (*la reina de la noche*). The beauty pageant as a cultural form in Venezuela, as in many other places, provides a platform from which contestants, producers, and audience members can project ideas about who they are to a broader (sometimes imagined) public. This is the *scenic* order of magnitude to which I refer in my articulation of the politics of scale of beauty in Venezuela; the creation of platforms, stages, runways, and other sites from which Venezuelans can project glamour and beauty onto real or imagined audiences. But more than the stage is important here; the *making* of queens for the stage is a process of producing sexual subjectivity, as much for the contestants as for the stylists who work most closely with the contestants. Through this process, feminine spectacle centers itself in the magic of glamour, opening a contingent space of projection and possibility that allows its bearers to be queen for a day.

What does it take to become a *miss*? This chapter looks at the beauty pageant as a site for the mediation of gendered performance through a set of ritual forms that project local actors onto a global stage. We will look at three moments in the production of different subnational pageants in Venezuela to think about how the form of the beauty pageant creates possibilities for its participants, and how it serves as a site of contestation and deliberation about aesthetics, authority, and, ultimately, power. We will visit two quite different beauty pageants, both held in an out-of-the-way region of Venezuela, the coastal area of eastern Venezuela popularly called Oriente. One is a pageant created and staged by gay men (*maricos*) and *transformistas* during carnival in the town of Carúpano.[1] The other is a *casting* for the Organización Miss Venezuela (OMV) held in the region, which I will call Miss Oriente (Miss East).[2]

By examining the beauty pageant as a ritual form, an approach proposed by the authors of the first book to take beauty pageants "seriously" in anthropology, *Beauty Queens on the Global Stage* (Cohen, Wilk, and Stoeltje 1996), I will extend the consideration of the beauty pageant, glamour, and center-periphery relations begun in chapter 2. While the previous part addressed the role of the pageant in place-making and (trans)national processes, this chapter focuses on local and out-of-the-way manifestations of social relations in the two pageants I describe. I provide some context for these out-of-the-way beauty pageants, show what it takes to make a *miss*, and describe how the pageant comes to mean something to its participants and audience.

In looking at these two distinct pageants, both held in a region of Venezuela that has historically been a challenge to the consolidation of the nation, I consider not only the role of the pageant form in the production of sexual subjectivity but also what I am calling *beauty pageant democracy*—that is, the way the beauty pageant becomes a site for the performance and contestation of the politics of representativity. It is a place where we reveal our cultural expectations about deliberative processes. The pageant has also become a way that Venezuelans from many different walks of life negotiate and respond to processes that at the very least make places such as Oriente appear peripheral and also often manifest very real forms of structural and physical violence.

Beverly Stoeltje proposes an approach to the beauty pageant as a "modern secular ritual event," in which she traces three elements that frame specific manifestations of the beauty pageant: "The *evolution of the 'form'* runs through time, incorporating influences of specific sociopolitical contexts; the *'discourse'* includes the language of the performance itself, but also that of any texts concerning it, including those used by the media, and especially the oral traditions which circulate informally; the *'organization of production'* refers to the organization of forces and energies necessary to materially produce the event, including the decisions concerning the rules, the form, access to the performance and the selection process for determining the outcome" (Stoeltje 1996, 16; my emphases).

While chapters 1 and 2 discuss the evolution of the form and the broader discursive environment in which the pageant operates, this chapter focuses on discourse within pageants as they are being staged, and on the *production* of beauty pageants in Venezuela. I start in Carúpano, at a carnival beauty pageant featuring *maricos* and *transformistas* called La Noche de las Luciérnagas (Night of the Fireflies). After presenting the context for the La Noche de las Luciérnagas pageants I observed, I discuss an eruption in beauty pageant democracy and its ensuing drama. Then I will move to another pageant in the region, one that was held as part of a national casting call for contestants in the national beauty pageant. The *casting* of Miss Oriente gives us more examples of beauty pageant democracy and shows the kinds of sexual subjectivities produced through the making of a *miss* and the staging of beauty pageants. So to Carúpano it is.

La Noche de las Luciérnagas

Carnaval in 2003 was a somber occasion. The Opposition general strike that began in November 2002 had led to a sharp decrease in tourism throughout the country, and no one was in the mood to celebrate.[3] By February 2003, the strike was petering out, the Chávez administration was denying it had ever happened, and the Opposition leadership would not acknowledge that the strike had not attained its goal of forcing Chávez out of power. But the informal economy, and much of the formal economy, was returning to business as usual, and *transformistas* worked steadily on Avenida Libertador during this time.

Tourism, however, was the last thing on the agenda of most Venezuelans, as evidenced by nearly empty long-distance buses and deserted resort areas. Undaunted, I asked several *transformistas* I had met on Avenida Libertador where they went for Carnaval. Very few were planning trips out of Caracas, but many said the best place for *transformistas* during carnival was Carúpano, a town on the eastern Caribbean coast of Venezuela in the state of Sucre. Oriente is a part of Venezuela that appreciates *transformistas*, they told me. The girls mentioned a big beauty pageant that was held every year, the contestants all *maricos* or *transformistas*. The queen of *La Noche de las Luciérnagas* was celebrated, they told me, paraded through the town of Carúpano throughout the Carnaval festivities. The audience, they told me, was huge, and, oddly, *straight*. This was not a pageant for *maricos* and *transformistas* alone. Apparently, Carúpano has a lot of love for *mariqueras* (queening) during carnival. As they say, "sin *marico* no hay carnaval" (without a *marico*, it's not carnival).

Carúpano was assigned the distinction of having a *carnaval internacional* designation, that is, a Carnaval worthy of international tourism, in 1966.[4] A bustling seashore town, Carúpano boasts much more than its legacy as a folkloric tourist destination. A few miles outside the city limits is the site where Columbus first set foot on the South American continent. Carúpano was a major port of the colony of Tierra Firme that trafficked cacao and coffee. There, in 1816, Simón Bolívar declared the end of slavery in what would later become Venezuela (García Díaz 1996). In the waning years of the nineteenth century, Carúpano became the site where the first transatlantic cable connected South America with Marseilles, France. The presence of the telegraph at the beginning of the twentieth century turned Carúpano into a bit of a metropolis at the time, as it became a beach destination for elites from Caracas who could reach Carúpano by steamboat from the capital city. Carúpano is now known for its natural gas, fishing, and cement industries. The historian and journalist Luis García Díaz summarizes the history of Carúpano in the following way: "This twentieth century has been one of boom and downfall for Carúpano, one of prosperity and poverty, illumination and darkness. History now presents us with a town frustrated in its development, with a significant lack of progress [on the part of the nation] in terms of public services and education, and with governors and mayors with no sense of progress or pride. A town that after living shining years has until now been sunken in poverty, unemployment and grave failures in health, education and other social factors" (1996, 78; my translation).

Carúpano, in many ways, is close to what Anna Tsing has called an "out-of-the-way place" (Tsing 1993). While it is not as out of the way as the Meratus highlands (or even the Orinoco Delta just a few hours east — see Briggs and Mantini-Briggs [2003]), this small city on the Peninsula de Paria has made itself a "place" in *criollo* (Creole) consciousness by brokering an exchange: the natural resources of an export economy in return for news, communication, and goods from Europe.[5] Carúpano vacillated between center and periphery throughout its modern history, and its status seems to ebb and flow with the Atlantic currents.[6] There have been several attempts to promote tourism as a way to generate economic activity throughout the twentieth century. Now it seems halfhearted. While a tourism industry does exist in the city, planning and infrastructure do not support it — during a normal Carnaval the city is overrun with tourists and it is nearly impossible to find a place to stay. Plastic bags and other garbage sit on curbsides and whip in the ocean breezes. Hotel pricing is speculative during this time, and accommodations range from tiny rooms in *pensiones* (guest houses) to aging hotels reminiscent of the oil boom of the 1970s and 1980s. One development dwarfs them all — an early 1990s luxury hotel that stands nearly empty most of the year, testimony to the more recent attempts to rejuvenate a tourism economy.

On the advice of my *transformista* informants, my research assistant Gaston Torres Marquez and I boarded a half-empty bus blasting with air-conditioning. We left Caracas in the middle of the night. Teeth chattering, we awoke to sunrise over the fish market in Carúpano, where women fry *empanadas de cazón* for travelers. I had no idea what we would find, or if this legendary pageant even existed. Gaston and I spent the rest of the day trying to find a trace of the pageant. The elections for Carnaval Queen for girls were going on, I was told. But this was not the pageant we were look-ing for. As we passed a liquor store, I spotted a colorful poster advertising a big show at the Centro Italo-Venezolano, a private club on the outskirts of town.[7] "Luciérnagas: Noche de Estrellas," it read. From the poster we tracked down the organizer, known as "El Pulgoso," who generously al-lowed us to observe the preparations and attend the pageant.

LUCIÉRNAGAS BEGAN IN THE late 1980s as the house party of a well-known and respected gay man who lived in Carúpano. As the party outgrew the house, it spilled out onto the street. Eventually the founder, Carlos Vera, had to block off the street and take out permits for the event. At first, as I was told by both the current organizer and the emcee of the event, Vera would present what he saw as the best costumes at the party, where invari-ably some men would parade in women's clothing. This presentation, over the years, became a more formal competition. Eventually it took the form of a beauty pageant, modeled after the popular national beauty pageant. This is not surprising; Venezuelan gay men often appropriate the Miss Venezuela pageant into their signifying practice, taking on the names of current and past beauty queens or running pageants of their own. What is surprising about the Luciérnagas pageant is that the audience is not other gay men—the event caters to a predominantly heterosexual crowd that gathers in Carúpano for Carnaval.

Sandy Juraxis, a resident of Carúpano, hairdresser, and lifetime queen (*reina vitalicia*) of Luciérnagas, got her name because she has been around for so long. *Juraxis* comes from the movie *Jurassic Park*; she's considered a dinosaur in Carúpano, having been crowned in 1989. When I interviewed her in 2004, she looked to be in her late fifties—I didn't dare ask her age, which would have been incredibly rude. She has since passed away, and I am very grateful for the time she spent with me one afternoon after the pageant. We sat in her hair salon, Peluquería Sandra, on a sleepy street near the Plaza de Colón a few days after the pageant (see figure 3.1). She cut hair as we talked, and she entertained a few relatives who had come to visit from Caracas for the Carnaval celebration. Her small dog, a beloved Yorkie mix, circled around our ankles in the weary afternoon. Sandy was in her slippers, peroxided hair pinned into rollers. As she buzzed the hair of one of her regulars, a middle-aged man, she explained why the pageant is called Noche de las Luciérnagas:

FIGURE 3.1 ·
Glamour in an out-
of-the-way place.
Peluquería Sandra,
Carúpano, Vene-
zuela. Photo by
the author, 2004.

SANDY: Well the luciérnaga is, let me tell you, it's a bird. And since
   they say that one is a "bird . . ." Because *maricos* are . . .
OCHOA: A bird?
SANDY: Yes! That's a bird, it's a bir—. . . a, like an, an insect. That
   shines. Haven't you seen those, those little bugs at night that
   shine like this? Well, those are the fireflies.
OCHOA: And why is it used to talk about this pageant? What does
   that mean?
SANDY: *Marica* . . .

Her customer steps in to help out. Sandy is constantly exasperated by my
questions:

CUSTOMER: Excuse me for interrupting.
SANDY: No, no, go ahead.

CUSTOMER: As I understand it, it must be that the firefly is an insect that shines with its . . . how should I say it? Vulgarly, its ass.

OCHOA: Ah.

CUSTOMER: So I imagine that if they call it Night of the Fireflies, it's because they [here he uses the feminine form, *ellas*] are going to . . .

SANDY: Shine!

CUSTOMER: To light up the world with their butts, get it? Right? That's how I understand it.

The luciérnaga (firefly) is like a *marico* in that it comes out at night and lights up the world with its ass. From house party to block party to regional event, Luciérnagas began to increase in scale, and as its scale and reach grew, it became formalized as a beauty pageant. In early 2003 Vera was murdered at his home, in what is widely regarded by members of this community to be a homophobic hate crime. This left El Pulgoso, Vera's heterosexual business partner, with the rights to put on the Luciérnagas pageant. This resulted in a lot of drama the years that I observed the pageant, but it also made very clear to me the stakes of producing glamour in an out-of-the-way place.

Rather than appealing to authenticity or tradition for authority, as the Carnaval celebration has done in the past, the gathering begun at Carlos Vera's house gradually grew to produce a spectacle that required another kind of authority. It took on the form of a beauty pageant as a domain that *maricos* were highly proficient in and familiar with, while at the same time producing legibility on a national level (since local legibility and recognition was not forthcoming) for these activities. This is how I came to hear of the pageant in Caracas. A local historian I interviewed was insistent on the point that Luciérnagas was not part of the authentic Carnaval in Carúpano, that it represented the influence of outside commercial interests on this tradition.[8] What is true is that Luciérnagas produced an important kind of visibility for gay *carupaneros* (residents of Carúpano) while mobilizing a discourse of the metropole in an out-of-the-way place—by invoking extralocal authority in a hostile environment that ultimately cost Carlos Vera and Sandy Juraxis their lives.

The beauty pageant works as a form of glamour, creating a platform on which many kinds of Venezuelan women (including ciswomen and *trans-*

formistas) and gay men can produce momentary authority. The beauty pageant form is what makes this kind of power possible.

The Beauty Pageant Form

Beauty Queens on the Global Stage brings together ethnographic analyses of beauty contests from many different contexts. Stoeltje argues that these contests take on specific forms that mediate: "Beauty contests qualify unambiguously as local forms that also exist in a hierarchy linking the local to the global. A popular institution where power installs itself and produces real effects, the beauty contest is, however, embedded in a discourse that declares it frivolous or 'simply' entertainment, thereby masking relations of power" (1996, 18–19). The form of the beauty contest can be appropriated to produce local meaning while it maintains its ties to extralocal events and authority, as we saw in the postcard beauty contests to elect Señorita Venezuela in chapter 1. Stoeltje argues that as a global phenomenon, beauty contests depend on their legibility within a hierarchy of representation that privileges the global over the local, but requires mechanisms for local implementation. The beauty contest, however, does not work in the same way as other globalizing processes to structure local implementation — it depends on the collective participation and signification of local actors for its production. Unlike setting up a distribution channel for Coca-Cola or siting a McDonald's, which are decisions that can be made by a few powerful actors, the production of a beauty contest relies on multiple actors with differential positions of power in the process, as well as an audience. This production also relies on convention: the beauty contest is a story that unfolds over the course of the contest and through its medium, which must be legible to its participants and spectators, but which also must conform to the representational conventions set out by participants' previous experiences with this form. The form of the beauty *pageant* (one kind of beauty contest) has allowed it to proliferate on a global scale. A beauty pageant is a staged event that requires an audience, and, throughout the twentieth century, televisual mass distribution at its highest levels. Local beauty pageants rely on the conventions of mass-mediated pageants at the national or "world" levels, yet there is room within the reproduction of this form for local variation and appropriation.

The Luciérnagas pageant is based on the template of the Miss Venezuela and Miss Universe pageants but is also adapted to Carnaval conventions. Usually this involves an opening act in which contestants parade before the audience and judges and perform a choreographed dance; the presentation of contestants one by one to the audience and judges;[9] various musical and dance acts that provide transitions for costume changes; a showcase of local talent, such as musicians, lip synch artists, or comedians; and an emcee (*locutor*) who provides an overall narrative for the show. Also included are ethnic or national-costume and bathing suit competitions, which also require contestants to parade before the judges and audience. In Luciérnagas, the national-costume competition takes the form of a parade in colorful feathered Carnaval regalia (*fantasía*). Carnival-regalia designers and performers from around Venezuela and Carúpano provide one of the transitional acts. Previous titleholders and local celebrities, such as beauty and Carnaval queens will also be invited to the stage and honored, sometimes performing transitional acts. The judges pare down the contestants into a semifinal, usually half of the original number of contestants, and the show ends with the coronation of the *cuadro final* (the runners-up) and the coronation of the Reina de Luciérnagas (Queen of the Fireflies). She is subsequently paraded through the streets of Carúpano in a Carnaval "float," often consisting of the organizer's aging Jeep decorated with ribbons, signs, and crepe-paper flowers (see figure 3.2).

The Luciérnagas pageant draws *maricos* and *transformistas* from all over Venezuela. Participants travel to the pageant, often in groups, and stay at local houses, *pensiones*, or hotels, where the group works on preparing the contestants for the pageant. In groups work is divided by specialty: hair, makeup, costume, and choreography and runway walk. Often there are extended groups of friends who travel with the contestant and provide advice or running commentary. Rehearsal time is very short—the pageant is held on a Saturday night, and often participants arrive on Friday or as late as Saturday morning. During the two times I observed the pageant, rehearsals were held on Friday afternoon, Saturday morning, and Saturday afternoon. Contestants (and sometimes even show choreographers!) don't know what the routines will be until they arrive at rehearsals.

The show runs between four and six hours, and often doesn't start until well into the night, lasting into the early morning of the following day. For the two days of Carnaval celebrations following the pageant, the Reina de Luciérnagas is paraded around town on the back of the organizer's pickup truck, or some other suitable vehicle, following contingent after contingent of revelers dancing behind enormous sound systems. The Reina de

FIGURE 3.2 · La Noche de Las Luciérnagas. Photo by the author, 2004.

Luciérnagas returns the following year to crown the new reina, and during her tenure she can make guest appearances at gay-oriented beauty
pageants and clubs in the surrounding area and in different cities around
Venezuela. The Luciérnagas pageant is also televised on the local television
station, TúTV, although the station has no role in the production of the
show.

The Luciérnagas pageant follows the national and transnational pageants in many respects: the presentation of contestants, the conventions
of dress in the different segments of the competition, the presentation of
musical and dance acts, and the production of spectacle. Unlike "straight"
pageants, Luciérnagas has a parallel structure to the local-global hierarchy
of the national pageant. Luciérnagas does not provide any path to national
or international recognition for its producers and contestants, and in general the pageant does not advance their careers or possibilities for social
mobility.[10] While the social location of Luciérnagas (and other gay beauty
pageants) differs significantly from that of the "straight" pageants, the
form of the Luciérnagas pageant is very close to the hegemonic form, including the use of television broadcast.

As the history of beauty contests in Venezuela illustrates, the pageant is not the only form of beauty contest — early contests in Venezuela involved print media and did not take the form of events with a copresent audience of spectators or live broadcast. The beauty *pageant* in Venezuela has, importantly, taken the form of a mass-mediated live broadcast, following the convention of the international pageants, particularly Miss Universe.[11] The *pageant* form, according to Stoeltje, facilitates the connection between local systems of value and hegemonic ideals: "Beauty pageants serve to legitimize the perspective of the status quo with regard to the immaterial powers of young females, publicly identifying them as signs of social and civic institutions, including the family and the business, the community and the nation. The ritual contest in which young women compete against each other for the title of queen serves to link the individual contestants to the sponsoring institution as a representative of it, creating both an ideal standard by which to judge women and defining women's role as a sign of an institution to which she is responsible" (Stoeltje 1996, 14–15). As a ritual, the pageant produces institutional position, reinforces hegemonic values, creates women as symbolic representatives of an institution, and brokers relations of power. For Stoeltje and her coauthors, the beauty contest legitimates group values: "As universal and diverse as beauty contests are and as varied as their cultural and historical contexts tend to be, what they *do* is remarkably similar. . . . These contests showcase values, concepts, and behavior that exist at the center of a group's sense of itself and exhibit values of morality, gender and place" (Cohen, Wilk, and Stoeltje 1996, 2).

Stoeltje's model may explain the participation of young women and hegemonic social actors in the ritual event, but it fails to explain the social function of nonhegemonic pageants such as Luciérnagas. What are the implications to an understanding of the "modern secular ritual" if we consider actors who simultaneously subvert and reinscribe the hegemonic meaning of the event? What institutional positions, icons, and power are the participants of Luciérnagas producing for themselves and their audience? Stoeltje's model inscribes "legitimizing the perspective of the status quo" as the primary function of the beauty pageant ritual. In the case of Luciérnagas, it is hard to say exactly what the status quo is. Certainly hegemonic notions of femininity prevail, but these are not inscribed on the bodies of people sexed female at birth. As such, the participants subvert expectations of gender and gendered performance. Often participants are ridiculed when they fail to accomplish femininity. It could be argued that ridiculing people sexed male at birth when they fail to accomplish femininity reinscribes hegemonic notions of femininity, but this would not account for the social legibility and (marginal) legitimacy conferred on successful participants. Certainly participants in the Luciérnagas pageant do not gain social legitimacy through their involvement. They do not, as Stoeltje describes of the Miss Snake Charmer Queens of Sweetwater, Texas, become more employable or marriageable, and they do not become symbols of the sponsors of the pageant (who don't sponsor individual contestants but rather the event) or of the institution of femininity. So what, socially, do Luciérnagas contestants gain from their participation in the pageant? If we consider the function of the beauty contest as a secular ritual that produces social legitimation, these benefits might include recognition of participants' ability to accomplish femininity, or actual social legibility as women (for those contestants who are *transformistas*), or even the social legitimacy of being the winner of the pageant and parading through Carnaval.

However, if we consider that there may be other functions to the beauty pageant form besides social legitimation and institutionalization, these may explain the participation of so-called illegitimate social actors such as *maricos* and *transformistas*, who may or may not be seeking legitimation (let us not presume that people who are delegitimized in the distribution of power always seek to be legitimated). Luciérnagas contestants I interviewed in Carúpano and Caracas reported that the event was an important way for them to *project themselves out onto an audience*, to show the world how beautiful or fabulous they are. This formulation stems from an *internal* sense of legitimacy that then requires the cultivation of a public composed not of the discrete audience of Luciérnagas, but of the circulation of people in different queer-friendly spaces around Venezuela. At the same time, this publicity is also an integral part of *femininity* (see chapter 6 for an elaboration of the idea of spectacular femininity). But beyond gendered subjectivities, the pageant also produces *modernity*: La Noche de las Luciérnagas is not only concerned with harnessing the feminine; it is also concerned with the production of multiple modern subjects and social legibility. In this expanded argument, the pageant works to allow *maricos* and *transformistas* to broker a global, mass-mediated form of modernity and produce prestige, (temporary) local authority, and legibility, which may or may not produce legitimacy.

This authority is highly contingent, however, and is in constant negotiation during the pageant. The Luciérnagas pageant of 2004 in particular became a site for the deliberation and contestation of ideas about democratic representation, fairness, and justice. The drama that emerged revealed a deep contestation between the producer of the event and the *maricos* and *transformistas* who participated in its staging.

Beauty Pageant Democracy:
A *Zaperoco* in the Luciérnagas Beauty Pageant

Scandal is an important part of the beauty pageant form. Almost without exception, some kind of scandal erupted either backstage or during the staged proceedings of every pageant I attended in Venezuela. Often this kind of scandal is called a *zaperoco*, a falling out of order. Though actors in these scandals—whether they are contestants, producers, performers, audience members, families, or even people who hear about it the next day—often appear surprised, actually *shocked*, at the eruption of scandal, the predictability of scandal at beauty pageants suggests that these are not random eruptions. Scandal manifests in different ways, but in the pageants I observed in Oriente, scandals revealed the workings of decision-making processes and the expectations that actors had of these deliberations. Most often, there was a running commentary about the fairness of the election of the queen—either that the crown was bought and paid for or that the deliberative process (judges, coronation) had been tainted.

At Luciérnagas in 2004, the *zaperoco* erupted at five in the morning when it was alleged that the emcee of the event, Arikler, disregarded the decision of the judges to crown the queen he preferred (who happened to be a Carupanera), a young *transformista* who could have passed as a contestant in a hegemonic pageant. Contestants were confused, uncertain whether they should be on the stage or not and who had won. Audience members booed and eventually stormed out of the venue, disgusted that their will—and the judges'—had been thwarted. Arikler had to make a quick exit, and some audience members almost came to blows, throwing bottles in frustration. Several of the contestants refused to receive their runner-up sashes and also stormed out. We all had to run to the buses that took the contestants back to their residences under a hail of bottles and insults.

I began to ask myself why, if this was an event about spectacle and entertainment, audience members were displeased with the ending. The spectacle that they had paid to watch had extended well into the early morning hours, but the undemocratic end to the proceedings frustrated audience members. This left even the event organizer—who had already made his money on ticket sales—unhappy with the outcome of the pageant. But the micropolitics of this situation went even further than this single event. This drama had to do with the fact that the event organizer, a heterosexual man who was the business partner of Vera, clashed with Arikler, a very flamboyant gay man who complained that the organizer was making all of his money and not compensating the *maricos* who worked to put on the spectacle.

Sandy gives me the scoop:

SANDY: Well the story is that the one who was the queen . . . the ones that they put as queens were not the queens, they were the runners-up, and the ones that were the runners-up were the queens.

OCHOA: But according to whom?

SANDY: Miss Monagas was the queen.

OCHOA: Mmmhmm.

SANDY: And . . . Miss Distrito Federal, she was the first runner-up. Miss Zulia was the fourth runner-up but they put her as the queen. And that's why that *zaperoco* emerged there.

OCHOA: Mmmm!

SANDY: When the other *pato* [faggot, in this case Arikler] saw that *coroto* [thing], that paper [with the judges' decision on it], he said, "*Ay diós mío!*" And she [meaning Arikler] tells me, "Come and look at this." I tell him, "No, *marico*, you are going to burn yourself." [*Laughter*]. And those *maricos* were *pissed*. . . . I came home. After that, I don't know what it was they did or what they didn't do, because I hit the road and came home. Because behind a *marico* here it's going to blow up. . . . *Ay, no, mi amor*, that has nothing to do with me!

Sandy just wanted to get out of the way of the scandal that ensued. Despite her allegiance to Arikler, she did not want any part of the controversy. She chalks it up to competition and pettiness among *maricos*.

SANDY: You know that *maricos* are terrible. *Maaarico* is terrible! Every *marico* is a character.

OCHOA: You mean Arikler?

SANDY: No, all of them! One thinks one way and the other one thinks another.[12] She is more perverted than the other one, the other one wants to be more beautiful than her. That's not like, you might say, that's not a . . . *united* family. No sir.

Despite the infighting, it was very clear there was a disagreement among the judges, the producer, and the emcee, which resulted in Arikler's changing of the results using the only power he had in the situation—his role as announcer of the crown. In this, we see a *marico* act of resistance. What had started as a *marico* dream became a huge commercial event that had been taken away from *maricos* through the murder of its founder. After the death of Vera, ownership of the event transferred to the only institutionally legible relationship he had left behind: his business relationship with El Pulgoso, coproducer of the event. In some respects, Arikler's act of resistance was an act of mourning, and an act of defiance that purported to reinforce the *marico* aesthetics that Arikler believed were being ignored in favor of a heterosexual aesthetic that ridiculed contestants, or, worse, was bought by the highest bidder. But in practice Arikler's actions served to disappoint audience members and anger the event's producer. As a political move, this scandal on the stage was not effective—in the end it resulted in El Pulgoso vowing never to hire Arikler again. Sandy explained that the judges' panel was rigged:

OCHOA: But the one that won this year is from Carúpano, right? I mean the one, the one that was on paper as, the one they [the judges] had declared queen, Miss Zulia.

SANDY: Yes, from here. She was a contestant last year. And came in as fourth runner-up. The year Barbara won.

OCHOA: Yes.

SANDY: And this year too she was going to be fourth runner-up. But they put her down as queen. Because she had family on the judges' panel.

OCHOA: So it was because she had family in the judges' panel, so how . . .

SANDY: *And* some friends from TúTV also.[13] The judge from TúTV was her friend.

OCHOA: Ah, so he was her friend. . . . The judges weren't impartial.

SANDY: No, what do you think? It couldn't be.

In this explanation, Sandy invokes a common reason for dissatisfaction with beauty pageant democracy, undue influence on the judges' panel, either based in family, friendship, money, or a combination of these. But there is a clear negotiation of aesthetic principles that is going on in this *zaperoco*, one in which *marico* and *transformista* aesthetics are becoming usurped by the desires and gazes of a heterosexual public that doesn't know how to appreciate them:

> OCHOA: Ah, but so Arikler told me that it was like . . . El Pulgoso had picked who was going to be the queen, but it makes no difference to him, right? I mean he, it's more likely that the judges picked . . .
> [*Sandy reenacts the* zaperoco, *narrating it from Arikler's point of view*]
> SANDY: No! [It doesn't matter if it was] the judges or Alfredo, but what pissed off the other *marico* is . . . because, you're the owner [*dueña*] of the spectacle, . . . [you ask,] "What happened here, what's this?" . . . Now you see that you go this way, because in reality, in reality it's not up to you. You can't leave *that* [Miss Zulia] up there as queen. . . . *Diós mío!* . . . I'm getting out of here!

Arikler, as the feminized owner (dueña) or director of the spectacle, was the person who got all the *maricos* to participate and make the show happen. According to Alfredo (El Pulgoso), who sat down with me a few days after the event, there are plenty of other *maricos* who would be thrilled to put on that show. Arikler was trading on value that Alfredo realized he could undermine. Alfredo had already had to replace the primary artistic director of the show, Vera, who had been murdered the year before. Still, Arikler's judgment is the authoritative one in that moment, since he is the producer of the show who guides and shapes the *marico* aesthetic, the thing the audience comes to watch. As Arikler learned, *marico* aesthetics will only get you so far. But it's a fine line between *marico* and queen, as Sandy sees it. If a *marico* wants to win a beauty pageant, she has to conduct herself like a queen:

> OCHOA: So then why . . . why wasn't Zulia good to be the queen?
> SANDY: Ah?
> OCHOA: Zulia, why not, why didn't she deserve the title of queen?

SANDY: That *marico* doesn't conduct herself like a queen [*Ese marico no tiene porte de reina*].

OCHOA: She doesn't act like a queen?

SANDY: Nooo . . . and people who go to a pageant, that's just like . . . haven't you ever seen a Miss Venezuela pageant?

OCHOA: Aha.

SANDY: You haven't, you haven't . . . ?

OCHOA: Yes, I've seen it.

SANDY: You've never seen a Miss Venezuela?

OCHOA: Yes, of course.

SANDY: Aaah . . . well there are such beautiful women there, what do you think that [Zulia] . . . no, she couldn't win there.

OCHOA: So you mean she's not . . . beautiful enough?

SANDY: She *couldn't* win.

One of Sandy's family members, a woman visiting from Caracas, tries to explain it to me:

VISITOR: Not for the beauty, but because she doesn't carry herself . . .

OCHOA: Ah, her behavior.

VISITOR: Exactly.

Sandy explains it to me by contrasting the aesthetics of *marico* pageants with the expectations of straight judges, who presumably can't read *maricos* and have no idea what it means to conduct yourself as a queen. Straight businessmen are particularly ill suited to the task of understanding these distinctions:

SANDY: In those *marico* pageants you can't put, how can I say it, you can't put a lawyer, or a director of whatever, or a minister of over there or . . .

OCHOA: What, as part of the judges' panel?

SANDY: Because on the judges' panel because those people have no idea about . . . For them they [the contestants] are *men in costume as women*! They're not looking for the *qualities* of a woman who looks the most like a woman. Because you see them [the contestants], and they're horrendous. Didn't you see them during the day?

OCHOA: Yes.

She gestures to *transformation* as a key element in *marico* aesthetics—the ugliness of men by day is transformed into the beauty of a queen at night:

SANDY: Aha! So you can say, "*Ay, diós mío,* those are the things [*aparatos*] I saw during the day?" . . . They're not! I mean one has nothing to do with the other.

OCHOA: Aha.

SANDY: Aha, see? That is, you go out looking for, as they say, the qualities of . . . the one who has the most qualities of a woman. She is a woman. All the others are the ones that if you look at them, they're men. You look for a *woman.*

Here Sandy is using a tautology that appears often in the self-description of *transformistas:* a woman who looks like a woman. There is internal conflict in the pageants about the degree to which one could or should use cosmetic surgery, hormones, and other technologies to accomplish these "qualities" of a woman. Some narrate the unfair advantage that *transformistas* who have had breast implants and hormones have in the competition, while others describe the fundamental value as one of *transformation,* meaning you have to start with a man's body and transform it over the course of the competition. So I ask her:

OCHOA: But if one like Shakira enters the contest, for example, who has breasts and everything, eh, what happens, or rather, can she, does she have a chance in the pageant?[14]

SANDY: [*Thinking about* it] Noo, she's never entered. . . . You saw her there, right?

OCHOA: Yes, I saw her.

SANDY: Ah, but you saw her, right?

OCHOA: Yes, of course, I saw her.

SANDY: The body and the tits. What kind of person goes [*unintelligible*] there with a *coleto* [a rag in Venezuelan Spanish]? [Don't you know] what a *coleto* is for?

OCHOA: A what?

SANDY: The wig, didn't you see it? It was like a rag. [*Ochoa laughs.*] So you don't have your eyes open, you who are running around interviewing, talking, and writing? You have to have eyes for that!

OCHOA: Aha.

SANDY: That thing was a rag! That was like, take away her face and leave the body.

As the denizens of her beauty parlor and I laugh, Sandy fires up her clippers and gets back to work. Getting her digs in about the *transformista* Shakira (who had caused her own *zaperoco* the night of the pageant by threatening to cut another Shakira impersonator), Sandy reveals the secret for success for a pageant: it doesn't matter how great a body you have, if you can't carry yourself as a queen would, you have no chance. And it is the violation of this aesthetic that is the greatest offense: the one who can best carry herself as a queen should be the winner. A compromised judges' panel ruled by straight aesthetics that fails to capture the nuances of queenly carriage (as in the case of Miss Zulia) is an insult to the contest.

Luciérnagas, however, was only one of many beauty pageants where I observed the questions of democracy, repesentativity, and fairness. These ideas were in constant negotiation around many forms of aesthetics and power. If in the Luciérnagas pageant the key conflict was between *marico* and straight aesthetics in the shifting terrain of pageant ownership, in the national pageant and its regional *casting*, the key conflict was between the aesthetics of the center, in the form of the OMV and that of the periphery, in the form of local contestants and producers.[15] This negotiation was carried out with velvet gloves, often being a pleasurable reassertion of the primacy of OMV's vision of beauty in what is often called *el interior* (the provinces) of Venezuela. One key manifestation of this was the regional *casting*, a series of beauty pageants held in various regions of Venezuela to identify contestants for the national pageant. Though the *casting* took the form of televisual beauty pageants, they did not necessarily guarantee regional representation at the national pageant. As an event, they brought together and consolidated business partnerships between the OMV and its parent company, Venevisión, and OMV's advertisers. Ultimately, the *casting* reinforced the aesthetic valuations of OMV personnel and the media industry centered in Caracas.

The Coronation of Miss Oriente

Miss Oriente is the generic name I have given to a *casting* that took place in one of the metropolitan centers of this region.[16] The OMV ran nine regional *casting* in the year I observed them, and I attended six. The format of the events was quite predictable and involved a large venue with corporate sponsors. Contestants worked with local producers to participate in the *casting*, which required entrance and preparation fees. Many contestants sought sponsorship from small businesses in the area in order to compete. The events were treated as galas, with ticket sales, posh decorations, food and drinks, and fancy outfits all around.

What was very apparent from the composition of the judges' panel at the Miss Oriente *casting* was the relationship between social power and judging. The judges were often named as the result of business partnerships that had been established between the OMV or Venevisión and local retail chains. A few politicians were also appointed as judges. The panel of judges was composed of everyday businesspeople, not experts on beauty. The beauty experts who were in attendance were (quite strategically) OMV personnel.

The relationships between the audience, the contestants, the judges, and the OMV were often a site of contention: it was when these relationships broke down that drama happened. For example, when the audience favorite was not picked, postpageant conversations would involve mutterings about how the competition had been bought, or how the judges were ignoring the will of the audience (*lo que quiere el público*). None of these allegations were necessarily backed up with proof — they didn't have to be. These were expressions of participants' assumptions about the pageant's *representativity* and its *responsibility* to all participants. Interestingly enough, these assumptions were made without any explicit agreements between the OMV, the local pageant organizers, the contestants, the judges, and the audience. Audience members believed that they were entitled to have their *miss* represent them. When this did not turn out to be the case, they became frustrated. However, the discourse *and* practice of the OMV are never about representativity: they are not out to produce democratically elected *misses*. The job is to identify and train a Miss Venezuela who stands a chance of winning on the global stage: the Miss Universe and Miss World beauty pageants. Pageant producers and the director make this clear in no uncertain terms: no one else is fit to judge who should be in Miss Venezuela. In the practice of the OMV, the president of the organization has the final say over which contestants he will prepare for the Miss Venezuela pageant.

At the *casting* for Miss Oriente 2003, the OMV president Osmel Sousa selected three contestants to take back with him to Caracas for the national pageant. This was done with much fanfare, as if it never happened, but in fact it happened one or two other times over the course of the *casting* I attended.[17] The implication was that the contestants who weren't chosen were so compelling that rules had to be broken. Here's how it went down: We're in the cavernous grand ballroom of a luxury hotel. All day contestants, stylists, producers, and media mavens have been running around in preparation for the big event. Four hours after it began, we are about to witness the coronation of Miss Oriente. *Misses* are posed down the length of the *pasarela* (runway), perpendicular to the front stage. House music clangs, and the *misses* walk to the end of the *pasarela*, turn around, and walk back to the base stage. The announcer thanks the sponsors and judges, specifically the representative from Tiendas Traki, the major sponsor of this event. The *misses* line up on the base stage as the announcer revs up the crowd and calls Sousa to the stage:

> MALE ANNOUNCER: Let's see what the *people* have to saaaaay! [*Crowd cheers.*] Let's welcome Mr. Osmel Sousa with lots of applause. [*Louder cheering and applause, a new house song begins as Sousa comes up on stage with three flower arrangements.*]
> MALE ANNOUNCER: All right. Mr. Osmel Sousa has something to tell us. Let's see . . .
> SOUSA: [*Osmel Sousa begins softly. He's a bit difficult to hear at first. A hush falls over the crowd.*] All right, we came here to crown Miss Oriente. But I am not going to crown Oriente.

For a brief moment, the crowd is confused and quiet, unsure of what to make of Osmel's break from routine. Osmel throws the glittery sash that reads "Miss Oriente" to the floor and says: "Because here there are *three* women who can be in the Miss Venezuela competition . . ." The crowd goes wild. Osmel speaks, but no one can hear anything. He leads a blond, light-skinned contestant out and says, "Now . . . you." He next leads a darker-haired, darker-skinned woman out of the lineup to even more crowd noise: "You." He brings out a third, lighter-skinned, dark-haired woman, competing the trifecta of Venezuelan racial types in the world of beauty pageants: *catira* (blonde), *morena* (brown), *trigüeña* (dark-skinned). The winning *misses* pose, thrilled, with their arms bent at their sides, hands on hips. The other *misses* stand on the stage behind them, posed, but with their hands at their sides. The crowd blankets them in the white noise of their cheering. The announcer reflects as the winning *misses* sashay up to the front stage and pose: "Let's give the three girls a big round of applause. Participant thirteen, number twenty-three, and number twenty will receive their bouquets of flowers. What a surprise, eh?" He passes the microphone to the woman who is announcing with him. She's been there before, it seems: "Congratulations to all three of you. Don't be fooled, they are thrilled. I have also been there. Really, all of these three deserve to be in the Miss Venezuela [competition]. The male announcer chimes in, "You don't see that every day. Much luck to the three of them. Very well, ladies and gentlemen, we've arrived at the end of the evening. Let's say goodbye with a big hand; let's feel the emotion. [*Audience applauds and cheers*] Have a great night, and until next time. Thank you very much."

As a Europop remix of "What a Feeling" clangs, the event comes to a close. The *misses* remain on the stage, posing for photos as the audience clears out of the ballroom. Several things are going on in this scene. In terms of the overall narrative of the event, this is the culminating moment, the coronation of the queen, presumably elected by the judges, who are attentive to the desires of the people in the audience. The announcers are the intermediaries who are charged with soliciting and reflecting the desires of the audience members. The announcers work to elevate emotion and affiliation for the *misses* whom members of the audience would like to see win. They frequently appeal to *ánimo* (encouragement) and *emoción* (emotion). *Aplauso* (applause) also provides a way for audience members to register their enthusiasm and participate in the deliberations.

However, there is no illusion in these proceedings that the public is sovereign and able to determine who will be its queen. First of all, of course, queens are not democratically elected—they are monarchs! However the judges—who are clearly aligned with the capital necessary to put on the spectacle—are ostensibly the people charged with the determination of the queen. This too is merely ceremonial, for it is Sousa who will say which *misses* will be allowed to participate in Miss Venezuela. He says, "We came here to crown Miss Oriente. But I am not going to crown Oriente." In this act, Sousa affirms that what is important here is not the local crown but the opportunity to participate in the *national* competition. Miss Oriente is actually irrelevant, and the sash that identifies her is thrown to the side. What *is* important is who gets to go to Caracas and prepare to be Miss Venezuela. We interpret this as meaning that the people of Oriente who are viewing the pageant are excited to have three representatives, rather than one, at the national level. But in this competition, the *miss* who will go on to represent Oriente at the national competition is not identified. The other two will be assigned other states, and they will not necessarily be identified as having come from Oriente. Some of the competitors in this *casting* are not even *from* Oriente; they just decide to go to that *casting* as opposed to other *casting* throughout Venezuela.

What is thrilling is the departure from convention—the way Sousa personally comes in and throws out the rules in the best interest of the national pageant. The ritual drama that plays out here is that the beauty of the contestants has forced Sousa to suspend the understood rules of the ritual. This act cements his position as the "czar of beauty" in Venezuela. And so a ritual that performs a kind of audience-based spectacle of democracy by appealing to the public to express its wishes is ultimately—and very openly—a reaffirmation of the authoritarian nature of the magic of beauty.

If this were purely a question of identifying the young women who would be most successful on the national and international levels, the OMV could simply hold private *casting*, or work with modeling agencies, both practices it has done in the past. In 1999 the OMV switched to a regional and state *casting* system. The *casting*, as it was explained to me by my primary contact at the OMV, is important in terms of building excitement for the pageant and managing relationships with local pageant producers, who work with young women to develop them as contestants for the national pageant. These local producers often run modeling agencies that serve as both training grounds and agents for aspiring contestants. While the regional and state *casting* system elicits participation from people outside the immediate circuit of the OMV, and while it replicates the idea of democratic elections (which is why people in the audience get upset when it appears that there has been a miscarriage of justice), there is in fact a great deal of complicity with the authoritarian structures that produce the spectacle—the judges' panel made up of sponsors and the central figure of the president of OMV as the czar of beauty.

So, why go through the spectacle, the ritual of election, when in fact the practice of selecting the *misses* is so dependent on the opinion of one man? Well, Sousa does not put the pageant on by himself—there are other interests at play. A *casting* allows for these interests to cohere around a process, so local beauty promoters, designers, sponsors, and contestants, as well as their friends and families, have a narrative for collective participation in the process. Although Sousa ultimately has the final word in many cases (and is respected for it), the participants, the entertainers, the promoters, the stylists, and the audience make the pageant happen. In this sense, the jury members are afforded an honorary status by the OMV and the pageant organizers, but there are no illusions that this is a sovereign process that will select the competitors for the national pageant, or even that the competitors selected at a local *casting* will in the end represent the states where they were selected. The *casting* are an important mechanism for participation for a highly centralized production structure that otherwise creates little room for public participation.[18] Spectatorship is the point of the local *casting*, hence the spectacle. What is interesting here is that the spectacle takes the form of mock democracy, using the language and logic of political deliberation and determination (election, representation, fairness, justice). Spectacle in this case conditions not only relationships between participants, audiences, and producers; it also has implications for subject formation. It is to this process that I now turn, in which young women are transformed into *misses* in the dressing rooms and styling studios of the *casting*.

Producing a *Miss*

The *misses* parade before the judges in formation. They are all uniformly dressed, and they all stride in the well-known *pasarela* walk: legs long, hips swaying from side to side. Their arms rise and fall along with their stride. They look directly at everyone and at no one. The *misses* smile, baring their teeth, for as long as possible before dryness makes them press their lips closed, briefly moisten, then smile again. Sometimes petroleum jelly is applied to the teeth to maintain this smile. All kinds of *arreglitos* (little fixes) are made to produce this moment: ears that stick out too far are glued back, and makeup is used to shade large features and enhance small ones for the lights. The *misses'* bodies are the product of a conscious project of transformation, molded into the idealized form through diet, exercise, posture training, and, of course, cosmetic surgery, which is not uncommon at this stage.[19]

The contestants walk in unison and spread out across the stage, standing on green circles that have been placed there to maintain the *misses'* symmetry in front of audience and judges. It is very hard to describe the motion of *misses* in writing. This medium may not do justice to the way a *miss* walking her *pasarela* reorders time, the way in unison they glide across space and line up, all arms and elbows and legs. The *pasarela* walk is not really about showing off one's breasts, hips, or buttocks. It is much more about legs and arms, not the torso. If anything, hips are what make or break a *pasarela* stride, but not because they are the object on display.

What, exactly, *is* on display in the *pasarela* stride of a *miss*? Obviously the woman is displaying herself. Maybe she is displaying radiance, youth, or energy? But the hips are important because they power the legs; the hips position the legs exactly where they must be for the audience to fully view the stride. I think that more than any kind of protagonism, what a *miss* displays is her degree of conformity—her ability to conform to a minutely detailed standard of beauty, and yet channel a sort of selfhood through that form. This is called, sometimes, "personality," "attitude," or, in Venezuelan beauty pageants, *destacarse* (to make one's self stand out from the crowd).

What is sought is a gliding, stable motion at the head and shoulders, a swinging motion at the hips and arms, and a precise and limited trajectory at the feet, stepping one in front of the other to form a single line of paces. This is called a *tumbao* in Venezuela. It means, essentially, "cadence," but it also refers to the movement of the buttocks and hips. *Tumbao* is a racialized term in the Caribbean, often a quality attached to Afro-Caribbean women, as in the famous Celia Cruz song, "La negra tiene tumbao" (The Black woman has cadence). Venezuelan *misses* have to be careful not to have "too much" tumbao, but to definitely have enough. And while we might read the semiotics of such a restrained trajectory as giving us a message about the role of women in the symbolic world, this would not exactly explain what it means to enact this ritualized form of walking in a successful way: to have good *pasarela*. When a *miss* has good *pasarela*, this means she walks smoothly, without hesitation. It means that she dominates the stage even as she is performing exactly the same movements as everyone else: somehow she does them more fully, more confidently, in a way that gives her audience more of a sense of who she is. This also means that the arc of her motion is perfectly symmetrical, timed precisely to fall in rhythm with the music playing (or with some imaginary music playing), and that her hips glide side to side like a pendulum, legs crossing slightly in front, as if swiveling on a moving pivot. There is a sense of being in control of the motion (that is one reason why you can't have "too much" *tumbao*), but not being too robotic. *Miss pasarela* is distinguished from runway-model *pasarela* in the simple sense that the woman is trying to sell herself rather than the designer's clothes. It was explained to me on many occasions that *misses* do not make good fashion-runway models precisely because their training teaches them to project an individual sense of self.

In order to produce the *miss* who walks with the right amount of attitude, there exists the correct *tumbao*, the "projection" that pageant producers and judges look for, and an entire apparatus of production. This apparatus works not only on the physical form and stylization but also on creating a state internal to the subject, which creates the outer projection that stylists call *una mujerona* (a giant, imposing woman). At the Miss Oriente *casting*, I was allowed to observe and videotape this process.

From *Niña* to *Mujerona*

Gaston and I are directed to a room in a hotel. We board the elevator in the lobby with a young blond woman in tight jeans. We are going to the same floor, so we guess from how she looks that she might be a contestant. She smiles and cracks her gum on the way up. Gaston asks her if she is in the pageant and she says yes, she is going to get her makeup done. We head for the same room, where Jesús, a *maquillador* (makeup artist), is working with his assistants to prepare the *misses*. Two young women sit on his bed, looking bored and clutching their cell phones. Another woman is in the makeup chair, where the shades from two hotel lamps have been removed to provide the light of naked lightbulbs on either side of the mirror mounted to the wall. Yet another contestant sits in a chair by the bathroom while Jesús's assistant teases and blow-dries her hair. Upon seeing the three of us enter, Jesús screams out: "¡Puuta! ¡Ahora te tengo que hacer los labios de nuevo!" (You whore! Now I have to do your lips again!)

Gaston and I peer into the room from behind the woman from the elevator. She laughs, walks in, and plops herself down on the bed, ignoring everyone and dialing her boyfriend on the cell phone. The hairdressers chuckle. Some of the *misses* look a bit uncomfortable. The contestant blows Jesús a kiss. He smirks as he continues his tirade, muttering: "Coño de la madre eres una prostituta" ([Expletive about your mother's genitalia], you are a prostitute).

The contestant chats with her *novio* (boyfriend), oblivious to Jesús's insults. He goes back to applying face powder to the *miss* in his makeup chair, performance of righteous indignation complete. The evening goes on like this, punctuated with outbursts and laughter and the sound of blow-driers while beauty queens in curlers slouch on the bed and in the chairs.

Jesús is over the top. He and his hairdressers provide a running narration as they assess the *misses'* skin-care and makeup practices, outfits, hairdos, *pasarela* styles, smiles, ears, noses, work done, physiques, and attitudes. They clearly prefer *misses* who are not shy, and who do not cringe at the most crass remarks. At one point, Jesús, a flamboyant *marico*, rubs his crotch on a *miss's* shoulder as he applies her makeup, joking with her about how she likes it. He builds her up, sexually, narrating her sex appeal and her ability to control men through it. As another hairdresser in the room describes it to me, this is the process of converting *niñas* (girls) into *mujeronas*. A *mujerona* is aware of her own sexual power and knows how to use it. *Maricos* are her allies, tending to her and teaching her the ways of man-eating.[20] Although this process makes some contestants uncomfortable, it is accepted as part of the preparation for the pageant.

Many of the men I met openly identified as gay, homosexual, or *marico*, and treated the *misses* like platonic girlfriends—sexual tension, in the sense that the *misses* might be interpellated as the objects of sexual desire for the men who surrounded them, was nonexistent. Sexuality, however, was very present. In the banter between hairdressers, makeup artists, and *misses*, there was a great deal of queening, solidarity around *novios*, sexual advice, and sexual interpellation. By sexual interpellation, I mean that the *peluqueros* (hairdressers) and maquilladores produced *misses* as sexual subjects through their banter. Specifically, they produced *misses* as insatiable and promiscuous sexual subjects, whatever their actual sexual practices may have been. This production was about creating a *mujerona* who could walk down the *pasarela* in an imposing and sexually dominant way. I never observed the management of Miss Venezuela taking part in this production of *mujeronas*; this talk was reserved for the "locker room"—the chairs where *misses* got their makeup and hair done. Overt sexualization of the *misses* was antithetical to the official discourse of the OMV and the pageant organizers. However, the process of production was imbued with overt sexuality and sexualization. This process of sexual interpellation produced *mujeronas*.

Conclusion

From *luciérnagas* to *mujeronas,* this chapter has explored the ways beauty pageants in Venezuela produce opportunities for Venezuelan women to become queen for a day. The beauty pageant form, as a ritual form that connects local realities to transnationally mass-mediated discourses, produces sites of negotiation and conflict, and requires the production of particular kinds of subjects to project themselves onto the global stage. By visiting two beauty pageants in the Oriente region—the eastern Caribbean coast of Venezuela—I demonstrated the principles of glamour outlined in chapter 2 that allow Venezuelans located in out-of-the-way places to call down the authority they can summon from the transnational discourse of beauty. Beauty pageant democracy—or the idea that beauty pageants serve as a site where we project our ideas of democracy, representativity, and fairness—allows us to examine the conflicts and negotiations inherent in the dramas and *zaperocos* that regularly erupt during beauty pageants. Finally, I have described what it takes to produce *misses* who walk authoritatively on the national and global stage. In the next chapter, I explore another stage, this one a street in Caracas that *transformistas* have turned into a site of mythic projection over the course of decades.

Pasarelas y Perolones

TRANSFORMISTA MEDIATIONS ON

AVENIDA LIBERTADOR IN CARACAS

Mi nombre es Venezuela. Soy una *transformista*. Trabajo aquí en este *nightclub*. Es mi medio, pero no es mi meta.

My name is Venezuela. I am a transformista. I work here in this nightclub. It's my medium, but it's not my goal. —VENEZUELA, the *transformista* protagonist of *Las* TRANS *de Caracas* (1981; translation mine)

Venezuela is the star of the documentary film *Las* TRANS *de Caracas*, directed and produced in Caracas by Manuel Herrera and Miguel Manaure. She begins her opening monologue with this epigraph, having just finished a seductive lip-synch performance of the 1980 Irene Cara hit song "Fame." As the camera approaches Venezuela, she is drinking at the bar where she has just performed, bathed in red light. She puts down her drink, stares deeply at the camera, and introduces herself. The club, which is her medium and not her goal, is one of many that have existed and passed into oblivion in the Sabana Grande district of Caracas. It is where she drinks, performs for tips, probably stays off the constantly policed streets, and quite possibly does sex work. At the end of the film, Venezuela takes her coworkers from Avenida Libertador to the close-by fountain at Plaza Venezuela, in a scene I discuss in chapter 2.

By the time I got to Caracas, the club that Venezuela declared her medium but not her goal was long gone. Venezuela had passed away years before, although her fame lived on. Another generation of *transformistas* had ascended and yet another was coming up. There were other clubs in

Sabana Grande that provided a place to relax, respite from the police, and a stage for the interpersonal drama of *transformista* survival. Most of the *transformistas* I met didn't do shows in the style of Venezuela, although a few did, only now to the songs of Monica Naranjo, Britney Spears, and Shakira. They went to the bars that would let them in, and some of the *transformistas* did sex work a few blocks up the street on Avenida Libertador. In my attempts to contact *transformistas* and other transgender women to talk to them and observe their self-fashioning practices, I was able to encounter them at various sites: hotels, apartments, bars, *peluquerías* (beauty salons), NGOs, and on Avenida Libertador. These different sites gave me very different pictures of *transformista* survival and social life.

I have focused my observations on one of these sites. A large avenue in Caracas, Avenida Libertador, is a place where *transformistas* do sex work.[1] Although this is not the only site of *transformista* sex work or *transformista* presence in Caracas, it is one of the most visible. All of the people I asked about the presence of *transformistas* on the Avenida communicated that they had "always" been there — *toda la vida*. For most of my interlocutors, who don't remember a Caracas without Avenida Libertador, this is indeed the case. But the existence of Avenida Libertador is relatively recent, and on this street, history only goes back to the 1960s at best. How did the *transformistas* get to be on Avenida Libertador? Very few people I asked had an answer; *transformista* presence on Libertador seemed totally logical to them. Indeed, we could say that *transformistas* are a kind of tradition on Libertador. If you want to find a *transformista* sex worker in Caracas (and you have a car), the place to go is Libertador. *Transformista* visibility is inextricably tied to the practice of sex work on Avenida Libertador.

This "simple" description of one of my field sites quickly led me to some important questions: Why was it that everyone in Caracas seemed to know where to find transgender sex workers? Why were *transformistas* so visible on this avenue, and how did they get to be a natural part of this urban landscape? I soon began to understand that *transformista* occupation of this space says as much about the space itself as about the dynamics of being a *transformista* sex worker. I approach the question of *transformista* use of Avenida Libertador with the basic assumption that *transformistas* had good reasons for being there, and that their consistent use of this space for sex work — from at least the late 1970s to the present — indicates that there are important advantages to doing sex work at this site.

The question that led me to this line of research was, essentially, how it is that *transformistas* come to stand on Avenida Libertador to do sex work? In observing the work they perform as well as their presence on the street, I found many tactical reasons for the selection of this particular site. The *transformistas* I asked told me that the reason they work on Libertador is because that is where *transformistas* work when they do sex work; that is where the clients are. But beyond this practical knowledge, the performance of sex work on Avenida Libertador is overdetermined by various factors. The specific advantages that Avenida Libertador affords *transformistas* in this work include, ironically, public visibility. *Transformistas* use Avenida Libertador as a stage from which to project an image that provides both a kind of sex work marketing and a certain fame, or perhaps notoriety. These strategies of projection are part of *transformista* survival skills, and they are conditioned precisely by what Avenida Libertador *means* to the inhabitants of Caracas, and to the nation of Venezuela.

The site can be described in a few different ways: an *impressionistic* sense of the space—what it felt like to be there; a *physical* description of the site; and within the context of the social geography of Caracas. I also describe this space, and *transformista* occupation of it, through two lenses: the different *sites* they occupy on the avenue and the *stances* they employ there. *Transformista* occupation of Avenida Libertador creates a kind of public visibility that *transformistas* can and do use strategically.

An Impressionistic Portrait of Avenida Libertador

Avenida Libertador is a large and confusing place, with the sound of rushing cars everywhere, lights and shadows, and a palpable tension evident to lone pedestrians in the evening. I was warned many times that Avenida Libertador was a dangerous place, and that I should avoid it. I considered these warnings and took precautions to ensure my safety and that of my research assistants. On my first visits to the Avenida, I became acquainted with the two features I named in the title of this chapter: *pasarelas* (pedestrian bridges) which bear the same name as the runway walk I described in chapter 3, and *perolones* (paddy wagons driven by the Policía Metropolitana). The PM regularly rounds up *transformistas* on the Avenida. I approached my first visits to Libertador very tentatively because of the concerns that many of my collaborators expressed for my safety. This is how

I initially approached this place, accompanied by my research assistant, Antonio Borges. Eventually, the tension and fear of moving through this space dissipated as I became a more regular visitor.

Libertador

At first I came up to her carefully. Walked down familiar Solano Street, past the boys working the corner, the girls with their butch *papis* watching their backs, clustered in little groups, fixing each other up to look nice. Past the solemn storefronts of the gay bars, concealing the *escándalo* (scandal) they hold inside. Antonio and I stepped cautiously up the block and set foot on Libertador for the first time. It was quiet. We looked first east, then west. No one around. We hugged the walls of the Hotel Crillon and walked half a block until shadows and the unknown scared us back. A little plaza sat back from the sidewalk, ready to be the scene of a knifing. Half a block west we saw two *transformistas* working. The younger one sat on a nearby kiosk, watching and learning while the other, a *veterana* (veteran of the Avenida), posed on the sidewalk for oncoming traffic. We talked for a little while. It was there that I learned to stand with my back to the traffic, so she could keep an eye out for what was going on.

Before long we crossed over to stand on the *pasarela*. From there, on the bridge between the two local lanes, the veterana could see cars and police coming from a long way off. I asked her vague questions as she looked east. Antonio tried to show her how to use a condom. She said she already knew, and scanned the horizon for clients, police. Our conversation lulled. Antonio and I, wide-eyed, drank in the hiss of passing cars, the insect hum of the sodium lights, the orange glow on the pavement, the rush of traffic on the lanes below. Beneath all that, the silent hush of broadleafed trees. The heat dissolved my skin into the orange black around us, and I was only eyes, blinking and trying to interpret the dancing lights. The veterana's shriek opened my ears: "¡El perolón!"

She shouted in the direction of her friend across the street and rushed us down the stairs that led to the express lanes. A few steps down she said, "Wait here." Then she slowly climbed back up the steps. I craned my neck to see. "Get down," she hissed. The stairs strobed yellow with the flashing lights of the perolones that passed over us. She came back down. We kept quiet for a few seconds. The stairs stopped flashing and she went back up for a look. Cracked a joke with her friend on the other side of the *pasarela*. She told us when it was okay to come up. We four stood in the middle of the *pasarela*, express traffic streaming below, the girls laughing, trying to explain to me what *el perolón* meant. The veterana looked tired after it had all passed said, "I'm too old for this"; then she headed home. Antonio and I went back to friendly Solano, chests pounding after our first encounter with Libertador.

Physical Description

Four central arteries feed into the broad avenue at its westernmost end, where it is primarily an expressway with three lanes eastbound and westbound. Near Plaza Venezuela, there are off-ramps on the expressway to three local lanes on either side. These local lanes intersect with many side streets in the Sabana Grande district, which is where *transformistas* begin to occupy the Avenida. This part of Avenida Libertador runs for about half a mile between Plaza Venezuela and the neighborhood of La Campiña. There are wide sidewalks on either side, as well as pedestrian bridges over the expressway about twenty feet below; here *transformistas* stand and encounter clients in passing cars. Bridges over the expressway provide an easy way for a potential client to circle the Avenida. This configuration continues for about six blocks, and then the local lanes merge down to the express level, and Avenida Libertador continues through a shopping district, finally connecting to the Distribuidor Altamira, which feeds traffic north into Altamira and east and south onto the freeway system.

Map 1 shows the area where *transformistas* worked on Avenida Libertador while I was in the field. This stretch features six *pasarelas* (figure 4.1), which have stairs (figure 4.2) leading to the lower, express level (figure 4.3).[2] At this site along the avenida, several things converge: Libertador becomes more pedestrian friendly, with large sidewalks and slower local lanes in both directions, as well as the *pasarelas* that join the north and south sides of the avenida; the residential Sabana Grande zone begins; and the public space of El Centro becomes the privatized space of the east side. Those who might find scandal, glamour, and pageantry more interesting often recoil at the kinds of mundane details that produce this site (literally concrete and rubble), but it was these details that helped me make sense of how this site is even possible, and understand what it means to the city of

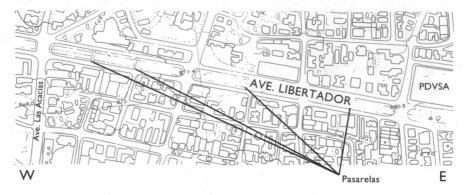

MAP 1 · Approximate area of *transformista* occupation, Avenida Libertador.
Illustration by the author, 2004.

Caracas and to *transformistas*. But first, I should describe the social geography of Caracas and the place of Avenida Libertador within it. Then I will turn to the history of the Avenida itself.

Avenida Libertador in the Social Geography of Caracas

To explain the social geography of Caracas, I employ three axes: east and west, north and south, and height. The social geography of this city of approximately six million is infinitely more complex than can be represented here, but I will make some general observations. These general categories tend to work more in the imaginary than in actual practice, in which class-differentiated zones are striated throughout Caracas. As I describe in chapter 2, the social geography of Caracas is variegated, similar to a leaf striated with pigments. A few blocks north of Avenida Libertador, *ranchos* (improvised working-class and poor housing built without permits) line the ravine atop which the Quinta Miss Venezuela, the house where Venezuelan beauty queens are groomed for international success, is perched. This produces a social landscape in which poverty and luxury coexist in an uneasy intimacy, where the needs and desires of communities take form in creative and complex ways. The part of Caracas where *transformistas* work is itself stratified, and the sex-work zones for both *transformistas* and cisgender women sex workers abut one of the largest and most opulent mall and hotel complexes in the city.[3]

FIGURE 4.1 · A pedestrian bridge
(*pasarela*), Avenida Libertador, Caracas.
Photo by Gustavo Marcano. (top)

FIGURE 4.2 · Stairs, Avenida Libertador,
Caracas. Photo by Gustavo Marcano.

(above, left) FIGURE 4.3 · Avenida
Libertador, Caracas, as seen from a
pedestrian bridge (*pasarela*). Photo
by Gustavo Marcano.

Socially and economically, Caracas is divided at El Centro into a west side (considered to be more working class and poor) and an east side (considered more middle class and elite). As a thoroughfare, the primary purpose of Avenida Libertador was to connect the elites moving to the east side of Caracas with El Centro, an area that became marked as a dangerous, impoverished place, but that is also the administrative center of the nation. Before the construction of Avenida Libertador in 1966, *transformistas* and cisgender women's sex work primarily went on in El Centro. After its construction, Avenida Libertador became a new kind of space in the social geography of Caracas, one that would soon be occupied by sex workers. The east-west axis of Caracas is a very clear marker of class. Indeed, my transit of this boundary on a regular basis proved a source of anxiety to some of my middle-class friends who lived on the east side. I had always been told about the legendary danger of Caracas by my mother, aunts, and uncles, who experienced Caracas as Colombian nationals, some of whom were working without papers in Venezuela. Caracas held great dangers for them — they saw it as a very uncivil place, where people were rude, arrogant, ungrateful, and treacherous. The representation of the west side that I got from most middle-class caraqueños (residents of Caracas) was one of uncharted horror. My pragmatic questioning about what it was I might lose or be threatened by did not appease their concerns. In their eyes, as a foreigner, I was fresh meat for people looking to rob. The specter of violence loomed just beyond the robbery but was never really named. There were moments, however, when it felt as though people were telling me that if I got out of the Metro any further west than the Capitolio station (in El Centro), I would somehow instantly vaporize! This sort of fear, which is very difficult to argue against (much like the rhetorics of national safety, capital flight, democracy, and terrorism), was a kind of membrane that I had to permeate in my travels across Caracas. Not being very familiar with the social map of Caracas, I could feign ignorance of people's concerns for a while, but when I had been around long enough to know better, my mobility was explained, in fact facilitated, by my privilege as a foreign investigator and an anthropologist.

The east side of Caracas provided another sort of boundary maintenance, primarily through the privatization of public space: this was evidenced by the increasing popularity of shopping malls as social venues and the campaigns to police the Chacao district of Caracas. At gay clubs on the east side and in Sabana Grande, this was done through a strict door policy that required dress codes and put me in the same boat with the *transformistas* by excluding *machas* (butch women), although certainly not as often as *transformistas* were excluded from these clubs. I experienced not only the exclusion faced by *transformistas* and *machas* but also exclusion based on skin color when I attempted to enter several establishments with friends who are dark skinned. Race and class certainly play a large part in the production of this social geography, and in the production of beauty and nation in Venezuela.

Given the thick membrane of fear and policing that envelops both the west side and the east side of Caracas, the ease with which one can transit from one side to the other is striking. The Metro, buses, and cars all pass through these zones, leading me to believe that the boundaries are indeed imagined and not necessarily spatialized, or rather that discourse and practice diverge here. It seems significant that *transformista* sex work is at its most visible precisely in the transition between east and west.

At this transition point, local traffic moves more slowly on the street level. The Sabana Grande zone begins, with more residential buildings that communicate to the sidewalks of Libertador. Traffic gets backed up heading east because of an incomplete section of the thoroughfare, and the public space of El Centro, the Bellas Artes district, Plaza Venezuela, and Sabana Grande becomes the privatized space of Chacaíto and Chacao — by the time you get to the Chacao district, businesses and shopping centers line the street, and apartment buildings are more set back, or on side streets. The giant shopping malls of Centro San Ignacio and El Sambil, which dwarf most malls I have seen in California, loom large, fashionable and orderly. *Transformistas* position themselves at the transition point of all this movement of humans, capital, and power from the old, public part of Caracas to the newer, more private part. *Transformistas* are well positioned to attract both wealthy east-side clients and working-class clients from El Centro and the Sabana Grande area. You can tell this mostly by the kinds of cars people drive — newer cars head east in the early evening, older cars west.[4]

THE NORTH-SOUTH AXIS

North and south are significantly less marked in Caracas than are east and west. Libertador is in the north-central area of the Caracas Valley. To the north of Libertador, various residential areas abut El Avila natural preserve, and La Cota Mil, a highway that rings the north side of Caracas. *Transformistas* I talked to reported being driven to this dark and lonely highway when in police custody, and being left there, sometimes without clothes, to find their way back.

Immediately to the north of the sex-work area of Libertador are several residential zones with shade trees, which serve as cover in the night for those evading police custody. These quiet streets are very different from the noisier and more trafficked Búlevard de Sabana Grande to the south. The street one block south of Libertador, Avenida Francisco Solano López, is an important site for male sex work and some sex work performed by cisgender women. In the five-block stretch between Calle Negrín and Las Acacias, I regularly encountered groups of friends who did sex work together, mostly young gay-identified men and women in butch-femme lesbian couples. There were approximately fifteen individuals that worked this way on this street, negotiating with passing cars and disappearing into the gay bars on Solano or down a block to the Búlevard de Sabana Grande when police came by. I regularly saw them on the walks that I took with my outreach assistants to visit *transformistas* on Libertador. These individuals did not work up on Libertador, they said, because *transformistas* would get territorial.[5]

A block south of Avenida Casanova flows another feature of the Caracas landscape: the river, El Guaire. When I first encountered it, I didn't think much of it. I thought it was a sewage overflow, a smelly, streaming, gray-brown torrent that separated the more commercial Sabana Grande area from the more residential Bello Monte zone. I began to understand what El Guaire means to the Caracas landscape after encountering it at two other sites: in the imaginary, as a threat that *transformistas* reported they received from police and other antagonists (that the *transformistas* would be thrown into El Guaire), and on paper, as a threat that the anthropologist Patricia Márquez (1999) reports her informants, street kids living and huffing glue in Sabana Grande, received when being antagonized. Mayoral campaigns have been launched with the promise to clean up El Guaire, which now flows along cement banks under the highway, hopelessly opaque. Sewer lines jut out of improvised homes built along these cement banks, pouring out directly into El Guaire, which becomes a visible and odorous marker of the impossibility that six million people might make this valley their home. El Guaire is where the excess of Caracas's modernity flows. To be threatened with being thrown in El Guaire is to be equated with garbage.[6]

HEIGHT

A final axis on which to consider the social geography of Caracas, and the place of Libertador within it, is the factor of height.[7] There are two forms of height as a social axis in Caracas: skyscrapers and mountainsides (*cerros*). Just as Caracas is deeply divided in terms of class on its east-west axis, so too is it divided by height. Tall residential complexes tower over the Caracas valley, facilitating incredible views of the cityscape, El Avila (the enormous, verdant, sleeping mountain that forms the northern boundary of Caracas), and the gorgeous Caribbean sky. These towers are protected by elaborate security systems, requiring several keys and magnetic gadgets to unlock, and there is sometimes the constant presence of security guards (*vigilantes*). During my time in Caracas, these security systems sprung into action through residents' groups that took precautions against the specter of looting in many buildings on the east side. The phrase I often heard repeated was *van a bajar de los cerros* (they will come down from the mountainsides). This imaginary of urban looting has its roots in both the intense disparity of wealth and poverty one can find in the Caracas valley and in the memory of El Caracazo, a 1989 uprising against structural readjustment policies in Caracas.[8] During El Caracazo poor people did come down from the mountainsides to protest and loot. But they primarily did this to the west of Caracas in other poor neighborhoods (these might be distinguished from the cerros by greater access to urban infrastructure such as electricity, sewer and water lines, and paved roads).

Throughout the political polarization of the first decade of the twenty-first century, residents of the privileged areas in the east of Caracas mapped the outrage of El Caracazo onto the supporters of President Chávez, whom they considered to be dangerous, armed, and angry. Chávez supporters certainly employed this aesthetic in their own projections into national media, but property owners on the east side had less to fear from angry crowds (whether they were Chávez supporters or not) than did residents of El Centro, where property damage did occur during volleys between the two sides. The implementation of security measures for middle-class and elite residential towers and subdivisions during the periods of social unrest in 2002–3 demonstrated this height axis: the poor from the mountainsides needed to be locked out of the towers, while the middle class and elites retreated up as their primary refuge. Ground level was the zone of conflict: the street, the Plaza de Altamira, Puente Llaguno, and even the highways were prone to disruption and danger. Avenida Libertador was also subject to this change in social dynamics. Over the course of my work there the *transformistas'* use of the avenida changed in response to political developments.

What I call *elite height* are the high-rise housing and commercial complexes that stud the valley of Caracas. *Poor height* refers to the improvised housing on the mountainsides that surround the valley, the cerros. A third kind of height to consider is what I call *state height*—large administrative and housing complexes built by various administrations. Specifically, I am using *state height* to refer to the housing projects of the 1950s and 1960s (called *bloques*), such as 23 de Enero and Caricuao, the monolithic administrative center at Centro Simón Bolívar, and the public-private development of late 1970s to early 1980s, the Torres de Parque Central, two identical towers that rise in the north-central west of the Caracas Valley.[9] This state architecture serves various purposes: housing people, administrative offices, and mixed commercial-residential-government offices. State height approaches the style of elite or middle-class height.[10] Working-class or poor height is of a completely different nature: it involves finding purchase along the rocky terrain of the cerros, negotiating a space with one's neighbors, and improvising infrastructure connections (often including unregulated electric and water hookups). Security takes the form of small windows, metal doors, and flimsy locks, and having family or friends who are present on the premises, as I learned by talking to and visiting *transformistas* who live in rancho-style housing. Strikingly, many *transformistas* I interviewed said that they preferred to live in ranchos because these were communities that were more accepting of their presence.

These three axes provide some context for how Avenida Libertador is situated in the social geography of Caracas. The history of the avenida itself provides some insight into how the site comes to exist as a manifestation of modernity in the physical landscape of Caracas. In the next section, I will describe how Avenida Libertador came into existence and what this means about modernity in Venezuela.

Modernizing the Caracas Landscape:
The Avenida Libertador Project

"Avenida Libertador nace con la democracia" (Avenida Libertador is born with the democracy). This is what I was told as I began to inquire into the history of the place in Caracas most associated with *transformistas*. An odd place to start, it seemed to me at first. It is striking, if not ironic, that the avenue where *transformistas* do sex work is named after Simón Bolívar, the liberator of the Americas and father of the Venezuelan nation. I was at first confused by the marriage of the chronologies of urban development and democracy in this description. What does one have to do with the other?

Avenida Libertador, like democracy, was the result of a long labor that was conceived of and incubated in dictatorship. Avenida Libertador, like democracy, emerged from the same parent: that impulse toward order and progress known as modernity. In the transition from dictatorship to democracy, the Avenida Libertador project became a manifestation of the democratic government's ability to produce "una gran avenida para una gran capital" (a grand avenue for a grand capital) (see figure 4.4).

It will be fourteen years from the construction of the Avenida to the first evidence I have of *transformistas* using the site for sex work.[11] Though the construction of steel and concrete is often not the subject of analysis in studies of gender and performativity, as I looked deeper into the production of the most visible space inhabited by *transformistas* in Caracas, I became fascinated with the story of its construction. Fueled by a desire for modernity and a need to demonstrate progress as much as by the logistical concerns of facilitating transportation across the east-west axis of Caracas, the Avenida Libertador project tells us as much about modernity and gender in Venezuela as do the *transformistas* who put it to uses other than those for which it was intended. For this reason, I will spend some time detailing the long process through which it was constructed. Those who are bored by concrete and rebar may wish to move on to the glamour that follows, and would be none the worse for it. However, the section that follows serves as a reminder that all glamour must be projected from a platform somewhere and through a particular medium.

The construction of the Avenida established its place as a hallmark of modernity in the urban development of a newly democratized Venczuela of the 1960s. I take this chronology from various sources, specifically reports of the construction project in the *Boletín del Colegio de Ingenieros*

una gran avenida
para una gran capital

caracas hacia su cuatricentenario

avenida libertador

FIGURE 4.4 · "Una gran avenida para una gran capital" (A grand avenue for a grand capital). *Boletín del Colegio de Ingenieros de Venezuela, 72.* January 1966.

de Venezuela (Venezuelan College of Engineers) from 1966 to 1971, and from the annual reports (*Memoria y cuenta* [Memory and account]) of the Venezuelan Ministerio de Obras Públicas (Ministry of Public Works, MOP) from 1959 to 1967.[12] According to the MOP's volumes of *Memoria y cuenta* from the period, construction began on what would become Avenida Libertador in 1957, the final year of Marcos Pérez Jiménez's dictatorship before he was deposed by a coup on January 23, 1958. The 1966 *Boletín* article reports that more than two thousand feet of the western section was built, but construction was stalled because of problems with the expropriation of land for public works.[13] The democratic coup continued work (slowly) on the Libertador project after coming to power in 1958.

The MOP inherited an administrative structure attuned to the needs of a dictator, and a stalled economy in the postdictatorship. At this time, the MOP was seen not only as an engine of progress but also as a driving force in the economy. This view of the MOP continued in the volumes of *Memoria y cuenta* from the 1960s, and the national government made several attempts to provide people employment through public works. In the *Memoria y cuenta* published in 1960 (for fiscal year 1959), the minister at the time described an abysmal administration problem as the national government's attempt to get the economy moving again:

The Provisional Government as well as the Constitutional Government have tried to solve the unemployment problem, and to this end, have undertaken the construction of hundreds of projects, the majority of them in the interior of the country. In the rush to begin these projects as quickly as possible, many were started without the necessary studies and budgets completed; without the required technical and administrative organization; without enough money in the budget, for which it was necessary to resort to additional credits. In terms of the construction of schools, some were [decreed] without having previously chosen the site, and without knowing if it was the most convenient site. (Ministerio de Obras Públicas 1960, viii; my translation)

In February 1959 the legislature passed the Plan de Emergencia o de Obras Extraordinarias (Emergency Plan or Special Works), which charged the MOP with putting some 28,000 people to work to regenerate the economy. All of these workers were paid salaries through the plan, but the MOP could only put 14,000 of them to work, and complained bitterly about the quality of their work in the *Memoria y cuenta*. Although expenditures were made on the Avenida Libertador project, the MOP's attention to it languishes from 1960 to 1962.

President Rómulo Betancourt continued work on the project, and built more than 3,600 feet of the avenida on the east side. Some of this construction may have taken place between 1960 and 1963, but it appears that by 1963 the MOP had changed its administrative practices to create a four-year plan, in which Avenida Libertador is highlighted as a project for completion by 1966. The format of the *Memoria y cuenta* changes to be more project based and visual — one-page summaries of each project completed or in progress fill the pages of the dense books for these years, each with a photograph and diagram of the project. Page after page of rising structures or smooth pavement show a Venezuela constructing itself out of rebar and asphalt. From the "Obras urbanas" (Urban works) sections of these reports, it is clear that the landscape of Caracas was changing to be more automobile centered, with great concern for the Sistema Vial Expreso de Caracas (Caracas Express Road System), the highway system with its spiraling access ramps that circle the valley.[14] The Avenida Libertador project becomes one of the markers of progress in a Venezuela that believed it was constructing its modernity both through democracy and through public works.

In *The Magical State: Nature, Money, and Modernity in Venezuela*, Fernando Coronil (1997) describes this attitude in Venezuelan public administration throughout the twentieth century. Coronil argues that Venezuelan political and state cultures have been understood to emerge from the dictatorship of Pérez Jiménez to the present. Coronil's work is to root the expectation of a state that magically provides modernity in the long history of Venezuela, specifically with the emergence of the petroleum economy in the early twentieth century, during the time of the dictator Juan Vicente Gómez. In *The Magical State*, Coronil discusses a specific project to develop industry in Venezuela: a tractor assembly plant, created in the Carlos Andres Pérez administration, which never went on to produce any tractors. Coronil is interested in the cultural logic and political economy of this project, which was seen as a giant flop. We can see this same kind of "magical" logic in the post–Pérez Jiménez MOP that completed the Avenida Libertador project. The MOP's own narrative positions public works as an engine of progress in Venezuela, not only for its infrastructure but also for its stalled postdictatorial economy.

Progress and Order: The Aesthetics of Urban Development in Mid-Twentieth-Century Caracas

The Avenida Libertador project came to symbolize progress for a democratic government in several ways.[15] The first was by its ability to signify modernity through order in concrete and asphalt; second, by its magnitude; and finally, by the ways the renovated MOP administered and completed the project. Avenida Libertador changed the way traffic moved on the east side of Caracas by cutting a broad, straight line through what had previously been local streets in Parroquia el Recreo, through to the Chacao district and Altamira. Even as late as 1970, the project continued on its mission to bring order to Parroquia el Recreo, at least part of which is described as being in a state of "total absence of urban and social planning" (Colegio de Ingenieros de Venezuela 1971, 49). In the late nineteenth century, this area was arranged spatially as a series of haciendas, ringed with workers' housing. As the population of Caracas spread eastward, more *quintas* (middle-class and elite extended-family dwellings) and ranchos (improvised dwellings for working-class and poor inhabitants) were built. In 1886 the Ferrocarril Central de Venezuela, a railroad between Caracas and Petare, was built through this area, very close to what is now Avenida

FIGURE 4.5 · A montage of development and disorder,
Boletín del Colegio de Ingenieros de Venezuela, 127. February 1971.

Libertador (Troconis de Veracochea 1993, 179). As population density increased in the Caracas Valley, this area developed into blocks of quintas and barrios of ranchos. Over the years these quintas and ranchos became more established, and when the Libertador construction project came through, some were displaced. Expropriation of land was considered to be one of the biggest obstacles to progress during the Avenida Libertador project (Colegio de Ingenieros de Venezuela 1966, 22).

These *Boletín* representations of Avenida Libertador show how developers imagined a contrast between the modern (*criollo* [Creole], middle-class, middle-aged, male) engineer and the poor (darker-skinned, female, young) occupants of the barrios around the recently constructed Avenida Libertador. In the lower-right corner of the montage in figure 4.5, a shirtless child carries a bundle up a hill strewn with honeycomb bricks and debris. Above that image is a photo of a ramshackle rancho set against a backdrop of construction rubble. A child leans from the door. This rancho actually has an address posted on it—Zona D 52—which indicates that there was planning or ordering at some level. The rancho also appears to have an electrical wire running to it from up above. A small structure of concrete debris, wood, cardboard, and zinc roofing, it is considered inappropriate for human dwelling—"unhealthy living," as the caption states. To the left, engineers and planners inspect the scale model of the project that is intended to address the poverty and disorder of the pictures on the right. Ironically, the disorder of concrete rubble and construction debris is likely the result of construction of either the Avenida or apartment buildings nearby—the order that is being contrasted to this disorder may in fact be what produces it.

The juxtaposition of these pictures—the grown engineers in suits and ties towering over a model of the housing projects under discussion and the young children dwarfed by rubble at the site of the proposed construction—communicates a particular kind of nostalgia. It is almost as if the engineers are saying: "We were once these boys; we must work to keep this from happening to any other boy." The ideas that progress is a human right, that no child should have to grow up in these living conditions, and that it is the responsibility of engineers and the state to provide humane living conditions drive this aesthetic of order and progress. However, in this case it is certainly no more than a driving narrative. The residents of these dwellings were most likely not housed in the development that displaced them. These buildings were designated as part of a university housing and office complex for professionals, taking advantage of the zone's proximity to the Universidad Central de Venezuela and the Colegio de Ingenieros Venezolanos.

Another indicator that progress was measured in concrete and asphalt is the way the MOP reports its accomplishments on the project: by listing the number of meters of earth moved, road constructed, and paving completed. This accounting method changed in 1963 to include photos and diagrams of the projects under completion. In the *Memoria y cuenta* for fiscal year 1964, the four-year planning grid lists 12,000 feet as being completed through 1964, and an additional 7,500 scheduled to be completed in 1965. These volumes of *Memoria y cuenta* display page after page of smoothly paved roads vanishing into the distance.

The design of Avenida Libertador also accomplished a modern aesthetic: through its materials, specifically formed concrete (as opposed to stone, earth, or brick); through its straight, unadorned lines; and through its disruption of local foot traffic, made slightly more friendly by the addition of steel *pasarelas*. The avenue's size provides another marker of modernity: it is more than 150 feet wide and includes eight traffic lanes plus sidewalks and medians. Streets in this area were two to four lanes wide before this construction. A large trench had to be dug through Parroquia el Recreo, which created a chasm of speeding cars between the residential zone of La Florida to the north and the business district of Sabana Grande to the south.

The 1966 *Boletín* article heralds the opening of Avenida Libertador by calling it "una gran avenida para una gran capital." A long shot shows both the width of the avenida in the foreground and its length fading off into the horizon. Grandeur in this sense meant not only the size of the project but also the ingenuity of its designers and builders: its elegance as a solution to this particular traffic problem. This self-congratulatory article highlights several accomplishments: it is the third-longest avenue in Caracas; it has express and local lanes, affording the coexistence of fast crosstown traffic with slower local traffic; while it cuts through this part of town, the avenue's bridges and *pasarelas* maintain the integrity of the pedestrian and local traffic; its sixteen bridges running north-south are, according to the article, what make "this magnificent project one of the most functional arteries of the capital" (21, my translation); additionally, its underground infrastructure was constructed to provide for urban expansion, with water, sewer, and service lines laid in anticipation of future growth. In 1966 traffic counts for the Caracas metropolitan area, Avenida Libertador is listed as carrying 80,000 to 100,000 cars daily. This visibility provides a tactical advantage for *transformistas*, in addition to signifying modernity through the sheer number of people who must transit this part of Caracas. What I am trying to say here is that massivity is also a marker of modernity, especially if massivity is counted in people in cars and not in poor people.

A third way that the Avenida Libertador project signifies modernity for the democratic government is through the shift in administration that occurred in the MOP, and, in this transitional project, during the course of the construction of the avenida. As I have established, the Pérez Jiménez dictatorship began construction on Avenida Libertador. The transitional *Memoria y cuentas* heavily criticized the urban-planning and contract-administration practices of the Pérez Jiménez administration. It was not until 1963, five years after the democratic coup, that the MOP fully revamped its administrative systems and its reporting became more thorough than in previous years. Under the direction of Leopoldo Sucre Figarella, the MOP took on a more systematic planning process, carrying out urban-planning studies and developing a four-year plan, first presented in the report from fiscal year 1964. In this report, Sucre Figarella indicts the government prior to 1959 (which is of course Pérez Jiménez's time) for making poor decisions, creating a deficit, and "strangling" the economy (Ministerio de Obras Públicas 1965, I-1). The democratic MOP distinguished itself from its preceding administrations by providing what it considered a full accounting of its activities (*rindiendo cuentas*). This meant detailed progress and expenditure reports, as well as extensive sections justifying the methodology of studies carried out during the planning process. In addition, it was important to the democratic MOP to prove that under its administration, projects would be completed, and in a timely fashion. Under Pérez Jiménez, the MOP annual report was little more than a showcase for the government's construction projects.

By the time of the Sucre Figarella administration, the *Memoria y cuentas* had ballooned into three tomes — two larger books detailing works in the planning stage and works in progress and a slimmer book with accounting information. Avenida Libertador was one of many projects completed by the democratic MOP on its *plan cuatrienal* (four-year plan) from 1965 to 1968. Published in 1964, this plan followed Sucre Figarella's administrative reforms of 1963. The plan communicated a kind of accountability that had previously been uncharacteristic of the MOP. On the Avenida Libertador project, this meant the MOP charted all previous expenditures on the construction, then projected costs and the time line to complete the project. Once this time line was established, the MOP could return to it in later years to demonstrate progress. Work continued through 1965, and Avenida Libertador was inaugurated by President Raúl Leoni in January 1966.

Pasarelas: Transformista Strategy and Tactics on Avenida Libertador

I have to admit that I cannot place with certainty the first moment the *tacón* (high heel) of a *transformista* hit the concrete of Avenida Libertador. I have evidence of this occupation from at least the late 1970s. While I am certain that the dynamics of *transformista* experience on Avenida Libertador have changed during the last thirty years, the Avenida has been a site for *transformista* sex work for at least this long.

The Avenida is not the only option for *transformistas* to do sex work, although it is perhaps the most visible.[16] What marks sex work performed on Avenida Libertador in particular is its *public* nature. Avenida Libertador provides specific tactical advantages for the *transformistas* who work there: the facility of pedestrian-automobile interaction allows *transformistas* to work with clients in cars. There is a difference in scale that the *transformistas* use to make themselves more visible: there are fewer pedestrians here than in the more heavily foot-trafficked open-air malls and improvised markets dotting the Caracas landscape. On Libertador, a *transformista* alone or with two or three friends on the sidewalk stands out a lot more than she would if she were surrounded by pedestrians and market stalls. This is why sites such as Avenida Fuerzas Armadas, closer to El Centro, or Avenida Andres Bello, a block north of Libertador, are not optimal sites for *transformista* sex work. Too much foot traffic obscures *transformista* spectacle, while too much automotive traffic (such as on a freeway or a less pedestrian-friendly avenue) makes it less possible to slow down cars or negotiate prices. Too much automotive traffic also obscures *transformista* spectacle in that the women become too small for the landscape, more difficult to perceive.

In this sense, Libertador is the perfect balance of scale and traffic for both projecting one's spectacle and facilitating selective contact with other people (too much contact would be dangerous, resulting in more vulnerability to policing or violence from passersby). In addition, the tactical advantages of Libertador include the stairs going between the upper and lower levels of the Avenida, which can be used to evade pursuit from police or other individuals, either in vehicles or on foot; the *pasarelas*, which facilitate north-south movement when evading police in vehicles; the many residential side streets that connect to Libertador, which provide opportunities to hide or run away; the two levels of the Avenida, its on-ramps, off-ramps, and turnarounds, which allow cars to circle around the north and south lanes interminably; its proximity to several gay bars on Avenida Francisco Solano López (one block south) or the Búlevard de Sabana Grande (two blocks south), where *transformistas* can take breaks or stay off the street for a while. During the political conflict between supporters of the government and the Opposition, Libertador provided yet another tactical advantage: the protection of Chavistas against the Policía Metropolitana, who were under the control of the Opposition leader Alfredo Peña, the mayor of Caracas. The Chavistas were set up in La Campiña, in front of Petróleos de Venezuela, the nationalized oil company, which has its main office at the eastern end of the sex-work area of Libertador. In considering *transformista* presence on Libertador, two categories of description come most to mind: the various *sites* along this stretch of the Avenida and the different *stances* that *transformistas* employ on these sites.

The primary site of *transformista* occupation on Libertador at the beginning of my fieldwork was the *pasarela*. These walkways, designed to facilitate foot traffic between the north and south sides of the Avenida, also serve various functions for *transformistas*. They provide a buffer to create distance between the police and *transformistas*. If a police vehicle (such as the perolón) is approaching from one direction, a *transformista* can move to the other side of the *pasarela* to avoid contact. This function also facilitates contact with clients — if a client is spotted, then circles back, a *transformista* can more easily go to his car across the *pasarela*. *Pasarelas* also provide boundaries — if someone is occupying one *pasarela*, a *transformista* can move down the street to work at another one, safely keeping her distance from enemies. The converse is also true — the *pasarela* can provide a place for a group of *transformistas* to come together while they are working. But what I believe is the most important function of the *pasarela* is that it serves as a site for both visibility and invisibility.

The word *pasarela* recurred in one of my other field sites — the Miss Venezuela *casting*. *Pasarela* means, simultaneously, "aisle," "walkway," "runway," and "runway walk," as in the walk practiced by both fashion models and beauty queens. If a model has a good runway walk, you say, "tiene pasarela" (she has runway). So the *pasarelas*, so cleverly designed by the engineers of Avenida Libertador, serve as a site not just for *transformista* tactics but also for imaginary projection. When a *transformista* wants to be seen in traffic, she wanders out into the middle of the *pasarela*, and then back to the end, where she can make eye contact with potential clients. She walks slowly, emphasizing the movement of her hips, swiveling on her *tacones*, looking distractedly out at the street, at cars passing by, at the other *pasarelas*. At the end of the *pasarela*, she can stand fairly motionless and watch cars pass her by. *Transformistas* do not signal to cars to get their attention, they just stand on the end of the *pasarela* in a sort of pose and make eye contact with a driver when a car slows down. This is how the *pasarela* provides visibility.

If a *transformista* does not want to be seen, she will make her way down the stairs on either end of the *pasarela*. These stairs lead to the second level and are often used as escape routes. Sometimes the stairs are used as a way to meet up with clients once eye contact is made from the *pasarela*. The stairs themselves can become another site of *transformista* occupation. They are used to hide from police, as an escape route, as an alternative place to meet clients, and as a place to take a quick break. This way a *transformista* can optimize her visibility by displaying herself on the *pasarela*, but she also has a way to get out of sight when necessary.

Pasarelas are not the only sites for *transformista* sex work on the Avenida, but they are the most visible. Some *transformistas* prefer to work on the sidewalks of the Avenida, closer to side streets, which provide more shadows and reduce visibility. I tended to encounter older and more down-on-their-luck *transformistas* at these sites. *Pasarela* space is at a premium when there are many *transformistas* out working. The *pasarela* is also too visible for some *transformistas*, who may not like the way the street lights shine on them, or who fear detection by police and so shy away from such public visibility. These *transformistas* tend to work alone or with one other person nearby. The cisgender women sex workers I encountered on Libertador stayed off of the *pasarelas* and were primarily on the sidewalk, on the west end of where *transformistas* worked. These cisgender women stayed at that spot even when *transformistas* moved east to take advantage of the shifting politics on the Avenida.

As my fieldwork progressed and national politics began to affect the Avenida, many of the groups of *transformistas* that had previously worked on the *pasarelas* moved east, in front of Petroleos de Venezuela, where an encampment of Chávez supporters clashed with the Policía Metropolitana. *Transformista* occupation of Avenida Libertador was accomplished at several sites: *pasarelas*, stairs, sidewalks, and plazas. However, mere physical presence at these sites was not enough to impose *transformista* presence. *Transformista* stances were an important element in projecting an imposing presence on the Avenida.

STANCES

I observed two stances that *transformistas* took on Avenida Libertador to impose their presence: runway modeling, also called *pasarela*, and display of breasts and torsos. Runway modeling consists of a stylized walk along a length of *pasarela* or sidewalk, along with the turning and posing I describe in chapter 3. *Transformistas* would emulate the walk of runway models or beauty queens when moving from one place to another in publicly visible sites such as across a *pasarela* or along the curb. This manner of walking, which pauses and reorders time for a moment, differed from the pace of other locomotion on the avenida and called attention to itself. A long stride and swinging hips perched on platform heels catches the eyes of passing drivers and other onlookers. This shift in temporality, often described as elegance, distinguishes itself from the pace of other goings-on. It is, of course, consciously performative, and it serves to reference and produce femininity as well as producing distinction. But *pasarela* also references the larger national culture of beauty and glamour, and in this way provides an entry for *transformistas* into an aspect of Venezuelan national identity in public view. *Pasarela* stance makes *transformistas* immediately legible as glamorous women to passersby. While it is common knowledge that the glamorous ladies of Avenida Libertador are *transformistas*, this stance normalizes their visibility within the Venezuelan aesthetic of beauty and femininity, if even from a distance. It makes them a visible and legible part of Caracas street life.

In addition to runway walking, *transformistas* also often stand still and pose. Occasionally, in these poses, some *transformistas* will open their shirts up to bare their hormone- or surgically enhanced breasts. Sometimes a *transformista* will remove her top altogether and go bare breasted. This practice of displaying the body to potential clients also generates *transformista* visibility, and constitutes the second stance I have identified. Displaying breasts and the torso serves several purposes on the avenida. Breast display occurred at very specific sites: at the ends of *pasarelas* and along the sidewalk in front of Petróleos de Venezuela—both sites where *transformistas* could avoid police. Ostensibly, this stance is used to market the commodity that *transformistas* are selling—their bodies. It is also a display of one visual sign that marks them as women (not just feminine appearing, but physically, carnally female), and thus reinforces *transformistas'* authenticity as women. Further, baring the breasts and torso scandalizes passersby, who are almost exclusively in cars, and creates a spectacle. The spectacular nature of this *transformista* stance can be seen in the cars full of people, sometimes entire families or groups of friends, that slow down and stare at bare-breasted *transformistas* in the evenings. *Transformistas* blow kisses or yell insults back at the cars. I never saw any business come of this interaction with groups in cars, but it was certainly part of the performance of being a *transformista* working on Libertador, even though not all *transformistas* engaged in this activity. When I asked a *transformista* who bares her breasts why she does so, she told me that she had to show off her "talents," essentially saying, "if you got it, flaunt it." It is important to note that this stance differentiates *transformistas* from many cisgender women sex workers, who do not risk public nudity in this way.[17] In this sense, it also marks and produces *transformista* space along the Avenida. By directly flaunting the local ordinances in a highly visible way, *transformistas* are asserting that they are in charge of the space — that they can stand calmly and display themselves and police can't do anything about it.

ACTIVIST STANCE

A third stance that I want to introduce is what I call *activist stance*; this is an emerging stance on the Avenida from what I can tell, and it involves more traditional forms of activist advocacy, such as condom distribution and a recent demonstration. I include my own presence on the Avenida under this category. The effectiveness of activist positioning at this site became clear to me on watching video footage of the first Vigilia Trans (Trans Vigil), celebrated on June 25, 2004, on Avenida Libertador, where about ten *transformistas* and thirty supporters positioned themselves along the Avenida and displayed placards bearing their rights as defined in the Universal Declaration of Human Rights.[18] This video footage was provided to me by the group TransVenus de Venezuela, formed after my departure from Caracas by some of the people who helped me distribute condoms on the Avenida. In the video of the vigil, several *transformistas* stand in the middle of the street, blocking half of the lanes of traffic with a banner. They hold placards made by TransVenus, which have the excerpts from the Universal Declaration of Human Rights: the right to identity, the right to employment. As vehicles pass, one *transformista* begins joking with the passengers, holding out her sign to a passing van and saying "lee, papi" (read it, daddy). When a moped slows to look at her or the sign, she tells the driver "ve abajo" (go below), an allusion to the strategy of having clients circle the Avenida on its lower express level. Argelia Bravo, who is making the video for TransVenus, notices the police come up in their SUV. She says "ah, los permisos," and she and a physician who volunteered with TransVenus approach the police with the permits that they have secured to protest and block traffic. After this vigil, the health reporter Vanessa Davies interviewed the organizers and published two extensive articles about transgender and *transformista* life in Venezuela. The articles were published in *El Nacional*, one of Venezuela's newspapers of record; one of the articles focused on Avenida Libertador (Davies 2004a, 2004b). I point to these two stories to suggest that the visibility that *transformistas* use for their survival on Avenida Libertador can also be used to draw attention to the violations faced by *transformistas* and other transgender people in Venezuela.

Transformista Mediation

I would like to return to the quote from Venezuela: "Mi nombre es Venezuela. Soy una *transformista*. Trabajo aquí en este nightclub. Es mi medio, pero no es mi meta" (My name is Venezuela. I am a *transformista*. I work here in this nightclub. This is my medium, but it is not my goal). In my work with *transformistas* in Venezuela, I was struck by this fierce sense of unconditional belonging in the nation—whether or not it was happy to have them. How, I wondered, do *transformistas* make a place for themselves in Venezuela? I suspect that they employ what I call *mediation* to project their presence in the national imaginary. Mediation is defined by the Spanish Colombian communications theorist Jesús Martín-Barbero as "the function of a medium, which mass culture fulfills day by day: the communication between the real and the imaginary" (1993, 56). By *mediation* in this case I mean the tactics that *transformistas* employ to project their mythic beings into the urban, and ultimately the national, imaginary. By using the mass medium of the mass transit that has trafficked Avenida Libertador for decades, *transformistas* have built a reputation for themselves as available, desirable, and dangerous. At this site on the juncture of power and modernity in late twentieth-century Caracas, *transformistas* have carved out a persistent place to project themselves into the national imaginary. *Transformistas* use Avenida Libertador for a variety of tactical and symbolic purposes. Through this use, and the public visibility it provides, *transformistas* are doing work on the order of symbolic projection: establishing a place for themselves in what it means to be Venezuelan and live in Caracas. Though it was her medium but not her goal, Avenida Libertador gave the *transformista* named Venezuela—and many others before and after her—the platform from which to project herself into the world. In the part that follows, we will turn to the third order of magnitude in this analysis: from the stage to the body itself.

PART III. On the Body

5

Sacar el Cuerpo

TRANSFORMISTA AND *MISS* EMBODIMENT

Yo gasté un dineral en este rostro, mi amor.

I've spent a fortune on this face, my love.
—LA CONTESSA, from an interview conducted in 2004;
my translation

Aceitigallo

The long-term occupants of a Caracas residential hotel have painted the walls a bright green with orange accents and put up posters with messages of friendship: Garfield, Piolín, Sylvester the Cat. I sit on the corner of a squeaky queen-size bed in the modest room. A television in a cage is bolted to the wall above me. It blares with the sounds of the afternoon cartoons. Modelo, the queen and enforcer of Avenida Libertador, relaxes on her bed, smoking and laughing at the *comiquitas* (cartoons).[1] Beside her on the floor sleeps a girl; you can only see her peroxided hair poking out from under the sheet she has wrapped around her. Long night. Long story how she ended up on the floor next to Modelo. On the bed the *transformistas* Norkeli and Carolina chatter about some *loca*[2] they saw last night on the Avenida. I ask Norkeli how she gets her breasts so full and round.

"Me inyecto aceitigallo" (I inject *aceitigallo*), she replies. I think that aceitigallo is the name of another hormone, one of the litany that *transformistas* recite when I ask them how they form their feminine bodies.

"What is that, aceitigallo?"

"Gallo. Gallo. Aceite Gallo" (Gallo. Gallo. Gallo Oil).

"¿*Aceite* Gallo? Isn't that bad for you?"

"No, no," says Norkeli, shrugging it off. When I get home, I confirm it: Gallo is the brand of olive oil that I have in my kitchen, a pretty gold tin with a rooster on it.[3]

In this moment I am acutely aware of the ways that *transformistas* imagine and produce their bodies. Norkeli's nonchalance in telling me that she injected olive oil under her skin to achieve her breasts was striking, but this is not an uncommon practice among *transformistas*. It initially struck me as a very dangerous practice, and, indeed, the injection of foreign substances into the body can cause discomfort, infections, and tumors, and at times it may lead to amputations. Not to mention that it is pretty uncomfortable to do to one's self or one's friend. That Norkeli would be so cavalier about this practice marks a key way in which she relates to her body. In this chapter I reflect the logic of the body in which one comes to be so nonchalant. When placed alongside the daily hail of bottles, insults, and aggression to which most *transformistas* are subject, the idea of injecting olive oil under your skin seems somewhat minor. Indeed, as part of a project of fashioning one's body with the technologies that are available, it may even be pleasurable after the initial sting wears off. It is important to see *transformista* logics of the body in their full social context before projecting a universalized sense of the body and its limits onto the choices that *transformistas* make about their bodies. It is also important to place *transformista* logics of the body within a broader social context that includes the logics of hegemonic bodies. For this reason, I place the inquiry concerning *transformista* bodies alongside one about *miss* bodies, specifically on the topic of plastic surgery and other technologies of bodily transformation.

The logic of the body is the way the body makes sense — it encompasses the principles that govern how people understand their bodies in the world. Some of this is based on the experience of the body, what one understands one's body as capable of tolerating through experience. Some of it is based on social ideas of the body. Elizabeth Povinelli's (2006) analysis of the medical response to a boil on her shoulder as she crossed several borders reveals the differing logics of the body that frame the ways she and the people around her experience and interpret the boil.[4] This boil is understood as highly contagious and threatening anthrax in the United States and Canada, and in Australia it is taken as a normal part of inhabiting the social space she has transited. She uses this example to argue that these ways of seeing the boil are reflections of a system that leaves some bodies within a gray area of slow death, or "rotting" (32). Povinelli calls this way of paying attention to the fate of the flesh "carnality" (7). Similarly, I explore the social contexts that give meaning to the ways *transformistas* and *misses* produced their feminine bodies in Venezuela during the time of my fieldwork.

This chapter is based on interviews I conducted with *transformistas*, *misses*, and plastic surgeons about the process of transforming the body. The logic of the body I encountered among *transformistas* in Venezuela includes a strong notion of *nature* as both inherent and in need of collaboration in order to allow it to emerge. Medicine, in the form of plastic surgery and hormones, is a collaborative technology, correcting natural defects, such as unattractiveness, age, and unsatisfactory profiles. This is very similar to how plastic surgeons and *misses* described the relationship between these technologies and the body. The capacity to submit (or not) to medical authority defined the boundary between legitimate subjects of medical treatment and those seen as illegitimate, what Charles Briggs and Clara Mantini-Briggs call the line between "sanitary citizens" and "unsanitary subjects" (2003, 10). This logic, I argue, is bound up in the ideas of development and management that buttress the production of modernity in Venezuela. The notion of the development of the *self*, in the forms of both self-esteem and personal development, is deeply related to this way of understanding modernity in Venezuela. In these interviews, the way one felt about oneself formed part of the logic of the body that governed the sense of bodily transformation. The horizon of possibility enabled by one's body — the doors that one's body opened — also informed many of the ways *transformistas* and *misses* imagined bodily transformation.

While *transformistas* showed a broader tolerance for sometimes painful self-administered procedures, the idea of sacrificing and suffering for beauty was present for most of the people I interviewed. The logic of vulnerability is key here — a sense of what the body is capable or incapable of tolerating. This idea of vulnerability is wrapped up in the process of modernity in Venezuela, and in what Dean Spade has called "the distribution of life chances" (2011, 32). I have argued throughout this book that the process of modernity in Venezuela seeks to extinguish nonnormative subjects, such as *transformistas*. I will develop this idea further to encompass how modernity shapes the bodies of the Venezuelans in this chapter.

It is impossible to separate *transformistas'* experience of bodily violation from their ideas of what kinds of interventions their bodies are capable of withstanding. La Contessa, for example, narrated the extraordinary violence that she lived through in the 1980s in almost the same breath as she described the kinds of investments and interventions she had made on and in her body. The examples in this chapter eloquently show how these logics buttress the kinds of decisions people make about the management of their and others' bodies in Venezuela—whether they are *transformistas*, *misses*, or plastic surgeons. *Sacar el cuerpo* (bring out the body) was a phrase that came up in both pageant and *transformista* contexts, and it describes the use of technologies to allow the feminine body to emerge. Here I explore the production of *transformista* and *miss* bodies through the logic of *sacar el cuerpo*.

Sacar el cuerpo, as a *transformista* logic of the body, reflects a broader discourse of carnality in Venezuelan modernity, one that also emerges in the production of *miss* bodies. This logic of the body in Venezuelan modernity is produced through the horizons of gendered possibility, the line between sanitary citizens and unsanitary subjects, and the relationship between technologies and bodies through somatechnics such as plastic surgery and hormones. While *misses* and *transformistas* may at first appear socially distant from each other, the logic of *sacar el cuerpo* unites the productions of femininity on their bodies. As the examples in this chapter demonstrate, *transformistas* and *misses* "bring out" their bodies in the discursive climate of Venezuelan modernity, negotiating its limitations and excesses as they make their ways in the world. Examining carnality—the constitution, maintenance, and destruction of flesh—in its full context reveals the powerful ways that bodily practice and social discourse are interconnected, and this examination refutes a universalizing, first-world tendency in gender performativity and embodiment frameworks.

I offer a methodological discussion of the ways we ask questions about the relationship between social discourse and bodily practice. Framing this inquiry within gender studies more broadly, I chart a course through Harold Garfinkel's concept of ethnomethodology and his analysis of a subject he calls "Agnes," and then I discuss feminist ethnography's proposal that we ask questions about how bodies come to matter in various local contexts. I end my discussion of methodology by outlining recent approaches within transgender studies that propose we consider gender as an empirical question.

After the discussion of methodology, I describe in more detail the nature of plastic surgery as I encountered it in the lives of *misses* and *trans-*

formistas in Venezuela. I employ the concept of somatechnics to explore the mutually constitutive relationship between technologies and bodies in the production of femininity in Venezuela. I then expand my analysis of the interviews I conducted with plastic surgeons, focusing on the production of medical authority through the idea of sanitary citizenship. I move to a discussion of the production of modernity in Venezuela through the project of harmonizing the body, both in plastic surgeons' proposals that "science" is against commercial interests, and in the ways they see plastic surgery as a form of management of both bodies and patients' desires. The idea of developing the self emerged in several ways throughout these interviews, particularly as this related to the therapeutic justification for plastic surgery. I discuss this idea of development through the themes of voluntarism, self-esteem, and the intervention of third parties. I conclude this chapter by returning to the idea of *sacar el cuerpo* as it was articulated in my interviews with *transformistas*.

A Note on Ethnomethodology

I employ Garfinkel's notion of "accomplishment" in my construction of the idea of *the accomplishment of femininity*.[5] Garfinkel developed this concept in his *Studies in Ethnomethodology* (1967), in which he details his work with Agnes (a pseudonym), a patient of the Gender Identity Clinic at UCLA who sought a sex-change operation. In Agnes, Garfinkel found an intriguing challenge for ethnomethodology, and indeed thought of Agnes herself as a "practical methodologist" (180) because of the way she reported studying the behavior of women in order to herself "pass [*sic*]" as a woman. For Garfinkel, ethnomethodological observations were an important method for attending to the detailed practices involved in producing femininity, and these observations were also useful in considering interview data. An ethnomethodological approach seeks to observe the logic that grounds particular statements and practices observed in social interactions. I approached the backstage preparations for beauty pageants and my interviews with plastic surgeons in this chapter ethnomethodologically, attending both to the performances inherent in these moments and the logics on which these performances rested. Ethnomethodology was useful in mapping out some areas of inquiry for this research, but its commitment to agnosticism in observations and the presumed positionality of the ethnomethodologist as naive outsider were insufficient to fully connect these practices and statements to the processes of gender and racial formation that mark the Venezuelan nation.

The ethnomethodological approach was useful in considering the terms on which people engaged in the project of shaping their bodies. Essentially, this concept refers to the practices, gestures, and underlying assumptions implemented to achieve legibility as a feminine subject. Garfinkel engaged Agnes within a clinical environment, concerning himself with endogenous ways of producing meaning—what "passing" as a woman meant to Agnes, not to the people around her. What an ethnomethodological approach allows is an emphasis on the practices involved in the construction of an everyday gendered performance. All of us, as gendered subjects, engage in the accomplishment of gender. This concept allows me to focus on the minute details of the practices we use to achieve legibility in a particular gender. More important, it put me in the dressing rooms of the Miss Venezuela *casting*, and suggested that in addition to observing the spectacle of the show, I also needed to observe the process of applying makeup, doing hair, and dressing. From this location, I was able to observe the unique relationship between pageant contestants and pageant producers (including organizers, stylists, coaches, and other *casting* personnel), who are key to my findings in this book.

I extend ethnomethodological inquiry into the realm of what Povinelli has termed "carnality." While Garfinkel's approach was primarily concerned with the *performance* of gender, carnality is an important part of passing: without a convincing feminine flesh or form, any performance of femininity displayed by Agnes would be unconvincing.[6] Garfinkel does not fully explore the importance of bodily transformation to Agnes's passing; he instead focuses on identity-based concerns, such as Agnes's creation of her "female biography." Povinelli's carnality demands attention to the social condition of the bodies being observed. In this approach, a *transformista* or *miss* body does not make sense without an understanding of the social forces acting on it.

Carnality requires an apprehension of the discursive climate that produces bodies as well as subjects. This approach allows me to account for what Garfinkel presents as a confounding factor. Agnes submitted herself to Garfinkel's analysis in order to obtain sex-reassignment surgery, explaining that she was "intersexed." In an appendix to this chapter in *Studies in Ethnomethodology*, Garfinkel cites Robert Stoller to reveal that, in fact, Agnes had been taking her mother's birth-control pills since she was twelve years old (1967, 285). Agnes had also obtained breast implants before approaching the clinic, another sign that the "treatment" she was undergoing was not her only strategy to feminize her body.

Using carnality to read between the lines of *Studies in Ethnomethodology*, I see Agnes engaging in the same kinds of creativity and resourcefulness that *transformistas* employ in their projects of transformation; Agnes works medical authority to shape her body according to her vision. Agnes's approach to Garfinkel and Stoller themselves was an extension of the practical methodology that so impressed Garfinkel — one that plumbed the sexological logic of the body for its collaboration in her project of becoming.[7] Only by attending to carnality does this become apparent in the case of Agnes. In the spirit of Agnes, and many others before her and since, I seek to do justice to the resourcefulness of *transformistas* managing their own transformations.

A *Transformista* Logic of the Body

Transformistas consider the body a site of transformation, and they have a very specific ideology about how this transformation takes place. The contemporary *transformista* notion of transformation is different from the binary and radical notion of transformation many might be familiar with. Transformation is of course not as abrupt as revolution, but for most of us transformation implies a poetic transition from one state to another: Larva becomes chrysalis becomes butterfly. The ideology of transformation that many of the *transformistas* I interviewed in Venezuela articulated was a bit different. To them, transformation is what they *are* — they embody it. And transformation operates through a specific process: *sacar el cuerpo*. To cause what is already there to emerge. To bring out the "desirable" features one notes about one's self using technologies such as posture, gesture, clothing, makeup, hair treatments, hormones, strategically injected substances, silicone, and other kinds of plastic surgery, even transnational migration. This sense of gender transformation differs from the familiar notion in the realm of transsexualism, that of changing the state of the body to concur with the gender identity that resides in the mind — the use of technologies of the body and psyche to address "gender dysphoria." For *transformistas*, gender is always already in their bodies. The task of a *transformista* is to enable its emergence.

Transformistas use various technologies to *sacar el cuerpo*, to bring out desirable features in their bodies as part of their feminizing process. The *transformistas* I worked with in Caracas used olive oil, baby oil, saline solution, and water injections to round out breasts and hips. Silicone injections were less frequently reported, but I do know of *transformistas* who have migrated to Europe and have since had silicone injections done. Breast implants were considered both a feminizing practice and an investment for moving up in sex work. These were often professionally or semiprofessionally implanted—in other words plastic surgeons or people who presented themselves as plastic surgeons implanted prostheses in operating rooms. *Transformistas* have developed a folk medicine around hormone administration that involves large and frequent doses of various forms of birth control available over the counter in Venezuela.[8] While at first I was surprised by the kinds of substances *transformistas* use to shape their bodies, I learned to record this information with little reaction or judgment. Shock and judgment do quite a bit of work to produce social distance—the distance between a body hegemonically conceived of as human and one thought to be monstrous. The luxury of shock in receiving this experience of the body is one of the things that sets *transformistas* apart from many sexologists and endocrinologists I interviewed, who often expressed shock or outrage when I asked them about *transformistas*' self-administered feminizing regimens. While there is cause for health concern for many of these procedures, these medical professionals used their concern and shock to exclude *transformistas* from the category of therapeutic subjects, delegitimized them with the label "false transsexuals," and disavowed themselves of any medical obligation to assist *transformistas* in their feminizing processes.

Sacar el Cuerpo

Transformistas appropriate, innovate, and abstract technologies such as hormones and injections in order to "bring out" their female bodies. The phrase *sacar el cuerpo* suggests a relationship between nature and technology in which technology is employed to draw out what is naturally there and help nature express itself. This cultivation of the body, technology assisting nature, a Foucauldian ethics, profoundly informs the corporeal projects of *transformistas*, and, I believe, of other subjects in Venezuelan modernity.

In her discussion of hormones during an interview in the Propatria neighborhood of Caracas in October 2002, Paulina describes in detail how she received information about self-medication regimens and what their effects were.

OCHOA: How did you start taking hormones?

PAULINA: Because I met a friend who was already transgender; she was already a *chica de apariencia* [feminine-looking girl] who had been operated. She started telling me about them, and she would even give them to me for free back in those days. While I was working with her.

OCHOA: Did you take shots or pills?

PAULINA: Both, because we always had to have everything [that was available]. That's a treatment you follow. You get injections and you take pills. What I don't like is that it's for the rest of your life. I'm never going to stop taking hormones.

OCHOA: No?

PAULINA: No . . . I stopped taking them, and that's why my back came out. I have a photo from when I used to do sex work, and I was all skinny. I stopped taking the pills when she went to Germany and she got married, and my body starts re—. . . it reproduces itself as a man's body, the hormones go elsewhere . . .

OCHOA: So after she left you didn't take any more hormones?

PAULINA: No . . . but now I have Minigynon, the [contraceptive] pills, but I haven't been taking them because since I'm not working now well, that's money right there. Spending on shots. Because you have to take like five to ten shots in one day.

OCHOA: Every day?

PAULINA: That you have to inject yourself.

OCHOA: How much does that cost?

PAULINA: Ginecosid costs like sixteen hundred bolívars [about US$1.50 at the time] per shot. And Cycloesterin costs like thirty-five hundred bolívars [about US$3] . . . for the box; it's like thirty-five hundred for the box.

OCHOA: So, how do the hormones affect you?

PAULINA: Look, I get very affected by the pills. Yes. Because they stick to the walls of my stomach and it's a lot of vomiting but . . . yes, you do see a good result . . . taking hormones, because

it helps you manage your body hair, and it goes, it like polishes
every angle of one's body, it goes along making it more feminine.

In Paulina's account of her transformation, I see a regimen that exacts
a high price: nausea and vomiting. But for Paulina, the transformation
is worth it because this regimen brings out the body she has within; the
regimen polishes the feminine aspects of her body and deemphasizes the
masculine. Paulina does not narrate this as a battle in the way that one
transgender woman's mother did when she invoked Simón Bolívar to describe her daughter's project of transformation: "Si se opone la naturaleza, lucharemos contra ella y haremos que nos obedezca" (If nature is
opposed, we will fight her and make her obey us). Instead, for Paulina, it
is a routine that helps her manage her body. And it is this management of
her body, her "art of existence," that we can read as a mediation of modernity in Venezuela. The potentiality of a *transformista* body comes not from
her liminality in terms of gender but from how she is able to exist within
a space of violence and death, to negotiate its excesses, and to make her
body out of these excesses.[9]

Gender as an Empirical Question

In order to understand how *transformista* and *miss* bodies are mediations
of modernity in Venezuela, I have found useful a recent approach to asking
questions about gender. Various authors in transgender studies have proposed that we begin to think of gender as an empirical question. Following this approach, gender itself is an empirical question, one that requires
us, in ethnographic projects, to observe the categories in use in gendering
practices (see Jagose and Kulick 2004). David Valentine outlines the use-
fulness of such an approach in delineating the categories operating in a
field site, in this case the "ball culture" of New York City: "In the constel-
lation of performative categories available at the balls, there are, indeed,
strict distinctions between fem queens (male-bodied feminine people),
butch queens (male-bodied masculine people), butches (female-bodied
masculine people), and women or lesbians (female-bodied feminine per-
sons). But the divisions, strictly enforced as they are, are seen at the balls
to be united by the category 'gay'" (2004, 218). Valentine elaborates on
this idea extensively in his later *Imagining Transgender* (2007). Spade and
Wahng expand this idea of gender as an empirical category to attempt to

account for relations of power and coloniality. Wahng's interpretation of the situation of Korean sex slaves for the Japanese military in the Second World War suggests the national and colonial dimensions of gendering practice:

> Although born female, [Korean sex slaves] were configured as sub-human entities with superhuman strength—as Amazons and "sanitary toilets"—in the Japanese nationalist imaginary. . . .
>
> In contrast, Japanese women, including Japanese military prostitutes during World War II, were for the most part represented and representable as reproductive, feminine supports for the reification of Japanese masculinity within the field of civility comprised by Japanese nationalism. Because Korean sex slaves were reterritorialized as subhuman, they were factored out of an economy in which representable and recognizable genders circulated within Korean as well as Japanese fields of civility and respectability. In fact, several former sex slaves attest that they do not experience their gender as similar to that of "other women" who have not undergone sex slavery and militarized bastardization.[10] (Spade and Wahng 2004, 244)

This approach to the study of gender refuses the isolation of racial, colonial, and gender categories from one another and reveals the complex and mutually constitutive social formations that produce subjectivity in these systems.

In the context of Venezuela, this approach demands that I contextualize the development of Venezuelan femininities in their internal and external colonial-national relations, putting this work in dialogue with the literature on coloniality, race, and modernity in Latin America. As this project developed, I began to see that this work is about understanding third-world queer survival in the context of power relations that produce many people as "subhuman" subjects, in the words of Wahng, and subject us to physical, social, and economic violence.

This empirical approach to gender allowed me to hold two groups of people in very different social locations (*transformistas* and *misses*) within the same analytic frame. My stakes in making this analytic move have to do with the ways trans subjects have been studied in the past.[11] In much of the scholarly literature, trans subjects have often been figured as "concentrations of gender" (Kulick 1998, 9), subversive subjects who trouble gender (Butler 1993, 1999), materializations of "category crisis" (Garber 1992; Prieur 1998; Schifter 1999), or non-Western Others who denaturalize the Western gender binary (Johnson 1997; Nanda 1990; Roscoe 1991; Trexler 1995). Indeed, many of these studies (with the notable exception of Judith Butler's) start with the premise of describing transgender experiences, sometimes with an attempt to explain the presence of transgender people in the societies under analysis (in particular Jacobo Schifter, Annick Prieur, and to a certain extent Don Kulick). However, trans subjects remain isolated from the broader social context. This has changed somewhat with the emergence of the field of transgender studies, and with a queer move in anthropology that has produced work such as Martin Manalansan's *Global Divas* (2003), Gayatri Reddy's *With Respect to Sex* (2005), and David Valentine's *Imagining Transgender* (2007).[12] Following this queer turn, as well as Judith Halberstam's *Female Masculinity* (1998) and Eve Kosofsky Segwick's *Epistemology of the Closet* (1990), in parsing a taxonomy of genders relevant in this social world, I hold *misses* and *transformistas* in the same frame to reveal the Venezuelan logics of the body that govern the carnalities enfleshed in these relations of power. Ethnographic approaches to the body rooted in feminism establish an empirical approach to the question of gender while attending to the fate of flesh.

Feminist Ethnography and the Body

Feminist ethnographies of structural and political violence seek to account for the psychic and everyday residue of spectacular forms of violence, such as war and famine. The works of Nancy Scheper-Hughes and Veena Das have been important in this effort. Both refute the notion of violence as rupture, and through their ethnographic description they show how violence wears itself into the everyday, how hunger becomes a "lived experience," how it shapes the "body-self" (Scheper-Hughes 1992, 135). As Das eloquently asks, "What is it to pick up the pieces and to live in this very place of devastation?" (2009, 6). These approaches attend to the logic of the body in processes of modernity and colonization. Rather than understanding the body as a universal constant, as a psychic projection and material reality that remains intact and enduring, feminist ethnography shares with Butler a project of understanding materiality *itself* as a cultural construction. As Scheper-Hughes puts it: "The unquestionability of the body-self is, for Ludwig Wittgenstein, where all knowledge and certainty of the world begins. And yet it is difficult to imagine even the first, most 'natural' intuition of the body-self as unmediated by cultural meanings and representation. And so even at this primary level of analysis, the biological, psychological, and symbolic meanings of hunger are merged in the experience of bodies that are mindful and minds that are *culturally embodied*" (1992, 136).

Three feminist ethnographies, Diane Nelson's *A Finger in the Wound* (1999), Saba Mahmood's *The Politics of Piety* (2007), and Elizabeth Povinelli's *The Empire of Love* (2006), provide important critiques of Butler's logocentric approach through the empirical study of gender. Responding to misreadings of *Gender Trouble*, in *Bodies That Matter* Butler addresses the notion that her work ignores materiality. The constructivist misapprehension of her argument, she says, ignores the constructed nature of materiality itself, here in the concept of sex. Butler reveals both the normative power of a concept such as sex and the moments in its reiteration and reinscription when that normative power becomes vulnerable: "As a sedimented effect of a reiterative or ritual practice, sex acquires its naturalized effect, and, yet, it is also by virtue of this reiteration that gaps and fissures are opened up as the constitutive instabilities in such constructions, as that which escapes or exceeds the norm, as that which cannot be wholly defined or fixed by the repetitive labor of that norm" (Butler 1993, 10).

This approach to gender, and then sex, has inspired a great deal of empirical work, much of it in the area of the performativity of gender. But if we take Butler's argument about materiality into the field, we must weigh it in a social arena crosscut with competing and colluding social forces. Materiality, in Butler's sense, is an effect in and of itself, and it can be read as evidence of the workings of power. Diane Nelson's ethnography of body politics in quincentennial Guatemala extends Butler's argument about materiality and bodies to the negotiation of power and the state in Guatemala. Nelson's formulation, which she calls "bodies that splatter," contests the integrity of the body in the process of colonialism and civil war. For her, this approach is "an attempt to get away from the idea of either a primordial or a potential whole body — either of an individual or a body politic — and to focus attention on the wounded body, on constitutive differences and antagonisms" (Nelson 1999, 210). Nelson reveals the gendered, racialized, and ethnocidal differentials in the constitution and legibility of bodies in Guatemala. Nelson's examples are of friction points on and of bodies in relation to the Guatemalan state, sites of cultural anxiety that reveal the materiality of power in Guatemala. Nelson extends Elizabeth Grosz's (1994) notion of "body image" out to the "body politic," effacing the divide between the individual and the social body, between "the body" and bodies. Nelson's use of the term *splatter* where Butler uses *matter* is a response to the overwhelming focus on disembodied discourse in Butler's work. As Nelson puts it, "the term *splatter* emphasizes wetness and fluidity, insisting on the instability of bodies as carriers of meaning. A splatter leaves a wet spot, like blood, or 'stains' on a lineage" (211).

Nelson's use of Butler's argument about materiality helps me make sense of bodies in Venezuela through the lenses of coloniality and modernity. It helps me understand that Aceite Gallo is a way of understanding the body and its permeability that exists within the ways *transformistas* learn the social significance of their bodies. Within this context, Aceite Gallo may not seem excessive at all — and indeed makes sense as a choice for many *transformistas* — despite its very real health effects. Nelson's use of Grosz allows me to connect both *transformista* and *miss* bodies with the production of nation, and to attend to the discourses of modernity, such as voluntarism and nature, which mobilize intervention and transformation.

Mahmood's insightful critique of liberal feminist notions of agency in *The Politics of Piety* (2007) also employs Butler's argument about materiality. Mahmood quite effectively connects this argument to Butler's critique of agency. Through her study of participants in the women's mosque movement in Egypt, Mahmood uses the example of the cultivation of modesty and shyness as an embodied practice. While drawing a similar conclusion to Nelson, that bodies are the materialization of social processes, and that embodied practices can simultaneously hold both possibilities of agency and the contradictions of power, Mahmood's example reveals the limits of Butler's logocentric framework. Mahmood proposes that a "mutually constitutive relationship between body learning and body sense" (157–58) is operating in the cultivation of shyness and modesty. Butler's emphasis on signification and language is perhaps not adequate to analyze "formulations of the body that insist on the inadequacy of the body to function as a sign" (166), according to Mahmood. Here she shows that mosque participants "do not understand the body as a sign of the self's interiority but as a means of developing the self's potentiality. . . . *The mosque participants treat the body as a medium for, rather than a sign of, the self*" (166; my emphasis).

Mahmood's notion of the body as a medium is one that I have also considered through the idea of mediation in media studies. I am interested in convergence of the multiple senses of *medium*—the material, the spiritual, and the communicational. What does it mean then, to think of the *transformista* or the *miss* body as a mediation? First, it is to open up the question of how the body comes to mean in a given social context, but further it is to understand the processes and practices that produce that body as part of the social process of becoming.

Povinelli's approach to the body in *The Empire of Love* (2006) distinguishes between *corporeality* and *carnality*. In her chapter "Rotten Worlds," Povinelli contests Giorgio Agamben's idea of "bare life" and argues that Agamben doesn't account for the long, slow process of "rotting" to which some bodies are subjected. This rotting, living in a space of social death, marks the bodies of Australian aboriginal people and those, like Povinelli, who cohabit with them. When we make the body central to the question of gender, feminist ethnography gives us a way to pay attention to bodies in terms of their broader social meaning, while simultaneously contesting the tendency to abstract and universalize a sovereign or intact notion of the body. Further, it represents the carnal, messy, and enfleshed logics that an abstract approach can only hint at.

One incident during the production of the Miss Venezuela pageant made the carnality of *miss* bodies clear to me: It is the second day of shooting the *coletillas*, video shorts that will air for each of the *misses* as they are introduced in the buildup to the national pageant, to be held in two weeks. The pageant buzzes with *misses*, *maquilladores* (makeup artists), crew, and producers. Gisselle Reyes, the modeling authority of the nation and owner of Gisselle's International Models, oversees the taping of the modeling sessions, which combine photography with the video shoot. She stares intently at the video screen as the contestants pose, scrutinizing their two-dimensional forms.

Miss Yaracuy is waiting in chairs. She remembers me from the *casting* in Barquisimeto and smiles. The photographer begins the bikini session, directing Miss Yaracuy heavily in her poses: "Chúpate; sácate el cuerpo" (Suck it in; bring out your body). I notice deep bruises up and down Miss Yaracuy's legs. Her posing has rubbed off some of the makeup used to cover them. The bikini shoot ends and she goes in for a costume change and touch-up.

I ask the *maquillador* about the bruises. He says they are from *mesoterapia*, a kind of weight-reduction massage that is often advertised in shopping malls. And injections. Of what, he's not sure, but they go along with the massages. Several of the contestants sport these bruises, some with injection marks, some without. The *maquilladores* need to make sure they're all covered up.

Yaracuy emerges fabulous in a black dress. I ask her how she felt about the photo shoot. Fabulous. One of the stylists comes up to her and tells her that the dress looks amazing on her. It does. It is silk, crushed in a wave pattern. Spectacular. She turns around and he mentions he would only change one thing: take off that bra she has on. The strap is showing, he says, and it would not look lascivious.

"What would I use for breasts?" she responds. "Ah, you don't have breasts," says the stylist. I want to ask her if she is going to get an operation, but she is abruptly called away to makeup.

Plastic Surgery, Sanitary Citizenship, and Somatechnics

In both the *transformista* and *miss* contexts, the phrase *sacar el cuerpo* was used as a way to name the active participation of *transformistas* and *misses* in producing their feminine bodies. The Miss Yaracuy incident, in which the photographer issues this phrase as an instruction to his model, illustrates the everyday nature of technologies of bodily transformation and the unremarkability of an intervened body to the *miss* production process. When the stylist helpfully suggests removing the bra, both he and the *miss* understand her breasts as part of the construction of her image. Although the *miss* does indeed have breasts, the phrasing in this interaction reveals the shared understanding that her breasts are not truly breasts unless they are big enough, or, rather, that unaugmented breasts are not breasts at all. It is this unremarkability of bodily transformation, the willingness to submit one's self to surgical intervention, that marks *misses* as sanitary citizens. In this way, I would argue, *transformistas* also conform themselves to sanitary citizenship in their desire for plastic surgery. Their unwillingness to conform to the strictures of gender diagnosis, however, also marks them as unsanitary subjects. I turn now to a discussion of plastic surgery, as a primary site for the negotiation of sanitary citizenship for *transformistas*, *misses*, producers, and surgeons.

One of the challenges of this analysis was the difference in the ways *transformistas* and *misses* discussed plastic surgery. This was due in part to the kinds of access I had in the study—I was able to spend more time interviewing *transformistas*, while my access to the *misses* was limited by the logistics of the *casting* system and the rushed pace of production. This resulted in much more data on *transformistas'* ideas about plastic surgery and bodily transformation. At the same time, plastic surgery was such a routine element of the beauty pageant production system as to be almost unremarkable — it was no surprise to anyone that *misses* employed plastic surgery and were encouraged to make "fixes" (*arreglos*) to their bodies by Miss Venezuela producers. *Misses* and pageant producers were not centrally focused on plastic surgery; instead they were interested in the ongoing contest in which they were engaged. Osmel Sousa, the president of the Organización Miss Venezuela, is very matter-of-fact when discussing the question of plastic surgery, often the first thing he is asked by journalists. At times his response is provocative, indicating his nonchalance about the use of plastic surgery in the contest. A 2009 interview with ABC News illustrates this approach:

> As Sousa likes to say, "God created these beautiful women — but he also created plastic surgeons."
>
> Sousa is very open about the fact that women who train at his school get plastic surgery.
>
> "Every country does it," he said. "They just don't admit it. I do." (Kofman 2009)

In a 2000 interview with the curators of the *90-60-90* museum exhibition, Sousa contests the notion that the *misses* are produced. In this case, he minimizes the emphasis on plastic surgery in the beauty contest, however he still acknowledges its role in preparing beauty queens. The interviewer asks, "Can you tell us about the process of 'constructing a miss'?" Sousa responds:

> First of all you don't construct a miss. They are here because they are already pretty, because if they weren't, they wouldn't be here. Of course if you do have to do something to them, a surgical intervention, a facial fix, a reconstruction, well, what needs to be done is done. But, of course, that is done only to some of them. It's not like we're working in a clinic, please. I aim to do the least possible to them, but when it's inevitable, we have to do it. They're small surgeries, outpatient. These are not drastic changes at all. (Borges 2000, 14; my translation)

Another incident, which occurred during the national *casting* in the interior of Venezuela, illustrates both the nonchalance regarding plastic surgery among pageant contestants and the imaginary of social mobility and opportunity often attached to the idea of surgery. Inés is auditioning for Miss Venezuela in the Dallas of Venezuela, the business center of an oil-rich state that used to be cattle country and now has a lavish mall in the middle of a plain. She has been preparing for the *casting*, the way the Miss Venezuela organization selects its candidates from around the country. She says to be a *miss* is to be very disciplined: you practice and practice, and you have to manage your time. The contest is so all absorbing that there is no time for your friends, your boyfriend.

I ask her if she has had any surgery done. No. Nothing? She says she has not had to "fix" anything so far. But she'd like to. She wants to do her breasts, and profile her nose a bit. Nothing else. The boyfriend calls. She keeps telling him she is in an interview, but she keeps talking to him anyway.

I ask her, "What do you think about plastic surgery?" BUENISIMA. The best. It is the best solution God put in the heads of men.

Later she asks me about the *casting*; she wants to know what the other *misses* were like before this *casting*. I tell her what I have seen so far about the selection process. The other *misses* around us listen in.

"So there's still hope . . . that's why Miss Venezuela moves me." Yes? "Because . . . they operate on you for free."

"¡Ay, sí!" The other *misses* chime in.

"That's why!" exclaims Inés, laughing. "And for all the privileges you get just by being there." Another *miss* adds, helpfully: "Yes, because of all the doors it opens for you."

Plastic surgery is employed by both *transformistas* and *misses* to accomplish femininity and other life goals, such as social mobility or migration. As we will see in the interview data, plastic surgery is linked to ideas about nature and artificiality, opportunity and development, technology and excess. Informed by developments in transgender studies, I understand plastic surgery as a *somatechnology*, a technology of the body that is inseparable from the bodies it produces.

Somatechnics is a concept elaborated by Susan Stryker and Nikki Sullivan in the context of work on body modification. In the call for papers for the Transsomatechnics conference, the idea of somatechnics is employed as an analytic in transgender studies: "We understand the material intelligibility of the body (soma) to be inseparable from the techniques and technologies (technics) in and through which bodies are formed and transformed, and by means of which they are socially positioned and lived. The term somatechnics thus reflects contemporary understandings of the body as the incarnation of historically and culturally specific discourses and practices. It conceives of activities involving bodies — in medicine, science, law, information technologies, the arts, language, migration, racialisation, surveillance, state bureaucracy — as fundamentally constitutive of bodily being."[13] Sullivan elucidates the tenets of the somatechnics approach: "[Somatechnics] was recently coined in an attempt to articulate . . . the always-already technologised character of bodily formation and transformation, and the necessary material (or enfleshed) character of technology. The term somatechnics thus aims to supplant the logic of the 'and,' suggesting that modes and practices of corporeality are always-already, and without exception, in-relation and in-process: they necessarily transect and/or transgress what dominant logic conceives as hermetically sealed categories (of practice, embodiment, being, and so on)" (2009, 276).

Transformistas employ the somatechnologies of hormones and self-administered prosthetic injections. While *misses* also employ hormones to manage fertility, as well as diet and massage to manage weight, I do not focus on these here. The somatechnology that unites both *transformistas* and *misses* is plastic surgery, particularly (but not exclusively) breast augmentation.

I have tried to avoid presuming the given nature of the "transgender body" because the ways *transformistas* narrated and experienced their bodies seemed so deeply at odds with the ways I had encountered in the United States. The U.S. orientation of much of the emerging field of transgender studies has continually responded to a highly regulated medical authority to which gender-variant people have necessarily had to relate in order to gain access to the somatechnologies of bodily transformation. Medical authority functions differently in Venezuela, and in many other parts of Latin America. Differential regulation of both pharmaceuticals and medical practitioners has created opportunities for access to hormones and surgical procedures for Venezuelans. Readily available birth control without a prescription provides feminizing hormones, both to cis-women managing fertility and to *transformistas* managing transformation. Surgeons not necessarily governed by a strong accrediting organization can choose their affiliations in the manner that best suits their practices, thus defining their own ethics and standards, without the same fear of litigation encountered by their U.S. counterparts. Consequently, plastic surgeons can collaborate with media producers to modify contestants' bodies to conform to the demands of the media industry and provide access to breast implants for *transformista* patients who are not following the protocols for sex change at their discretion. The concept of somatechnics and somatechnologies have been useful analytics in considering the physical and social relations embedded in the technologies of plastic surgery and feminizing hormones.

In her discussion of plastic surgery and transsexuality, Bernice Hausman argues that plastic surgery is "highly subject to ideological appropriation" because it does not depend on a "terminological code," in the Barthesian sense (1995, 49). Hausman contrasts cosmetic surgery with endocrinology in order to establish this distinction: "Both endocrinology and cosmetic surgery function as medical practices in accord with descriptive discourses concerning the body's physiological processes: in this sense, they operate as terminological codes. Both are also governed by ideological systems of meaning concerning the form, function, and operation of sexual difference: in this sense, they operate as rhetorical codes. Yet endocrinology is more connected to its terminological 'mode' than is cosmetic surgery, whose main purpose is to change the human body, not to describe its functions. Thus, the latter medical specialty is more subject to ideological appropriation" (190).[14]

In taking this approach, Hausman cedes a kind of ideological purity to endocrinology that the biologist Anne Fausto-Sterling (2000) or Wahng (2009) would certainly refute. Hausman's discussion of plastic surgery focuses first on the evolution of the logic of "correction" in the profession as it was practiced in the United States in the early to mid-twentieth century. This section focuses exclusively on surgeries such as breast reduction, rhinoplasty, facial reconstruction, and breast augmentation, and the shift from a reconstructive to a corrective approach. The earlier, reconstructive justification for plastic surgery distanced itself from the "beauty business" by focusing on treatment for birth defects and accidents (Hausman 1995, 52). Hausman shows the shifts in medical and popular discourses that both elided "the distinction between the normal and the ideal" (56) and legitimated the desire for plastic surgery to "correct" minor differences while employing the goal of "patient happiness" instead of the functional goals typically employed in surgery (58). This, according to Hausman, moves plastic surgery off of its therapeutic moorings—a sign of its ideological appropriation—and places it in the realm of improvement. During this part of Hausman's argument, the use of plastic surgery by transgender, intersex, or transsexual patients is not raised—it is only in the context of genital surgery that Hausman invokes the transsexual patient. The transition in Hausman's argument is abrupt, relying on what she characterizes as the limits of the human body: "The technological capacities of plastic surgery and endocrinology offered physicians the ability to construct physiological normality both discursively and materially. Yet the human body sets certain limits on the efficacy of the plastic ideologies. Sexual organs are not equal under the scalpel, and the differences between the sexes constrain the efforts of the plastic surgeons to construct female and (especially) male genitalia. This fact forces us to consider the materiality of sexual difference and the effects of technology on cultural ideologies" (66). The sticking point in Hausman's argument is this notion of materiality, which maintains the genitals as the site of sex "change," and excludes transgender and transsexual subjects from participation in forms of "sex change" or gender confirmation not constituted through genital surgery.

This distinction does not bear itself out in the research I did in Venezuela. *Transformistas*, beauty pageant producers, and plastic surgeons alike employed the logics of correction and patient happiness to justify cosmetic procedures. For many *transformistas*, sex change was not the desired outcome of transformation. Somatechnics provides another way to think of the indexical dimension of the semiotics of sex, gender, and the body—and here I am invoking a Peircean alternative to Hausman's Barthesian approach, one that recognizes the carnality of the body while attending to its symbolic currency. If sex change is not a sign of transformation—that is, if *transformistas* don't need genital surgery to be the women they are, then the semiotics of sex, gender, and the body are more complex than those proposed by Hausman. They are anchored in the status of the body in its particular economy. This economy, in Venezuela, is governed both by the production of modernity and by spectacularity, as I will discuss in chapter 6. For this reason, *miss* and *transformista* logics of the body are interrelated and mutually constitutive, despite the social distance that separates them.

Notions of embodiment and corporeality are already embedded in somatechnologies such as plastic surgery and hormones. *Misses* are presented as ideal sanitary citizens, part and parcel with their willingness to submit their bodies to plastic surgery, to become the sculptural media, as it were, for the "modern Pygmalion," Sousa. In the same way, competing discourses of medical authority and voluntarism in plastic surgery practice police the line between sanitary citizens deserving of treatment and unsanitary subjects outside the purview of medical authority. *Transformistas* and plastic surgeons skirt the blurred boundaries of this line to accomplish their goals. *Transformista* and *miss* corporealities reveal important ideas about the status of the body in the sanitary regimes of modernity in Venezuela. Rather than seeing these bodies and technologies as unique to the experiences of individuals, it is important to understand the continuities in the ways both bodies and technologies are formed. Plasticity and artificiality are two logics that authorize the use of technology to shape the body and serve as limit tests for the always-present specter of excess—the body that has become monstrous in its plasticity. But plastic surgery, the primary tool discussed in this chapter, is not necessarily seen as artificial. Instead, *transformistas*, *misses*, and plastic surgeons describe and justify plastic surgery as a technology that collaborates with nature to improve patients' lives. In this environment, the transgender body, like the bodies of other subjects, "comes to matter" under different conditions and through different cultural logics. These logics become apparent when examining how *transformistas*, *misses*, and plastic surgeons describe and justify the process of bodily transformation. First and foremost, the discourse of modernity in Venezuela is grounded on a separation between civilization and *barbarie*—and in the history of Venezuela, hygiene is one somatechnology that has produced this separation with very carnal consequences.

Modernity, Hygiene, and Sanitary Citizens

Medical practitioners enforce what Briggs and Mantini-Briggs (2003) call "sanitary citizenship" on *transformistas*. Using their shock and outrage about the kinds of technologies *transformistas* employ on their bodies, many medical practitioners characterized *transformista* self-medication as a kind of unregulated excess that provided a limit test for the line between sanitary citizens and what Briggs and Mantini-Briggs call "unsanitary subjects." *Transformistas*, however, work this line between sanitary citizen and unsanitary subject, at times calling upon medical authority and technologies to legitimize their projects of transformation, and at other times rejecting medical expertise. While they are indeed excluded from the realm of therapeutic subjects because of their failure to conform to transsexual treatment protocols involving psychiatric, hormonal, surgical, and legal sex change, *transformistas* do not always let this get in the way of their projects of transformation. In this negotiation of medical authority, they do not differ much in their attitudes toward plastic surgery from *misses*, pageant producers, and the plastic surgeons who work on *misses*.

Sexologists and endocrinologists affiliated with the Centro Bianco, a well-known sexology clinic and training center in Caracas, practiced an earlier iteration of the Harry Benjamin Society's standards of care for gender reassignment, which recommended progressive reassignment, along degrees of reversibility, from social to hormonal to surgical to, finally, legal. These protocols have undergone much revision and are currently in their seventh iteration as the World Professional Association for Transgender Health (WPATH) Standards of Care for Gender Identity Disorders, last updated in 2012. The version of the standards of care practiced by Venezuelan sexologists and endocrinologists were, like many standards of care, based in the absolute belief that medical and psychiatric professionals were the best stewards of gender reassignment, and that gender reassignment was based on treatment for transsexualism, a process that is seen in Venezuela as completed through sex-reassignment surgery and integration into society as an individual of the "desired" sex. This approach clearly excluded *transformistas* from treatment.

The feeling was mutual. *Transformistas* did not see the need to consult sexologists or endocrinologists in their regimens, and only called on the services of plastic surgeons for implants and pharmacy technicians for some injections. *Transformistas* were not interested in medical scrutiny over their processes of transformation. In terms of bioethical considerations, I saw *transformista* self-transformation practices through the lens of harm reduction. When *transformistas* and other transgender women asked for information about feminizing regimens, I would supply it to them, using the Internet and the publicly available Tom Waddell Clinic protocols from the San Francisco Department of Public Health.[15] My background in harm-reduction work in HIV prevention and needle exchange prepared me to ask questions about hormone use and respond to informational concerns that the *transformistas* raised. But the questions of regulation and compliance with treatment for transgender people are very complex, particularly in an environment in which the "care of the self" is fraught with overlapping systems of valuing and devaluing, and keeping safe and doing violence to, certain bodies.

Many *transformistas*' decisions not to get genital sex-reassignment surgery render them illegible to sexological discourse, excluding them from the status of therapeutic subject. At the same time, *transformistas* themselves are interested in breast augmentation, but not so interested in genital sex-reassignment surgery. This manifested itself in an interesting way during the interviews with *transformistas*. In almost every case, when I asked about surgery, *transformistas* automatically assumed that I meant plastic surgeries such as breast augmentation, silicone injections, or rhinoplasty, not genital surgery. Here is an excerpt from my interview with Paulina:

> OCHOA: What do you think of surgery? Is it something you want to have done? And if it is, what do you want to have operated?
>
> PAULINA: I want to have breast surgery. Breasts, and . . . no other part of my body.
>
> OCHOA: Nothing else?
>
> PAULINA: Because I consider myself . . . I would have breasts done and maybe hips. To bring out the form a bit more [*para sacarle más la forma*], but no more, I wouldn't like that . . .
>
> OCHOA: Okay. Tell me a little more about that because in some cultures the genital operation is very important for a transgender woman's identity [*Paulina says "hmm"*], but it's not always that way in other cases.
>
> PAULINA: No, it's not like that because, look, I know like ten [girls] who have had genital surgery. . . . And I've seen that they kind of go crazy. They all have a trauma.
>
> OCHOA: Oh, because they operated on their . . .
>
> PAULINA: Because they had the operation and now they say no. . . . I have a friend who is a *señora* already, operated from top to toes, and she tells me no, don't do it, because it's frustrating to be with a man and not feel him. Because they cut your organs. So I prefer to have my woman's breasts, but that there doesn't matter. Anyway, it's just there for decoration.

Paulina voices a concern that many *transformistas* expressed regarding sex-reassignment surgery: the trauma of the operation and the frustration of losing sensitivity. Often this was described in the interviews as "going crazy." While this is not the experience of many transgender or transsexual women I've spoken to who have had sex-reassignment surgery, this is the perception that many *transformistas* have of this technology. For Paulina, having breasts and a shapely body is more important to accomplishing femininity than removing her penis or having a vagina, and she sees no contradiction between being a woman and having "that there." This would place Paulina squarely in Centro Bianco's category of the "false transsexual," making her ineligible for hormone or surgical treatment. It is important to also note that the costs associated with the protocols followed by sexologists in Venezuela are prohibitive for most *transformistas*, and also seen as unnecessary. The inability of medical practitioners in Venezuela to respect *transformistas*' ownership of their transformations creates an environment where *transformistas* seek other ways to meet their needs.

La Contessa, whom we met in chapter 2, described the sex-reassignment surgery she had in Ecuador. It cost her US$2,500. While she was initially happy with the results, she says that she has never been the same since, and that sometimes it makes her feel crazy. She found the doctor through an Ecuadorian friend she met in Italy, who gave her his phone number.

LA CONTESSA: I called, I called and talked to the doctor and I told him, "*Ay mira*, this is what I want. . . . I want an appointment with you and I want to have the operation, you tell me what I need to do." Then he told me what I needed to do. . . .

OCHOA: Did he ask you for your psych workup, all that?

LA CONTESSA: No because I was already . . . He asked me how old I was, and I told him I was thirty. He told me yes, before the surgery he asked me if I was sure of what I was about to do. "Yes I'm sure," and he interviewed me.

OCHOA: What was the interview like?

LA CONTESSA: The interview, he asked me if I was sure, that . . . It was like noon, and still at 3 p.m. He said, "Are you *sure* you want to do this?" I said, "Yes, I want to do the operation." "Are you *sure?*" "Yes." "Well then, if you're sure, sign this paper for me." And I signed the paper. That I was sure of what I was doing. That I wasn't some underage kid, understand? That I knew what I was doing. He told me, "You know that you won't be the same afterward, because that's a, we're going to cut off something vital. You can have a normal life afterward, but remember that it won't be like before, because [after the operation] it's no longer normal."

La Contessa was able to access sex-reassignment surgery by traveling across multiple borders and working with a surgeon who was willing to do the procedure without following the WPATH protocols, which require psychological counseling and long-term management of the transition. While she was happy with the results at first, she has complained of problems with the surgery since. The success of the procedure for her lies in her sense that she is now a complete woman, and is able to rest her authority as a woman on this sense of completion:

> What I wanted was to be a complete woman, understand me? Because each of us, I think that's the goal one can have, to be a woman one hundred percent. . . . I was happy because . . . now I didn't see that thing hanging there. I said, 'ay no, now I am a woman.' Now the only thing I need is my papers, and to act like so. Understand? And if an ignorant person calls me *marico* (faggot), or anyone calls me *marico*, tsk—imagine. I know what I have between my legs, and I know what I have in my mind.

The plastic surgeons I interviewed were aware to some degree of the protocols recommended for sex reassignment. Dr. Frances, who at the time represented the Sociedad Venezolana de Cirugía Plástica, Estética, Reconstructiva y Maxilofacial (Venezuelan Society of Plastic, Aesthetic, Reconstructive and Maxilofacial Surgery, SVCPREM), made it very clear that the society's statutes prohibited its members from deviating from these protocols. When I ask him what the society's professional ethics are regarding breast implants for male-bodied individuals, he responds:

> Well, plastic surgery can be done when and if the patient complies with all the requirements, of course, that *have* to be followed. That they are a patient, that there has been a study, that they have, well, met the criteria to be intervened, there's no problem placing breast implants if the patient will follow the process to then have a sex change. Okay? Because if they're just doing it for, for, because of poor orientation, or whatever, for trying to get more clients, I don't think that's—that wouldn't be very ethical on anyone's part, although it's not counterindicated. Every plastic surgeon is within

his rights to do it when and if it's within the ethical guidelines that, well, must be followed.

That is, we, the society, are not opposed to it. I haven't said the society is opposed to surgery on the male-to-female patient; no one's saying that. Simply put, patients must comply with the doctor's orders. So if suddenly the patient, or if you receive a patient, or if I receive a patient, before anything else, there has to be a psychological evaluation, or psychiatric. To see if the process will be followed. . . . Like the lady I was telling you about, she always said, "I've always felt feminine; I've never felt like a man."

Paramount in Dr. Frances's response are the authority of the clinician and the need for patients to comply with doctors' orders. *Transformistas'* unwillingness to subject themselves to these protocols excludes them as candidates for surgery. Only compliant patients are deserving of treatment. Others, according to Dr. Frances, have "poor orientation" or commercial interests in mind. He responds to requests to circumvent the protocols by asserting that patients who would do so are misguided and want to take shortcuts: "It's important that patients who want to do this know that this [requires] a multidisciplinary team, okay? You need a urologist, a psychiatrist, an endocrinologist, I mean, a lot of things. So, because it's such a long road, people don't want to follow that path. Now if you really want to do this, are you convinced that this is what you want to do, or not? Because once it's done, it's irreversible."

Similar to La Contessa's experience, Dr. Frances also needs absolute reassurance that the patient is *convencido* (convinced), sure of what they want to do. While breast implants are reversible, Dr. Frances understands them as part of a road that leads to sex change, which he understands as irreversible. The teleology of sex change is haunted by the clinical anxiety of castration, an anxiety that Lawrence Cohen (1995) describes as framed by an ambivalence between falseness and authenticity. Dr. Frances remembers the case of a transsexual patient who was going to have a sex change performed:

Another patient, a lady [*señora*], who—it was while I was doing my graduate work—a woman who had been studied by psychiatry, she had over ten years with psychiatry, endocrinology, she had a stable relationship, she had an adopted child, and she wanted, well, to have a sex change. It couldn't happen, even though she was complete, plastic surgery was in agreement, because, as I said, it's not that we oppose [sex change] or that we're strict. . . . And this patient met all the prerequisites. But then urology, the chief of service in urology, opposed it for religious reasons. . . . And that's where it stopped. And that lady, I don't know, because really that lady deserved to have her operation, because, well, she really was a lady.

As Sandy Stone documents in her landmark chapter "The *Empire* Strikes Back: A Posttranssexual Manifesto" (1991), clinicians managing sex change often rely on such narratives of feminine authenticity to grant patients access to procedures. Despite her appropriateness as a candidate for surgery, the urologist on the team blocked this patient's surgery. Frances regrets this because she is a deserving candidate, a *señora*. This stance allows him to defend this woman's need for the surgery while denying "reversible" procedures to the *transformistas* he sees as undeserving or noncompliant.

Breast augmentation, which is more accessible to *transformistas* within the borders of Venezuela, was the chief form of plastic surgery that *transformistas* expressed a desire to have. In fact, when I started asking about "surgery," I learned that I had to modify my questions to ask specifically about both cosmetic *and* sex-reassignment surgery, since most of the women I interviewed immediately assumed that I meant cosmetic surgery. Another plastic surgeon I interviewed, Dr. Gaviria, worked on both *transformistas* and *misses* in his practice. He reported that *transformistas* almost exclusively sought breast augmentation when they consulted him. Dr. Gaviria understood that the SVCPREM did not approve of plastic surgeons performing breast augmentations on male-bodied individuals outside the context of sex reassignment:

> OCHOA: Does the society of plastic surgeons have any ethical guidelines about this type of surgery?
> DR. GAVIRIA: They're not, they shouldn't be done. I don't know, it's not spoken of but we—. . . In fact, I am not a member of the society of plastic surgeons, not because of that, but because, well . . . But in effect that [policy], it's a strike against the doctor who does want to belong to the society. It stops you if you should decide you want to join the society. It puts the brakes on you.
> OCHOA: Why?

DR. GAVIRIA: Because they don't accept that situation.

OCHOA: So, openly they don't accept it.

DR. GAVIRIA: No.

OCHOA: How . . . ?

DR. GAVIRIA: Well like, as a statute of . . . that.

OCHOA: It's a statute.

DR. GAVIRIA: Yes. A change in the physique of an individual is not permitted, whether it's from male to female or from female to male.

. . .

OCHOA: So do you belong to any medical society?

DR. GAVIRIA: Well [of course], I belong to the International Society of Aesthetic Plastic Surgery.

OCHOA: Oh, okay, and they have no problem with . . .

DR. GAVIRIA: No, no.

OCHOA: . . . any statutes.

DR. GAVIRIA: The thing is, that society is not just plastic surgeons; it includes a whole series of specialties. Dermatologists, gynecologists, it's a bit more open in that respect.

The SCVPREM doesn't explicitly mention or prohibit a change of physique from male to female or vice versa, nor does the Federación Ibero Latinoamericana de Cirugía Plástica y Reconstructiva, the international body to which it belongs.[16] Despite the lack of an explicit prohibition, both Dr. Gaviria and Frances understand that the SCVPREM does not look favorably on such procedures. Dr. Frances's response to this is to insist that there is room within the statutes for change of physique within the protocols for sex-change treatment. If patients don't comply, they are simply not eligible for surgery. Dr. Gaviria is able to circumvent the authority of the SCVPREM because he does not have to affiliate with them in order to practice. At the same time, he justifies his stance by reaffirming the voluntarism of the patient, and espousing an open-minded approach that accepts the individual:

OCHOA: I've seen an attitude on the part of [sexologists and endocrinologists] that it's like plastic surgeons are sabotaging them when they operate on *transformistas*. What do you think of that idea?

DR. GAVIRIA: Well, look. You have to see that from another point of view. That I also, from the point of view of accepting the individual, of that experience, well I . . . They want the patient, or the person, to concretely, truly accept their new, their new sex. But what I've seen is that the majority of patients that come here, of that type of patient, they accept it, from the point of view of their physical transformation. But many of them don't reject their genitals. As a matter of fact, in my experience, no one has ever asked me if I know or have heard of anyone who [performs sex-reassignment surgery].

Dr. Gaviria sees this approach as part of the therapeutic nature of plastic surgery. Plastic surgeons, he asserts, exist to allow patients to "develop" themselves:

I think that we, plastic surgeons, we practice a specialization that is very different from other specializations. We should be a bit more open about these things. Accept the individual as they are, because indeed what we want is to benefit the person, from the point of view—no?—of health, because we are health-care providers. But of the individual's *mental* health. That he feel good about himself, we do provide that part. And if the patient feels good, with that attitude toward life, well, that's what's important for us. That he feels good how, and the way, he is. And that the individual feels good when he sees himself in the mirror and his self-esteem goes up, whether he's a man or a woman, or a *transformista*, or whatever.

While Dr. Gaviria describes his approach as an open one that honors patients' wishes for their own bodies, Frances sees plastic surgeons willing to operate on *transformistas* as simply interested in making money. When I ask him if he thinks it would be difficult for a *transformista* not following treatment protocols to get a breast augmentation, he says:

DR. FRANCES: Yes, possibly they would have a problem. They might not find someone who might. . . . But maybe they might, because of course there are people who, for money, you know how it is.

OCHOA: Of course, you do what you do . . .

DR. FRANCES: Yes, looking from the more commercial point of view.

Dr. Frances discusses this theme of commercialism extensively. The distinction between scientific motives and commercial motives is part of how Dr. Frances reinscribes the legitimacy of medical authority. This is as much about the aesthetics of science, or what he calls "harmonizing" the body, as it is about medical rationality.

Harmonizing the Body: Justifying Transformation

The themes that emerged from my observations and interviews with *transformistas, misses,* plastic surgeons, and other medical professionals reveal the rationales that are employed in justifying medical and self-administered interventions to shape the body into a legible feminine form. These rationales reinscribe medical authority as well as the voluntarism of people who employ such technologies to transform their bodies. As Diana Dull and Candace West argue, the central dilemma of cosmetic surgery involves "the evaluation of patients' complaints, the determination of what should be done about them, and the assessment of postoperative results" (1991, 54). In particular, Dull and West find that "the assessment of 'good candidates' for surgery [is made] in relation to normative conceptions of men's and women's 'essential natures'" (55).

Inquiring into the rationale and desire for plastic surgery, I also found ideologies of essential nature. However, the concept of nature extended beyond exclusively gendered notions of feminine essence into larger frameworks of nature and modernity in the maintenance of Venezuelan society and bodies. In my interviews, people of all genders were seen as justified in seeking plastic surgery to improve their lives, open doors, and develop themselves. It is impossible to isolate this sense of nature from the ideologies of modernity and development that have shaped the Venezuelan nation. Indeed, the producers of the Organización Miss Venezuela often narrated the process of refining Venezuelan girls into *misses* as one of production. As chapter 3 demonstrates, the beauty pageant is seen as an industry, which, like others in Venezuela, refines an available pool of raw material to produce a finished product for export to a global market. In this sense, the bodies of *misses* are subject to processes of refinement that exceed the kinds of therapeutic justifications employed by plastic surgeons in Dull and West's study.[17]

The primary critique leveled at plastic surgeons that operate outside the understood bounds of appropriate practice is that of commercial interest. In these interviews, the notion of commerce emerged as the limit test to appropriate practice and yet was simultaneously used to justify patients' desires to seek plastic surgery. The sense that plastic surgery was an investment was most clear in La Contessa's assertion, "Yo gasté un dineral en este rostro, mi amor" (I spent a fortune on this face, my love). While commercial interest is not seen as appropriate for clinicians, it is appropriate for *misses* and other people working in the entertainment industry, according to Dr. Frances. Dr. Gaviria extends this logic of career aspiration to *transformistas* as another rationale for intervention. The dichotomy around commercial interest reflects the idea that the clinician is expected to protect the patients, rather than profit from them. Surgeons who blur this line are, in the eyes of the SVCPREM, eroding the therapeutic and scientific endeavor of plastic surgery. Dr. Frances says:

> When you belong to the society, well you have to follow the statutes, to follow a series of rules that the society has. And even so we've had a lot of problems, kind of, because of the area of advertising. There are people who advertise [as plastic surgeons]. You've seen them in *Estampas* [the Sunday magazine of the national newspaper *El Universal*]; you see them in magazines . . . You should take some with you because they offer you villas and castles, okay? And many of those surgeons have been trained in good hospitals, but then they go over to the commercial side, saying, "Look, I'll do this for you, I'll do that." Understand? The society wants to prevent that, I mean, and tries to [go] more toward the scientific side, where you do research.

The ethical guidelines from Federación Ibero Latinoamericana de Cirugía Plástica y Reconstructiva and SVCPREM are very clear on this matter and prohibit excessive or misleading publicity. Clinicians who operate on the "commercial side" are not to be trusted. Dr. Frances sees them misleading patients who are interested in shortcuts: "So, that's the problem, that's how they fool patients, they're patients who . . . All patients in surgery must receive preoperative and postoperative treatment according to the regulations. But then [the surgeons say]: "Look, I can do it without bandages, without . . ." Lies. So those people, the people who are fooled by that, that's the problem." Operating outside the guidelines of the society is dangerous, according to Dr. Frances, because once you are on the commercial side, you don't keep up with advances in medicine. As an example, he cites collagen injections:

> At the beginning there was a collagen boom, but then there were complications, and the society and its members, well, you attend the conference and you know, "look, we don't use this anymore." So you stop using it. But because it's a simple procedure, then whoever sees the need for money or sees an opportunity, they employ that procedure. Even though it's no longer, let's say, it's not indicated, or it's in disuse. In the case of plastic surgery on breasts, at the beginning patients were injected directly in the breast with silicone. This brought on many problems. Later better implants were developed, such as the ones we now use, which are excellent and produce minimal complications. . . . So what happens? Well, plastic surgery, plastic surgeons evolved: "Even though I don't do injections, I'll use implants instead." But not these people; these people keep on injecting because it makes them money. And people want fast things, easy things, simple things, that don't take too much time. They want to look beautiful from one day to the next.

The fast and easy path sought by these hypothetical patients is one that circumvents medical authority. Plastic surgeons and the society must maintain this authority in order to maintain a sense of control over both the practice of and the market for plastic surgery. The SVCPREM's promotional materials reinscribe this authority and issue warnings similar to Dr. Frances's regarding those who promote aesthetic procedures outside the purview of the society. But science is an end in itself for the society, as this too is a source of legitimacy. Science, in this case, involves publishing investigations in journals and attending the meetings of the society. Science also signals a search for what Dr. Frances calls "harmony" that is, according to him, not profit motivated. In this way, the idea of science merges with artistic ideals.[18]

> OCHOA: How do you know what's harmonic?
> DR. FRANCES: Well, by bodily proportions. Like, you see a person, let's say, who has a particular kind of hip; well, that goes with a bust more or less of this form. That is, there's a figure, let's say, and various artistic concepts. In the plastic surgery specialization, you take a class called "Artistic Anatomy," and more or

less through that, you try to kind of focus it on the patients. Of course, as I say, always taking advantage of their unique traits.

OCHOA: So this is part of your coursework?

DR. FRANCES: One, yes, one part of it that you take. "Artistic Anatomy," it's the course about the proportions defined by painters for example. The nose is this big. Approximately, it's not that everyone should look alike. That is, the eyes have a specific dimension to them, the mouth, so much. The face is divided into three parts that are more or less equal, I mean, the ears are angled more or less like the nose. They're things that really you have to see in your patients, trying to find that . . . always the human body has a certain symmetry in the center. So all of that is what, well, what is beautiful.

OCHOA: Aha. Symmetry.

DR. FRANCES: It's all part of beauty.

In Dr. Frances's formulation, the primary motivation in performing plastic surgery on a patient becomes a search for an ideal, symmetric beauty. This allows Dr. Frances to account for plastic surgery outside a directly therapeutic rationale (that is, correcting a functional impediment) and transcend the "market" as a motivator. The market also intervenes in patients' decision making. Here the rationale that transcends the market is an artistic or scientific pursuit. Dr. Frances conflates the idea of science with the maintenance of medical authority. This authority resides in the community of surgeons willing to be regulated by protocols and statutes, aspiring to an ideal of harmony, and unwilling to compromise for profit. The tension between the desire of the market and the rationality of medicine also consistently emerges in the ways surgeons negotiate expectations with prospective patients and determine patients' eligibility for surgery.

Managing Nature, Managing Expectations

The theme of management places the surgeon at the center of plastic surgery: it is the surgeon who manages the body's "nature" into a more beautiful form, and it is the surgeon who must manage the unrealistic expectations of patients seeking plastic surgery. La Contessa puts the relationship of surgery to nature very plainly, when I ask her what she thinks of it: "It's something good because it helps you correct the defects that nature. . . . If nature gave you small breasts, plastic surgery makes them bigger. If [nature] gave you an ugly nose, plastic surgery will make it beautiful for you [te la embellece]. If you get wrinkly, plastic surgery rejuvenates you. Plastic surgery has its advantages: one hundred percent."

Dr. Frances sees the surgeon's role as a collaborative one, emphasizing the individual needs of each patient toward a principle of harmony. I ask him, "What is the role of plastic surgeons here in Venezuela in the process of visualizing and executing an aesthetic change?" He responds:

> Each surgeon has his own point of view, and I think that's very specific. But I think that we all have to agree that it's best to be in harmony. In other words, to harmonize the human figure. That is, to see each patient as an individual and not to generalize. It's not like: "I'm going to make all of them [breast implants] four hundred [cc, or cubic centimeters, the size of the implant]." Or, "I'm giving you five hundred [cc implants]," because not everyone is going to look good in that. So, you have to see patients, and according to the patient, for example their features. . . . I mean, Asian patients, well, they have Asian features. If there are patients, let's say, with Indian features, well, each one has their features that have to be conserved. Because that is part of their beauty. I start from the premise that everyone is beautiful. What happens is that people need to find their inner beauty, their outer beauty and one, well, one collaborates in finding perhaps what might stand out most [resaltar] in the patient. But I like that harmonic part, I mean, unharmonic things, I don't like.

Of course, this idea of harmony has been roundly contested, and Dr. Frances's answer even responds to these critiques in some ways by noting the specificity of racialized features and emphasizing individuality. But at the root of his understanding of the role of the surgeon is the sense of collaboration and emergence. The collaborative role of the surgeon and the search for harmony are ways to manage the features of the patient toward a desired outcome.

Dr. Gaviria sees his role as managing patient expectations, rather than achieving some kind of harmony. According to him, the role of the surgeon is "to guide the expectations that the patient has about what they are seeking, and that the patient is educated about what is realistically going to be done, and what, or how it might turn out after the surgery; that's our goal. Just that. And, well, giving them guidance around things that they want to do that can't be done. And things that maybe they want to do but won't turn out well." Surgeons have to manage expectations because patients come with an unrealistic sense of what can be accomplished surgically. The surgeon mediates these expectations by making sure the patient understands the clinical implications of the procedures they desire, by giving them a reality check. According to Dr. Gaviria, "Plastic surgery patients come in with high expectations. Because information in the media gives them an expectation that is different from the reality of what can be done. So we have to focus the patient on the results they will get from the procedure they will be getting, independent of what they might think it will be."

Dr. Frances bluntly suggests the kind of reality check some of his patients require: "All the women who come, come with high expectations to look better. It's only that, of course, when you have the body of a twenty-year-old woman, thin, or rather, who exercises, who takes care of her diet, and you put implants on her, well she looks spectacular. It's not the same for the person who doesn't have the same conditions for implants. Well, it doesn't look spectacular." He agrees with Dr. Gaviria: false expectations make poor candidates for surgery. He introduces the idea that these expectations are not just physiological, as Dr. Gaviria has put it, but also social and psychological. I ask Dr. Frances, "What about patients who are not ideal, who would be a bad candidate for plastic surgery?" He says, "Ah, well, those are, I think it's the majority. It's the patients who have . . . what do they call it? False expectations. They expect plastic surgery to solve a problem, let's say, an internal problem that can't be resolved. Or they have problems with their spouse [pareja], or, well, they're patients with a certain psychological trait, an underlying psychological issue. Those are not ideal patients. At all." In this way, Dr. Frances ascribes a kind of irrational desire to the patient who expresses psychosocial motives for seeking plastic surgery, however, psychosocial motives such as self-esteem and "feeling better about one's self" provide legitimacy for plastic surgery.[19] Despite the reliance on this form of emotional legitimacy for plastic surgery, Dr. Frances narrates a need to manage patients' emotional expectations of surgery.

The management of the patient's body and expectations function together to produce the surgeon as the arbiter and domesticator of nature and desire, centering medical authority as the ultimate form of rationality.

The surgeon says what is possible and what is not, despite the fact that the standards themselves are quite arbitrary and changing. Dr. Frances describes the change in the size of breast implants during the time that he has been practicing. This offends his principle of harmony, but it is part of plastic surgery now. Note, however, that he attributes the irrationality of breast-implant size to patient desires, not surgical decision making:

> Yes, [young women] are often looking for an increase in breast volume. An interesting fact is that as the years pass, the volumes increase; the demand is higher. When I was in graduate school, putting in a two hundred cc implant . . . it was something *gigantic*! Now, it's three hundred cc, two hundred and eighty cc, and that's small now. People want more. So it's horrible too because well, it's . . . For example, from my unique point of view, well, I think that the patient wants harmony. If you are a tall woman, with a good body, you can get an implant bigger than three hundred. Of course it looks good on you. But if you're a girl, one and a half meters tall, like the average Venezuelan woman, don't put in four hundred cc. I mean, it's gigantic. You're going to look deformed! But that's an issue, I don't know if it's advertising or television or, well, it's many, perhaps multiple influences that make it so a big bosom is a great thing, so they want to be big. It's really complicated.

In this statement Frances foreshadows concerns with the excesses of plastic surgery. The notion of deformity haunts plastic surgery practice and is a key concern for surgeons in managing patients' expectations of the results of procedures. It is the job of the surgeon to prevent the desires of patients from producing these kinds of excesses, as both Dr. Frances and Dr. Gaviria suggest.

Voluntarism, Self-Esteem, and the Ideal Candidate

Simultaneously, these plastic surgeons also place some responsibility for decision making around plastic surgery in the hands of patients. The surgeons do this by determining the appropriateness of patients as candidates for surgery. Voluntarism plays a key role in these surgeons' understandings of the ideal candidate for surgery. An ideal candidate should be decided (*decidido, convencido*) on the surgery, not induced (*inducido*) into it. Dr. Gaviria makes this distinction clear:

DR. GAVIRIA: I think we help those patients to accomplish, really what they are looking for. I haven't had a patient yet who has come back to get the implants removed. In fact, I have patients who have come back for bigger implants, and always all of them have had an attitude toward their, eh, their way of being, very conscious of who they are and they accept themselves as they are.

OCHOA: Do you mean *transformistas* or all your patients?

DR. GAVIRIA: No, all my patients. In general. They come with their minds made up [*decididos*]. What happens is that this specialization is different from others. We plastic surgeons do not impose ourselves on the patient; the patient is the one who takes — almost always — control of the procedure. We are like advisors, and we do the procedures, but we don't have the power to impose on the patient what we want to do to them. Because, since all of this is aesthetic surgery, the patient is the one who has to like the way they look and feel comfortable with what is going to be done.

Similarly, Dr. Frances describes the ideal patient who is *convencido*, who has decided on surgery for reasons that do not involve other people directly; she is having surgery to improve her self-esteem.

DR. FRANCES: The ideal patient, let's say, is the one who is convinced [*convencido*], who wants to have plastic surgery . . . of their own free will [*por voluntad propia*]. Not because "this way . . . my husband won't leave me," or "I'll get a spouse," or "people will like me more." No, I mean, I think the ideal patient is the patient who, from a position of self-esteem says, "look, I think I have a bit of . . . lipodystrophy; I think I have a small bust . . . and I want to look better and feel better about myself." That's the ideal patient.

OCHOA: Aha. So, they have more . . . realistic expectations?

DR. FRANCES: Yes, that they have their expectations, their self-esteem in good shape.

The idea of self-esteem is a key element of the therapeutic rationale for aesthetic surgery. Alexander Edmonds's recent review of this concept in *Pretty Modern* connects the emergence of this idea to a shift in political rationality in Brazil and globally (2010, 76). He sees its use as part of cultivating what Michel Foucault calls "the care of the self," and Edmonds proposes a political economy of self-esteem as it manifests itself in Brazilian plastic surgery (76). Interestingly, Dull and West (1991), and later Sander L. Gilman (1999), don't extensively focus on the emergence of this concept. Dull and West mention it as part of what surgeons propose is an element of a good candidate but don't fully explore the meaning of this idea in the surgeons' responses. Gilman at times lists self-esteem as a positive side effect of aesthetic surgery, but he chooses ideas such as happiness and psychotherapy to describe the therapeutic effects of aesthetic surgery. The two doctors I interviewed invoked "self-esteem" when describing the therapeutic effects of their work, and when characterizing appropriate candidates for surgery, similar to what Dull and West found. Dr. Gaviria, in particular, employs the idea of self-esteem to justify surgery for all his patients:

> I think that plastic surgeons, because plastic surgery is a very different specialty from others, we should be a bit more open about these things. Accepting the individual as they are, because in fact what we want is to benefit the person, from the point of view, not of health—because we're not health-care providers—but of the mental health of the individual. That they feel good about themselves, and we do provide that. And if the patient feels good, with an attitude toward life, that's what's important for us. That they feel good how, with what they are. And that an individual feels good when they look in the mirror, and their self-esteem goes up, whether they are a man or a woman, or a *transformista*, whatever they are.

For Dr. Gaviria, self-esteem is an important concern in all procedures, and this approach rationalizes his circumvention of sex-change protocols when it comes to giving *transformista* patients the breasts they are seeking. He extends the justification for plastic surgery to his *transformista* patients and frames his role in facilitating their bodily transformations as akin to the role he plays in all his patients' transformations. By separating breast augmentation from the idea of sex change, Dr. Gaviria is no longer bound by the protocols for sex change. The link between self-esteem and voluntarism (to be *convencido* or *decidido*) produces a good candidate for plastic surgery. The converse of this is that the patients who are induced are undergoing plastic surgery without addressing the underlying psychological issues that have led to their dissatisfaction, potentially creating a bad situation for the surgeon. Dr. Gaviria also understands that the ideal patient is convinced of the procedures he or she would like, and not induced by a third party:

> DR. GAVIRIA: The ideal patient of plastic surgery is the patient who is truly *convinced* of what he wants to have done. This is the ideal patient because the result they will have is what they are seeking. Patients who are induced into having a procedure are never happy with the procedure they have done.
>
> OCHOA: How do you know that a patient is convinced?
>
> DR. GAVIRIA: Well, because the patient, as I explained, when they discuss the procedure, the patient is clear about what he is seeking, and what they really want as a result. The induced patient is the patient that comes because her husband has another woman, or because she's seen as too fat, and so she wants to be more stylized because . . . there's always an affective problem in that, in which the patient doesn't know what [she] wants. Instead she comes seeking the solution to a problem that she thinks is caused by her looks.

The doctor begins to refer to the hypothetical patient in the masculine, but his examples reveal that he is imagining a feminine patient. Beyond the idea of self-esteem, Dr. Gaviria proposes that the influence of relationship and social factors are not conducive to a satisfied patient. He mirrors Dr. Frances's concern with the kinds of problems plastic surgery can't fix, and then concludes by saying, on the other hand, "there are other patients for whom the change in their looks opens a lot of alternatives."

In this Dr. Gaviria reveals the imagined possibilities of plastic surgery: no, plastic surgery doesn't resolve your problems for you, but then again, it might open some doors. These are the kinds of doors the *misses* in the *casting* system were thinking of: jobs in the media industry, particularly on national television. Indeed, models and actors are, for both doctors, a different kind of client, one in which influence is to a certain degree expected. Dr. Gaviria discusses the differences in his patients:

> Well, the general consultation with a patient is one where the patient comes in with some expectation. They come specifically seeking something. The *transformista* patient also comes in, as I

explained earlier, directly, to have a specific procedure, which is almost always breasts, a breast augmentation. And in the models, or people who work in television, modeling, it's changing the image. Induced almost always by the people with whom they work, the producer, the director, that is, who tells them that they have to improve their profile, that they have to improve certain things, take away certain lines, get a bit of an increase in breast volume, in the case of some girls, in order to work in television.

Both doctors discussed the emblematic example of a third party influencing a patient's decision-making process around plastic surgery: the Miss Venezuela pageant. Specifically, both doctors discuss the participation of Sousa in providing instructions to patients or even to surgeons regarding the changes he recommends. Dr. Gaviria mentions his experience working with contestants in the pageant:

DR. GAVIRIA: When we worked the Miss Venezuela, Osmel Sousa would directly let us know what they wanted to do to the patient: "Raise her eyebrows, fix her nose, make the point like this, give her bigger implants, reduce the [implant] volume, give her liposuction here and there." The patient would come, determined to have this procedure done, which was not what the patient wanted but what someone else wanted.

OCHOA: Aha. And those expectations of Osmel Sousa's, in the cases you treated, were they realistic or unachievable?

DR. GAVIRIA: Well, the majority of times they could be achieved, but sometimes not. But sometimes even though it wasn't what was called for, whether it turned out well or poorly, we had to do it that way because that's what they were asking for. That's why I didn't work much with them because, they, I didn't understand why he was going to tell me what to do . . . in terms of the patient.

OCHOA: And how did you find the patients? Were they happy to have the changes done, what they needed to be *misses*, or were they indecisive?

DR. GAVIRIA: No, no. What happened was that they came already with the, with that situation because he said that if they didn't have that procedure, they wouldn't get in [to the pageant], so they came looking for that . . . result. Which was to get into Miss Venezuela, or to get into a *casting*, or to do something else.

OCHOA: Aha, so for the hope of winning, not for something definite?

DR. GAVIRIA: Yes, and sometimes when the patient would come in on her own and we did what we thought was correct and what the patient thought was a problem area, well, sometimes he didn't like it and wouldn't accept them. So then you would have to, so he would send her to another plastic surgeon that . . . would do what he wanted to have done.

The way Dr. Gaviria frames it, plastic surgery is a tool used to shape contestants' bodies to the specifications set by Sousa. This sometimes contradicts the surgeons' recommendations, and yet pageant contestants must find a surgeon willing to perform the procedures required to enter or remain in the pageant. Frances notes that the SCVPREM doesn't look kindly on this kind of intervention, particularly when the instructions come from Sousa and not a plastic surgeon.

OCHOA: Does the [SCVPREM] have any professional ethics governing modifications done for the media industry, for work, let's say? . . .

DR. FRANCES: No, there's nothing prohibiting any of that.

OCHOA: So, if there are third parties, the classic example is the *miss* that goes to the Quinta [the Quinta Miss Venezuela, where the pageant is produced] and Osmel says, "trim this, take this off," and even though the *miss* hadn't considered those changes, she undergoes them because there is a third party . . .

DR. FRANCES: To get in [to the pageant], exactly, yes. Because the third party is the plastic surgeon. Because he [Sousa] has his surgeon there. Particularly, the society opposes this treatment, when there is a third party like this Osmel Sousa and there is no plastic surgeon. So then he's the one who says what it is that you are going to do. Perhaps if the plastic surgeon was more in charge and didn't let someone else intervene in the medical side, perhaps it would be better regarded. . . . I think that the person who should be giving their opinion in this case is the doctor. In order to improve a girl's beauty, let's say, of the ones who go there [to the pageant]. But I think that this kind of intervention from someone who isn't a doctor, it kind of interferes a bit with the, well, medical side, and then it becomes something more commercial.

Frances again invokes the divide between the scientific side and the commercial side of the enterprise — a boundary he is concerned with maintaining. Further, there is a point of conflict between the artistic vision of the pageant producer and that of the surgeon. What becomes clear is that participation in the media allows producers, patients, and surgeons to transcend the therapeutic rationale for plastic surgery, despite the fundamentally commercial nature of these kinds of bodily transformations. Despite Frances's objections to the commercial interests he imagines that *transformistas* seeking breast implants have (for "attracting clients," as he puts it), an economic rationale for plastic surgery that involves outside influence is possible as long as there is respect for medical authority.

Conclusion: *Sacar el Cuerpo*

The specter that haunts plastic surgery is the patient who seeks procedures outside the bounds of medical rationality, the patient who constantly pushes the limits of what "appears" human. Dr. Frances invokes it when he talks about the size of breast implants: two hundred cc, three hundred cc, four hundred cc . . . *gigantesco*. In saying this, he calls attention to the fact that the proportions of plastic surgery are constantly shifting; patients are measuring their bodies against proportions that change over time. What is reasonable in one era is ridiculous in another. Both plastic surgeons invoked this specter of monstrosity when describing the excesses of *transformista* technologies of transformation, specifically, those employed outside the authority of medicine. Both of these surgeons were aware of the kinds of practices Norkeli so nonchalantly disclosed that hot afternoon in the center of Caracas. For the surgeons, these practices confirm the irrationality of *transformista* bodies and exclude them from the realm of sanitary citizenship. Frances describes one patient who sought treatment in a public hospital:

> DR. FRANCES: In the hospital we saw a *transformista* patient.
> And he [*sic*] injected oil in his gluteus.
> OCHOA: What kind of oil?
> DR. FRANCES: Vegetable oil.

OCHOA: Vegetable oil? Aha.

DR. FRANCES: Yes. Well. A bunch of immunological problems—
I think he was HIV-positive as well. We couldn't offer him
anything because . . . it gave him multiple—like abscesses—
periodically on his body. We sent him to immunology and he
left the hospital, never came back.

Frances stops a beat for emphasis when he tells me that the *trans-formista* patient injected vegetable oil. He expects me to be shocked. I am not. Then he continues with the kind of medical distancing that allows practitioners of medicine to see patients as untreatable. The patient leaves the hospital untreated. Dr. Gaviria presents the case that shocks him with a bit of a different perspective, one that opens up a possibility of change in the way plastic surgery can relate to *transformista* patients:

OCHOA: I was going to ask you about the girls that come in already
somewhat transformed. They've taken hormones or injected
oil, as you told me; they're what I call self-medicating. In other
words, it's a way to adapt their bodies without the care of a doctor. What kinds of transformations have you seen, specifically,
and do these pose a problem for the health of these individuals
or not?

DR. GAVIRIA: Yes, well, before there was a lot of . . . disinforma-
tion because we were very few plastic surgeons who would work
with this type of patient. So they would do what you say, they
would resort to self-medication. So, a friend would say, "Look,
and these tits . . ." We've seen patients injecting even vegetable
oil, the kind you use for cooking. Mineral oil, baby oil, injecting
themselves. So in that case, yes, the lesions are significant and
irreversible. But I think the culture that they have about this has
been increasing, and now there are very few that one sees that do
these, these barbarities. The majority either seeks aesthetic surgery, a plastic surgeon to resolve their problems, or they inject
hormones to try to accomplish the changes they need. And it's
almost always breasts, or augmenting the hips, or more below,
changing the morphology of the masculine leg to a more feminine morphology, so they inject themselves there [in the leg],
then.

OCHOA: They inject, as you say, mineral oil or . . .

DR. GAVIRIA: Yes, baby oil, olive oil, vegetable oil, that . . .

OCHOA: And what's the biological effect of these injections?

DR. GAVIRIA: Well, the biological effect, the organism creates a reaction to foreign bodies, and at the beginning you see only the volume, and increase in the volume of the area because of the product [injected], but later you see complications—ulcerations . . . to the point that, I saw a young man [*sic*] in the hospital who, we had to amputate his legs because, for oil injections. He injected motor oil.

OCHOA: A *transformista*?

DR. GAVIRIA: A *transformista*. . . . I was doing my specialization in plastic surgery then.

OCHOA: People sure do come up with some things . . .

DR. GAVIRIA: Yes, yes, yes. Don't you see that before . . . before they didn't have those, because no, and there was no access to, to these things then so they would have to find whatever alternative they could. To change their form, their figure.

Dr. Gaviria approaches the issue of self-administered feminizing regimens as one of education, "culture," and access, allowing for the possibility of incorporating *transformista* feminizing projects into plastic surgery practice. Although he expresses medical concern about these practices ("barbarities"), he poses the problem as one of access to treatment, rather than one of patient compliance or noncompliance.

There is nothing inherently excessive in *transformistas'* desires to transform their bodies, but the social context in which they form their ideas about the body and the technologies they have to accomplish their transformations produce a context in which practices such as Norkeli's olive oil become completely logical and unremarkable. The logic of the body that the phrase *sacar el cuerpo* represents is one forged in Venezuelan modernity: one that produces medical authority by policing the line between sanitary citizens and unsanitary subjects, that understands medicine and technology as collaborators in the improvement of the self, and that provides a set of imaginary possibilities for women whose bodies conform to hegemonic national ideals of beauty. Physicians, sexologists, and surgeons are invested in maintaining medical authority, but they also collaborate with those whom they consider their patients to accomplish the desired aesthetic. In this context, women who participate in these imaginaries—

transformistas, misses, and others—place their bodies at the service of this feminine ideal, working with everything they have at their disposal to *sacar el cuerpo.*

We have seen the carnal and corporeal mediations of femininity and modernity on the bodies of Venezuelan women. Next we will look at another mediation: the ways that Venezuelans employ spectacle to produce femininity.

6

Spectacular Femininities

When I was a kid and my ma added the rice to the hot oil, you know how it sizzles and spits, it sounds kind of like applause, right? Well, I'd always bow and say *Gracias, mi querido público*, thank you, and blow kisses to an imaginary crowd. I still do, kind of as a joke. When I make Spanish rice or something and add it to the oil. It roars, and I bow, just a little so no one would guess, but I bow, and I'm still blowing kisses, only inside. — SANDRA CISNEROS, "Remember the Alamo"

In Sandra Cisneros's homage to gay Tejanos and other people who have died from complications of AIDS, the character Rudy Cantú talks about his fame and fortune in South Texas. Rudy describes how he changes when he gets up on stage at the Travisty, how he becomes Tristán, the world-class dancer, dancing it up with La Calaca, death: "Tristán holds himself like a matador. His clothes magnificent. Absolutely perfect, like a second skin. The crowd throbbing—Tris-TAN, Tris-TAN, Tris-TAN!!! Tristán smiles, the room shivers. He raises his arms, the wings of a hawk. Spotlight clean as the moon of Andalucía. Audience breathless as water. And then . . . *Boom!* The heels like shotguns. A dance till death. I will love you *hasta la muerte, mi vida*. Do you hear? Until death" (Cisneros 1991, 64).

Tristán is vital to Rudy's survival; the thrall that Tristán holds over the crowd is a symptom of his power—power to dance with death. But when he is not Tristán, when he is Rudy, the crowd is there. When he is not Tristán, Rudy dances differently with La Calaca, quietly, as he prepares his meal. Before an imaginary crowd, Rudy enacts an everyday, small spectacle, witnessed by no one but his stove. But what is this spectacle? To whom is it directed? And why, ultimately, does spectacle, whether large or small, appear time and again among gay men and transgender women in Latin American and other contexts?

So far I have described the ways *transformistas* and actors in the Miss Venezuela system produce femininities to various ends and through diverse technologies. In this chapter I consider the nature of spectacle as it relates to the production of femininity from the Venezuelan context. I do this by meandering through a conversation I partook in with two beauty pageant contestants, a stylist, and my research assistant during a makeup session for a Miss Venezuela *casting*. From this conversation, I engage Judith Butler's important work on the production of gender through performance. I ask: how does it feel to make a spectacle of one's self?

I propose *spectacularity* as a register on which to consider the performativity of gender and how spectacularity is used to produce particularly legible forms of femininity by *transformistas* and actors in the Miss Venezuela *casting* system. Of course, spectacle is not the sole provenance of femininity. Masculine spectacle, racialized spectacle, commodity spectacle, the spectacle of the Other, national spectacle, and myriad other forms of spectacle exist. For the sake of precision, I will parse out the definition of *spectacle* that I am employing, which focuses on performativity and mediation rather than ideology per se. More precisely, I propose spectacularity as a mode of signification and performative practice that is related to mass mediation. For example, the imaginary crowd of Cisneros's story, of Rudy Cantú's everyday, small spectacle, is an important component of spectacularity. Other elements, which I call *mode of address* and *interiority*, also attend to the performance of spectacularity. These elements reveal themselves as we move through the Miss Venezuela *casting* makeup session.

Michael Warner's concept of "publics" (2002) serves to lay some groundwork for my definitions of *spectacularity* here. I will propose some ways spectacularity might work within an analysis of the performativity of gender by engaging Judith Butler's treatment of "drag" as an example of performativity (1999), and I offer a few other examples. Butler's work on the production of gender through repetition and performance has provided an important framework for considering the relationships between discourses and bodies. When we approach these relationships ethnographically, the importance of accounting for context and the cultural specificity of signifying practices in Butler's framework becomes apparent.

By what processes do discourses materialize bodies? This has been a persistent question in my focus on the body. Spectacularity is an important dimension to consider in accounting for how gender is produced in and on the body within discourse. *Spectacular femininities*, then, are femininities that employ the conventions of spectacularity in their production.[1] The concept of spectacular femininities allows me to account for the role of mass mediation and spectacle in the production and authorization of certain aspects of femininity as I observed them in Venezuela. I witnessed how spectacular femininities are invoked and produced in two different contexts: on the street with *transformistas* in Caracas and during the makeup session of a Miss Venezuela *casting*.[2]

Spectacle and Gender in Cultural Theory

The topic of spectacle has been of significant concern to cultural critics, particularly those linked to the Frankfurt School, which characterizes spectacle as an instrument of mass distraction. It is worthwhile to review some key approaches to the notion of spectacle and the relationship between spectacle and gender. Specifically, I engage the work of Guy Debord, Mary Ann Doane, and Jean Baudrillard to map out my own definitions of *spectacle* and propose spectacular femininity as a way to consider the role of mass mediation in the performativity of gender. This is not a complete review of the copious amount of work that employs the concept of spectacle. Instead I contend with the specter of false consciousness and instrumentality that underlies the concept of spectacle, and I distinguish my own approach as located within processes of subject formation and survival. Thus, I am more interested in how people *employ* spectacle than in making claims about critical consciousness or political possibility.

Debord's *The Society of the Spectacle*, published in 1967, describes spectacle not only as a manner of distraction but also as the production of an entire society organized around the production and circulation of images and commodities: *the* spectacle as an ongoing realm of social interaction. Since this influential text was published, commentary on spectacle has proliferated in media studies and cultural criticism.[3] Debord proposes spectacle as an object, a social relationship. But this promising idea takes a different turn as Debord attempts to link spectacle to social power more directly. Debord asserts that "the spectacle is *capital* accumulated to the point where it becomes image" (1983, 17). In this formulation, resonant with Richard Dyer's analysis of stars as a kind of congealed capital (1986), it would seem that Debord's spectacle is just the sort of bridge between discourse and body that I have been seeking. However, with Debord we never seem to end up at the body. As an all-encompassing phenomenon, Debord's spectacle becomes a logic, a thrall. In *Comments on the Society of the Spectacle*, he likens the spectacle to the commodity: "Just as the logic of the commodity reigns over capitalists' competing ambitions, and the logic of war always dominates the frequent modifications of weaponry, so the harsh logic of spectacle controls the abundant diversity of media extravagances" (2002, 7).

Debord's characterization of *the* spectacle as an ongoing thrall is akin to the notion of the media industry, although for Debord, "the media" is not a sufficient category to understand the power of the spectacle. Perhaps, instead, this understanding of the spectacle is similar to an ongoing conversation or a fun cocktail party that has the power to make inconvenient things disappear: "When the spectacle stops talking about something for three days, it is as if it did not exist" (2002, 20). The spectacle then becomes a monolithic kind of power that blinds its spectators. Spectacle *becomes* reality. However, Debord's notion of spectacle depends on a passive spectator: "The attitude that it demands is the same passive acceptance that it has already secured by means of its seeming incontrovertibility, and indeed, by its monopolization of the realm of appearances. . . . It is the sun that never sets on the empire of modern passivity" (1983, 10).

This is where, despite my sympathy to Debord's argument about the discursive power of spectacle, we must part ways. Debord's objectival notion of the spectacle doesn't serve to parse out the lived experiences of people with respect to spectacle, nor does it allow for a complex understanding of spectacle as a cultural form, produced through specific histories, genres, and practices. A Miss Venezuela pageant might be considered the ultimate example of this kind of pacifying spectacle. But leaving it there, at the production of the illusion, ignores the vast amounts of labor, energy, desire, and preparation required to produce the pageant—the investment of its spectators and participants and the meanings these practices create. Treating spectacle as a monolith erases the universe of negotiations, commitments, and disappointments that take place as people make their lives within "the society of the spectacle." It is precisely this erasure in critical theory, which does violence to lived experience for the sake of ideological positioning, that motivates my own empirical project. We will have to forgo an objectival notion of *the* spectacle and instead look for other ways to understand spectacle.

Similarly, I have engaged two veins of cultural theory that use the concept of spectacle in the production of gender. In both of these cases, concepts of transvestitism and transsexuality are appropriated to describe ideological phenomena attendant to mass culture and gender. Mary Ann Doane (1982) and Jean Baudrillard (2002) employ transvestitism and transsexuality as allegories to describe the cultural processes they see at work in the ways audiovisual and cinematic media shape our lives. They each allegorize trans categories as a way to distinguish between the real and artifice. Indeed, both scholars are concerned with how mediated imaginaries of gender distort some essentially true reality.

Doane's landmark essay "Film and the Masquerade: Theorizing the Female Spectator" (1982) employs the idea of transvestism specifically to describe cinematic forms of cross-dressing. This usage appropriates the psychoanalytic category of transvestism, one of clinical diagnosis, as allegory. Doane's examples of transvestism consist of recognizably feminine actresses who wear men's clothing. She discusses the film *Adam's Rib* (1949), in which two women wearing men's clothing are objects of desire, while a man wearing women's clothing is the object of ridicule. Doane's imaginary of female transvestism presumes a female transvestite who is incapable of passing as a man, and who is significantly aware of the Otherness of masculine trappings: "The transvestite wears clothes which signify a different sexuality, a sexuality which, for the woman, allows mastery over the image and the very possibility of attaching the gaze to desire. Clothes make the man, as they say. Perhaps this explains the ease with which women can slip into male clothing" (81). Yet this "transvestism," which rests on an essential and enduring femininity, is a surface cross-dressing at best, only one of many forms of transvesting, and certainly not resonant with the experience of transvesting, even as defined in psychological diagnostic criteria (let us not even approach the experiences of people who wear gender-nonconforming clothing in myriad ways). The distance that Doane proposes exists between the female spectator and the masquerade — essentially, cross-dressing in one's own gender — is the site of lack: "The transvestite adopts the sexuality of the other — the woman becomes a man in order to attain the necessary distance from the image. Masquerade, on the other hand, involves a realignment of femininity, the recovery, or more accurately, simulation, of the missing gap or distance. To masquerade is to manufacture a lack in the form of a certain distance between one's self and one's image" (82). This presumes that, for a female spectator, the woman on the screen is somehow *like* one in some way that one can latch onto. In this formulation, what disappears is the "passing" transvestite (let's just call her the butch), as well as the gender-nonconforming female spectator. Also excluded from possibility is the male spectator who does not employ a heterosexual gaze, but rather one of desire and identification with the feminine form that Doane attributes to the female spectator, or, indeed, the transgender (woman) spectator who employs an identificatory gaze toward the femme diva. In the end, the gender math in Doane's formulation of the masquerade is too uncomplicated to account for the kinds of subjectivities and productions of gender I encountered in the field.

Jean Baudrillard similarly employs the "transsexual" as an allegorical category to develop his argument about the fate of gender and sexuality in the contemporary symbolic order, imbued as it is with technology, media, and viruses.[4] In an essay entitled "We Are All Transsexuals Now" (2002), Baudrillard invokes transsexuality to describe the "artificial fate" to which the sexed body is exposed: "The sexual has *jouissance* as its focus (*jouissance* is the leitmotif of sexual liberation), whereas the transsexual tends towards artifice — both the anatomical artifice of changing sex and the play on vestimentary, morphological and gestural signs characteristic of cross-dressers — what is involved is prosthetics and today, when it is the body's destiny to become a prosthesis, it is logical that the model of sexuality should become transsexuality and that transsexuality should everywhere become the site of seduction" (9).

It should be apparent that this formulation does violence to the people whose specter Baudrillard invokes to describe the paragon of artificiality, those who he sees as exhibiting "a carnivorous erotic ideology which no woman today would sign up to — except, precisely, a transsexual, a transvestite: they alone, as we know, live by the exaggerated, carnivorous signs of sexuality" (10). In a move similar to Doane's, he attributes this erotic ideology not only to transsexuals and transvestites but also to pop stars (his examples: Madonna, Michael Jackson, and the Italian porn star La Cicciolina) and ultimately, to all of us, as the title of his essay proclaims. While this claim is based on an incredibly distorted view of transsexuals and transvestites (perhaps including the very visible Latin American transgender sex workers of Paris, among others), Baudrillard is trying to sort out something important here—the relation between spectacle and gender. But because his perception rests on his fundamental approach to reality and artifice, the transvestite or transsexual of Baudrillard's argument can only be artificial because some originary gender claims prior existence. It is this same understanding of artifice that colors his well-known work in *Simulacra and Simulation*, in which he proposes a hyperreal, or rather "the generation by models of a real without origin or reality" (1994, 1). What is the status of this "real without origin?" Of the original? While this work has been very generative for thinking through the cultural permutations of postmodernity, it reveals an underlying anxiety, an approach to these cultural shifts that betrays a sense of loss.

Chela Sandoval describes this anxiety in postmodern theory in a discussion of the work of Fredric Jameson: "If, as Jameson argues, the formerly centered and legitimated bourgeois citizen-subject of the first world (once anchored in a secure haven of self) is set adrift under the imperatives of late-capitalist cultural conditions, if such citizen-subjects have become anchorless, disoriented, incapable of mapping their relative positions inside multinational capitalism, lost in the reverberating endings of colonial expansionism . . . then the first world subject enters the kind of psychic terrain formerly inhabited by the historically decentered citizen-subject: the colonized, the outsider, the queer, the subaltern, the marginalized" (2000, 27). Sandoval insists on accounting for historical processes of displacement in an understanding of the affective dimensions of postmodernity. She welcomes the postmodernist boys to the club of the decentered. In Baudrillard, the anxiety of decentering manifests itself in a silent mourning for the originary "real," an idea that he rejects as a possibility and yet reiterates through his insistence on a hyperreal. This response to the cultural shifts attendant to postmodernity affirms the hyperreal as the operative symbolic order with an insistence that produces as impossible the category of the "real." There is no real any more; we no longer have any access to it. In this way, Baudrillard fetishizes the hyperreal in his analysis while at the same time reifying the impossibility of the "real." And, like a typical Parisian fetishist, he heads straight for the most visible trans women in trying to work out his concerns. In the "We Are All Transsexuals" argument, transsexuals and transvestites represent the highest form of artificiality. And the violence of this is, of course, isolating the gender of trans people from the rest of gender, from the rest of "us." This begs the question: why is Baudrillard's claim about the "artificiality" of transgender people so easily digestible? Its transphobia is part of the answer. But it is also true that some, though not all, women employ the kind of aesthetic that Baudrillard is naming "transsexual." As I have argued thus far, this kind of hyperfeminine aesthetic is useful for negotiating many kinds of tricky situations. In Baudrillard's use of the transsexual, the universe of these possibilities is completely flattened in order to make a point about artificiality. Rather than allowing for the possibility that the original never was, Baudrillard must mourn its loss.

Contrast Butler's notion of the original in her theory of the performativity of gender to Baudrillard's models of a real without origin. In Butler we see a similar claim to Baudrillard's: *"gender is a kind of imitation for which there is no original"* (Butler and Salih 2004, 127; emphasis in original). However, Butler has no nostalgia for the original she names. Butler's concern is instead with the ways in which some notion of the original is produced *through* imitation. Her claim continues: "In fact, it [gender] is a kind of imitation that produces the very notion of the original as an *effect* and consequence of the imitation itself" (127). This formulation opens up the possibility of empirical projects to map these processes of production in different ways. And while the theoretical subject embedded in Butler's analysis does not stray far from first-world subjectivity and embodiment, this subject does provide an important intervention into the ways we think about gender. I will expand on Butler's approach in order to develop an approach to gender performativity that more closely accounts for media and spectacle.

Being Spectacular

What does it mean to be spectacular? Recall the flight attendant in the introduction. Was she being spectacular? The forms of femininity accomplished by *transformistas* and *misses* can be linked to spectacularity. What I mean by this is that both forms of femininity involve a kind of hyperfemininity intended for display, and they are created as the objects of an imagined masculine gaze.[5] Spectacular femininities, again, are femininities that employ the conventions of spectacularity in their production. This includes conventions of form such as genre, narrative structure, temporality, and archetype.[6] This also includes conventionalized gender formations—the tropes of femininity (in this case) that render the production of these femininities as highly legible. These have to do with morphology, affect, and iconicity and are always inflected with (trans)national discourses of race, empire, and corporeality. In order to understand how spectacular femininities work, we have to look at conventions of femininity as well as the ways these femininities relate to spectacle, and the media through which spectacle can take place.

We start with the place of spectacle in Butler's theory of the performativity of gender. This requires a bit of close attention to some distinctions embedded in the theory. In the 1999 preface to *Gender Trouble*, Butler writes about her tendency to "waffle between" two ways of understanding performativity: "Understanding performativity as linguistic and casting it as theatrical" (xxv). She argues that a speech act is both "performed" and "linguistic," and goes on to define the "performed" as "theatrical, presented to an audience, subject to interpretation" (xxv). While it seems contradictory to think of performance as being in any way separate from language, this distinction shows how Butler's formulation isolates spectacle in the context of the speech act. It is this spectacular register of the speech act that remains unaddressed in Butler's approach. But how do we get from the "performed" dimension of the speech act to the spectacle? Through Butler's own definition, which itself contains the elements necessary for media analysis: (1) "theatrical" — that is, staged, projected, the production of the spectacle; (2) "presented to an audience" — the mode of address of the performance and its forms of distribution; (3) "subject to interpretation" — in other words, the conditions and possibilities of reception.[7] These three elements, which mark a speech act as "performed" in the vernacular sense, are at the heart of a traditional sense of spectacle. The separation between the performed and the linguistic aspects of the speech act as identified by Butler suggests the traditional distinction between the everyday and performance. This distinction, of course, is one Butler argues against: performance is not just the theatrical; performance is the mechanism through which gender (an imitation without an original) is produced, through repetitive acts. But this "waffling," as she calls it, is a tension, an ambiguity around precisely the role of spectacle in the performativity of gender.

It is possible to argue that Butler provides a simple mechanism through which to include spectacle in the performativity of gender: the citation. The compulsory power of citation is very clear throughout Butler's *Bodies*

That Matter (1993). Citation is not a voluntary act; citation is an imperative for viable subjecthood, as she points out in the chapter "Critically Queer": "Femininity is thus not the product of a choice, but the forcible citation of a norm, one whose complex historicity is indissociable from relations of discipline, regulation, punishment" (232). Butler takes up the political possibilities of citation in a discussion of queer politics in the 1990s:

> Within queer politics, indeed, within the very signification that is "queer," we read a resignifying practice in which the desanctioning power of the name "queer" is reversed to sanction a contestation of the terms of sexual legitimacy. Paradoxically, but also with great promise, the subject who is "queered" into public discourse through homophobic interpellations of various kinds *takes up* or *cites* that very term as the discursive basis for an opposition. This kind of citation will emerge as *theatrical* to the extent that it *mimes and renders hyperbolic* the discursive convention that it also *reverses*. The hypberbolic gesture is crucial to the exposure of the homophobic "law" that can no longer control the terms of its own abjecting strategies. (1993, 232; emphasis in original)

While citation as a linguistic practice does hold some political possibility, Butler describes citation as part of a conscientious political strategy of resignification. This sets up a binary: either you have the oppressive imperative or the oppositional resignification. For *transformistas*, these lines are not quite so clear. Theatricality, as Butler defines it, involves miming and rendering hyperbolic a discursive convention. Spectacularity, as I am using it, refers to the ways in which the discursive conventions related to mass mediation are available for not just citation or miming but for all kinds of everyday performance.

The media, like the law, institutions, and medicine, could be said to provide yet one more source of these citational imperatives or political possibilities. Yet all of these fields have their specific histories and conventions. The kind of symbolic imperative (or resource) available for citation is unique to each field. Further, each of these fields has profoundly shaped practice in different ways—ways that are historically, geographically, and culturally contingent. Existing media and practices of spectatorship have shaped our localized understandings of the conventions of spectacle, modes of address, and conditions of reception. We all (along with the *transformistas* in the example I will give) employ these elements of spectacle in our signifying practices. What watching *transformistas* relate to a video camera reveals is the humor, skill, and irony with which they employ spectacularity. By moving through this argument about performance, theatricality, and audience, I am proposing that we consider spectacle as one register through which individuals can signify—a register that remains unaddressed in the theory of gender performativity. Our use of spectacularity in signifying practice, a complex and multifaceted form of citation, places us in a universe of symbolic resources and provides opportunities for imaginary projection beyond the material conditions in which we find ourselves. This kind of imaginary projection, as I have seen *transformistas* use it, also critiques existing material and symbolic regimes. Spectacularity, then, bears further description.

So then what makes something spectacular? Spectacularity, as I am using it, employs existing conventions of media spectatorship to signify beyond a semantic level of speech. That is, spectacular performance is the kind of performance Butler would call "theatrical." Only you do not have to be in a theater to be theatrical. How do we know when somebody is acting theatrically? I learned to identify this kind of spectacular performance on the street with the *transformistas* who worked Avenida Libertador. The following story exemplifies the second and third elements of Butler's notion of theatrical performance: the mode of address to an audience, and the ways in which the performance is subject to interpretation. After the story, I discuss the second element somewhat further as it relates to Michael Warner's concept of publics. Then I will discuss a second example from my fieldwork that addresses the first element: the staged spectacle.

The story is somewhat extended, but as a complete scene it captures the kinds of interactions *transformistas* had with the camera, and the humor and style with which they employed conventions of spectacularity. It begins one early evening in Caracas when I brought out on the street one of the video cameras that I was using to record beauty pageant *casting*. This was the first and last time I brought a camera along during the Avenida Libertador fieldwork, primarily because of the amount of attention it drew, from *transformistas* and in terms of the act of filming. I brought the camera to meet a group of *transformistas* who were getting ready for a procession that was to come through the area. The procession never came, from what we could tell, or the girls just decided to stay on the street and get down to work. We stayed on the Avenida through dusk and into night. The group, somewhat led by Shaidé, was animated.[8] Everyone was dressed to show off their bodies, in close-fitting crop or bikini tops and jeans that looked as if they were painted on, of the low-rise sort known as the "Brazilian" cut. As I turn on the video camera, Shaidé is cackling at something Andrea has said. Andrea motions to me to come closer and approaches the camera:

> ANDREA: Hey!
> OCHOA: Are we all going?
> VERÓNICA: Right here, here . . .
> ANDREA [*looking at the* LCD *screen viewfinder*]: How ugly they all look.
> SHAIDÉ, VERÓNICA, AND PILAR ALEXIS: Ay!
> ANDREA: Let me see how I look.

Andrea is still focused on the LCD screen and is now using it as a mirror by pointing the camera in my hand toward her and flipping the LCD screen so she can see herself. Shaidé says, to no one in particular but the camera: "Today, February 12 of 2003 we are all going to the Not One Step Back [*Ni un paso atrás*] march." *Ni un paso atrás* is the slogan of the Opposition to Chávez at the time. Verónica chuckles at Shaidé; Pilar Alexis is in the center of the screen. She keeps her eye on the camera and poses with shoulders back, smiles. Karla saunters across the screen in front of the girls and turns to look at the viewfinder with Andrea. Someone yells: "Aaaaaayyy!" Andrea exclaims: "Look at Pilaaarr!" Pilar Alexis lifts her arm up and does a "pinup girl" pose, bending at the knees and jutting out her ass. The high-pitched *aaayyy* spreads through the group. Andrea moves the camera away from the group so she can check her makeup in the viewfinder. La Bámbola jostles so she can have a look too.

> ANDREA: All right, let me see.
> LA BÁMBOLA: My turn! Ay how pretty . . . aaaayyyy!

Verónica, Karla, and La Bámbola all crowd into the frame with Andrea, push the camera away, and go offscreen. Someone says, *terrible!* La Bámbola screams and pushes in front of the camera so you can only see her teeth and silver lips with black lip liner: "Yo quiero saliiiir!" (I want to be in it!) Everyone laughs. The camera pans up and off, Andrea comes closer for another look.

ANDREA: Let me see myself.

OCHOA: Okay.

ANDREA: I can't *see* myself.

OCHOA: Fix yourself up, woman.

Karla jumps in front of Andrea, blocking her view. Andrea yells, "move!" Karla jumps off, laughing. Andrea shrieks, "Eeeeheeee! . . . That's better."

The jostle for camera time is both about the camera itself (particularly Andrea's relationship to the LCD screen as a mirror) and the social dynamics of the group. The fact that everyone is playing around is important — there is not a lot of sincerity about the use of these conventions, but they are what all of us slip into as the camera records. Andrea begins to fix her hair. La Bámbola starts yelling at Andrea offscreen:

LA BÁMBOLA: Hey, *marico.*[9]
[*La Bámbola's arm enters the frame to push Andrea off.*]
Marico, hasta cuándo? How long are we going to have to put up
with this?

La Bámbola jumps into the frame and assumes Andrea's place; La Bámbola begins to fix her hair, to everyone's laughter. I try to give some feeble direction, mostly to make sure I can keep track of everyone's name: "All right, for the archives, please present yourselves to the camera so . . ." A general chaos breaks out again. Shaidé stays at the center of the frame. From off-camera, Andrea shouts: "To Ishermann, speak Ishermann, a word for the cameras!" From the way Andrea uses it, it seems that Ishermann is the name of an announcer. She has already turned the video camera into a proxy for the press. Shaidé begins to effect an on-screen narrator persona:

Hello, good afternoon, we're here on the twelfth of February of
2003. We're going to the march in favor of the revolution in Venezuelan democracy — we, the transgenders of Venezuela. My name
is Shaidé and I will now introduce each one of the girls who work
here on Avenida Libertador.[10] First, we're going to call up Verónica.
Verónica, my love, welcome.

Shaidé has studied communication, and jumps at the chance to narrate. She employs the smooth conventions of an on-camera emcee or reporter, addressing her audience and expressing a self-consciousness about how she is received by affecting her language, choosing words like *elaboramos* and *transgender*, which are not commonly used on the Avenida. The camera pans to Verónica, who strolls on-screen. Verónica's affect is fairly exaggerated—she swings her hips out wide as she walks—and when she begins to speak, she does so a bit haltingly, trying to sound breathless: "Hello my love, my name is Verónica. I'm from here, from Avenida Libertador of the *transfor*.[11] . . . Well, I feel . . . beautiful, I mean, affectionate. I feel active, as a *transformista*, and that's how I want to be." She flips her hair back with both hands and swings her head for the camera. There is a lot of hair flipping in this entire interaction. It appears that long, luxurious hair is an important sign for the performance of femininity on the Avenida. Verónica concludes: "Thank you."

Shaidé chimes in: "Yes, thank you, Verónica. [*Verónica goes offscreen.*] Well, ladies and gentlemen, we're going to call up now one of the beauties of Avenida Libertador. She is considered the Venus for tonight, and she is, of course, Pilar Alexis." Several of the group members offscreen proclaim: "Leeeexxxiiii!" They applaud and the camera pans to Pilar Alexis, who is far offscreen, near the curb. She begins to walk over. Shaidé says, "Lexi, come over here, pose for the press." Lexi saunters closer in her black bikini crossover top and enormous breast implants. She is clearly the vixen of the group, showing the most skin at this point in the night, and more interested in what is going on at the curb than interacting with the video camera.

SHAIDÉ: Pose for the media.
ANDREA: Pose for the press!
PILAR ALEXIS: How silly.

Pilar Alexis runs both hands through her silken black hair, which cascades midway down her back. Then with one shake she flips the dark waterfall over her left shoulder and walks to the middle of the screen. She poses. She doesn't say much. Shaidé jokes offscreen about Pilar Alexis going to Los Angeles. Pilar Alexis stays quiet, smiling and posing.

OCHOA: Okay, we'll do a close-up from the bottom . . . to the top.
ANDREA [*to Pilar Alexis*]: Girl, but, you're straight out of a calendar!
[*Lexi pivots and does more pinup-girl poses.*]
OCHOA: Introduce yourself, love.

PILAR ALEXIS: Hello, I'm Alexis. [*She makes eye contact through the camera, flips her hair again, and glides offscreen.*] Enough!

She chortles and leans over onto Shaidé as the camera pans to both of them.

Shaidé says, "All right, now we're going to call one of the blondes, a gorgeous one of course, no less beautiful. And she knows who she is. Let me present to you . . . Andrea!" The group cheers and claps with laughter, and calls out her name: "Andreeea!" She saunters over from the curb, where she has retreated with Pilar Alexis. Andrea's voice is low, and streetwise. She speaks with a detached irony. "What do you want me to say? What I do for a living?" Andrea is making reference to the reporting of Erika Corrales, who at the time hosted a national scandal and gossip show called *En Caliente* (Hot Zone) on the Radio Caracas Televisión Network. The show taped on Avenida Libertador a few times, and Corrales would often dramatically confront *transformistas* and other sex workers on the Avenida with this question: What do you do for a living? WHAT DO YOU DO FOR A LIVING?

ANDREA: I am a prostitute on Libertador. [*She chuckles. Someone else laughs and says "Arrecha!"—fierce.*]
LA BÁMBOLA: Beautiful, queen, beautiful.
ANDREA: Okay, so what do you want me to say?
OCHOA: Present yourself.
SHAIDÉ: Present yourself.
OCHOA: How do you feel today?
ANDREA: How do I feel today? I feel divine and I feel young. Because I am still young.
OCHOA: And that's why we're going to the youth march.
ANDREA: Of course. That's why we're going to the march today. All of the girls here.

Having had her turn, Andrea waves goodbye and strolls offscreen. Shaidé resumes the narration, calling up an important trope of femininity in Venezuela: "All right, we're going to call up last year's Miss Venezuela, Miss Bambolaaa!" Offscreen, Verónica cheers La Bámbola on by saying "Hellooooooo!" La Bámbola stalks forward from the curb in jeans ripped to shreds and a paisley halter top. She pulls a band off her hair and shakes it loose in front of her as she walks. La Bámbola acknowledges her crown.

Several of the girls have copied her silver lipstick with black eyeliner, but her lips are perfectly done. She says, "Of course I am Miss Venezuela. Look at it, okay, make note of it." She flips her deep red hair over her left shoulder and turns to Shaidé.

SHAIDÉ: What gives, are we going to see it all right now, every-
thing, everything?
LA BÁMBOLA [*To me, ignoring Shaidé*]: What do you want me to
say?
OCHOA: Tell me your name . . .
SHAIDÉ: What's your name? "What do you do for a living?"
LA BÁMBOLA: Ah, okay, my name is Bámbola, and as you can see,
I am 90-60-90, Miss Venezuela 2002, my love.[12]

Andrea screams, in jest: "How *dare* you, insolent girl?" Someone in the crowd exclaims: "Aaaaayyy!" Andrea yells, "I'm the only one, and the one who will dispense with the crown among *transformistas* because no one else will ever be like me!" La Bámbola shakes her hair in front of her face as she speaks, then turns away from the camera. Andrea instructs La Bámbola: "But look at the camera . . ." La Bámbola whips around and gives the camera a piercing look. Andrea has to change midsentence: "Aaaaay!" Someone else says: "Ay, diva!"

Shaidé walks back on screen in front and resumes narrating: "Yes, the beautiful Bámbola. Last we're going to call up one of the other girls who is here, and she is . . . Karla!" Shaidé's enthusiasm for Karla is diminished, as is the group's. Karla herself is off at the curb when the camera pans and the group beckons her over, but with a deprecating tone: Andrea says, "Aha, come on. Get over here, *guajiro*!" Someone else says, "get over here, boy." *Guajiro* is a term used to refer to someone from the Guajira Peninsula region of northwestern Venezuela and northeastern Colombia, near Lake Maracaibo. The term is most commonly used to describe someone who is "wild" or "country" from that area, or an indigenous person from the Guajira cultural group. Note that all the *transformistas* I am interviewing are referring to this indigenous persona of Karla's in the masculine, deepening the level of insult (as she is already being deprecated for being country or indigenous), but Karla shrugs it off and puts up with it. She ambles over to the camera, laughing. She addresses the camera sincerely as Andrea continues the ribbing:

ANDREA: Hurry it up *guajiro*! . . . *Guaico* [a nickname for someone associated with the Yanomamö people], *guaico*. That's what they said. That's what Gina called her. She called her La Guajira.

OCHOA: Introduce yourself for the camera.

ANDREA [*Mocking*]: Hello, my name is Karla . . .

KARLA: Well, as you know, my name is Karla, I am from the city of Maracaibo and I am here in Caracas, right.

ANDREA: Prostituting yourself.

KARLA [*She cracks up at Andrea's constant interruptions to her introduction.*]: On Avenida Libertador. I'm here, feeling very fine, divine. Now we're going to go over to pose at that march for the youth, so, great, and I am here to be of service,[13] thanks.

She primly walks offscreen. While Karla is talking, Shaidé is asking everyone to come together for a group shot with the video camera. Once Andrea has called everyone together, Shaidé directs her attention to the camera once again. She says,

Okay, thank you. Thank you for being, eh, coming along with us, the Venezuelan transgenders, thank you for your support, for your solidarity, which is important. We are going to continue and present the entire group, what do you think? [*To the group*] Everyone get over here because they're going to take the group photo for the press!

The group assembles as the light in the plaza darkens. Some of the group members stand on a concrete circle that serves as a bench. A car trolls nearby at the curb; the men inside catcall to the girls as they assemble themselves for the "shot." They pose for a few seconds, then disperse. After the group photo, which is not a photo, some of the girls talk to the men in the car. Others hang out at the curb. In a while, everyone spreads out to different points on the *pasarelas* (pedestrian bridges) and starts to work. We never end up going to the march.

In this story, the *transformistas* hail each other and place themselves in discourse by citing conventions of spectacle. From Pilar Alexis's pinupgirl poses to Shaidé's smooth "girl reporter" narration, La Bámbola's Miss Venezuela, and even Karla's demure "I am here to be of service" (*para servirle*), each *transformista* employs a different mediated persona, or has one projected onto her by Shaidé or the group. The significant finding here is that each girl knows exactly how to use the convention she chooses. This is not, I would say, unique to *transformistas*, but it does some important work. To think about how spectacularity is productive, I turn now to another example, which employs the mode of address.

Welcome to the Audience

Michael Warner's use of the mode of address to "hail" his readers at the beginning of his article "Publics and Counterpublics" is an example of signifying spectacularly. Warner produces the object of his study in the first lines: "This essay has a public. If you are reading (or hearing) this, you are a part of its public. So first let me say: welcome" (2002, 49). In these sentences, he enacts a clever turn in the conventional mode of address of an academic essay, first by addressing the reader or listener directly ("If you are reading this . . ."), and then by interjecting an interpersonal mode of address ("let me say: welcome"). Warner's "welcome" is itself a felicitous speech act, in that it accomplishes its own proposition, placing the reader in the audience. In these sentences, Warner self-consciously invokes his audience and addresses it (us). As such, he is employing the conventions of reception to do some important work in this article. By hailing his reader or listener, Warner provides the first example of what "a public" might feel like. And it is a familiar feeling, if somewhat unusual for having been named.

The concept of publics is useful in considering reception studies, primarily because it allows us to critically think through questions of what has traditionally been called the audience. But reception studies can also inform the use of this concept, particularly in terms of the way it considers mass-mediated texts. Warner describes three senses of the noun *public*. The political sense is: "*The* public is a kind of social totality. Its most common sense is that of the people in general. It might be the people organized as the nation, the commonwealth, the city, the state or some other community." The theatrical sense is: "A public can also be a second thing: a concrete audience, a crowd witnessing itself in visible space, as with a theatrical public. . . . A performer onstage knows where her public is, how big it is, where its boundaries are, and what the time of its common existence is." And the textual sense is: "The kind of public that comes into being only in relation to texts and their circulation—like the public of this essay. (Nice to have you with us, still.)" (Warner 2002, 50; emphasis in original).

These second and third senses are different from the first in that they can be plural: the political sense is *the* public, while the second two refer to *a* public that is produced by these two different conditions of production, one scenic, or staged, and the other mediated through texts. Warner is most interested in publics mediated through texts and their circulation (the textual sense). While his second and third categories are distinct functions in his primarily textual endeavor, the theatrical and textual senses of Warner's publics, in much the same way as Butler's "performed" and "linguistic" dimensions of the speech act, are so blurred together as to be impossible to tease out when considering mass-mediated audiovisual spectacle.

The distinctions that both Warner and Butler make between performance and text or language rely on a logocentric framework, which stubbornly maintains the boundaries between words and flesh in spite of the work both scholars have done to break down precisely this binary in queer theory.[14] And while they both work to harmonize the binary, they ultimately stick to the text. This is a disciplinary decision, to be sure, but it is one that, for example, leads Butler to consider media texts such as novels and films, even an ethnography, as equivalent forms to examples of the everyday speech she invokes through experience, most evident in her use of drag as an example of the "constructed and performative dimension of gender" (1999, xxii). This flattening of forms of speech is at the heart of the frustrations with Butler's framework in terms of addressing racialization: if acts of speech are not embedded in the histories of colonization and racialization that have produced their contexts, they remain ecumenically available for argumentation without relation to these processes. The question of "what drag, where?" is paramount in considering drag practices as a set of examples. The queens represented in Esther Newton's *Mother Camp* (1970) are quite different from those represented in Jennie Livingston's *Paris Is Burning* (1992), and indeed, quite distinct from the communities and individuals that have been the objects of these representational projects. If we are to consider the performativity of speech acts, or the performativity of other acts of speech that are not in themselves speech acts, we must attend to the ways in which these examples of speech have been produced. The issue of mediation—particularly with respect to the debate over *Paris Is Burning*, in which bell hooks strongly critiques the film *as* a film while Butler argues the examples of speech *within* the film—is one of the things that gets lost in Butler's analysis of speech.

Speech acts are multidimensional. As Butler points out, the performative power of speech acts is not constituted by the words that are uttered (Butler 1993, 225). In the quintessential example of a speech act, that of a judge saying "I now pronounce you . . ." in a marriage ceremony, there is the authority of the person uttering the phrase and the citation of legal authority on which this phrase becomes binding. As Butler puts it, "It is the power of this citation that gives the performative its binding or conferring power" (225). But what happens to citation when it is mediated? That is, what happens when a speech act is performed in its local context, but then reiterated through a medium of diffusion? Does it signify differently?

Take the example of crowning a Miss Universe as a speech act: in the moment her nation is announced, and the crown is placed on her head, she is made Miss Universe by the authority — it would seem — of the Miss Universe Organization, Donald Trump, and NBC. But how is the performative power of this speech act constituted? What authority is cited in the conferral of the crown? While the corporate authority of the Miss Universe Organization and its owners is undisputed in this speech act and performed by a master or mistress of ceremonies contracted by this organization, the public of the pageant confers an authority as well, through its witnessing and recognition of the coronation.

In 2009 this public was estimated to be more than six million viewers in the United States alone; estimates of international viewership are unavailable, but the Miss Universe Organization boasts "an international audience of hundreds of millions of people."[15] The public of the pageant is constituted in various forms: the people attendant to its staging, the audience in the theater in which the pageant is held, the televisual audience, and now the Internet audience, but beyond these constituencies of attention, the public of the Miss Universe pageant includes everyone "within earshot," anyone who might have taken note of its occurrence. This is the fourth of Warner's principles of publics: "*A public is constituted through mere attention*" (2002, 60; emphasis in original). Warner's notion of attention, however, is fairly broad: "By coming into range, you fulfill the only entry condition demanded of a public. It is even possible for us to understand someone sleeping through a ballet performance as a member of that ballet's public[. . . .] The act of attention involved in showing up is enough to create an addressable public. Some kind of active uptake, however somnolent, is indispensable" (61). Without recognizing the scale on which Miss Universe is crowned, the nature of the public that lends its attention to this act, we lose the *dimensionality* of this speech act. Without scale, it becomes difficult to determine the significance of the speech act, whether it is uttered at one of the many gay and transgender beauty pageants held throughout the world or in someone's living room. All of these acts have significance; they signify, but they signify quite differently.

Mass-mediated audiovisual spectacle contributes another register on which to evaluate the productive power of speech: that of scale. Scale, in this sense, does not *necessarily* have to be mass mediated, but the "massivity" of mass mediation is a clear example of scale as a register for speech. Without this register, all acts of speech seem to float around in the same semiotic ocean, without the full weight of embodied context to anchor them. The ability to address a mass audience is an indicator of access to the means through which such audiences are constituted and addressed. When Shaidé and Andrea riff off of the conventions of address to a national Venezuelan or transnational Latin American audience, they are also using the massivity of this mode of address to hail an imagined audience, or to place themselves in a particular location in the world order, one that is clearly not resonant with the material conditions that surround them.

I follow Warner in suggesting that these conventions of address and the constitution of publics are hallmarks of modernity. Although these understandings and conventions may vary or be inflected with particular histories of spectacle, these are available as registers on which to signify. In employing these registers, we reach for and sometimes attain a bit of leverage. Even small-scale acts of speech have access to the register of scale as a mode of signification. In the example of the *transformistas*, the public is completely imaginary—the *transformistas* know that the tape will not be distributed. But it does not matter to them. They are still participating in a spectacle.

In addition to conventions, citations, and modes of address, spectacularity also employs a process of production—the mounting of a spectacle. This, of course, involves production processes, some informal and improvised (like the use of *pasarelas* as runways), some extremely well established. In well-established forms of spectacle, this process of production is often mystified, as I have discussed in previous chapters. Participants and producers in these processes employ techniques to accomplish the spectacle as intended. This was the case in the Miss Venezuela *casting* system. While I described the *casting* system in chapter 3, this example more closely describes how one contestant and a makeup artist narrate the process of making a spectacle of one's self. This process involves contestants in particular narratives and ideologies of interiority that are thought to produce exemplary forms of spectacle. In addition to accomplishing the correct body, the beauty pageant contestant must accomplish something more: a kind of attitude, affect, or performance that is thought to influence the outcome of the event. Whether or not a contestant is actually successful through these techniques is a different matter—the important thing is the internal state that the contestant disciplines herself to accomplish in order to reflect the desired outward state. This interiority is also a component of spectacular femininity. The following section describes one site of the production of a spectacular femininity—in the makeup chairs during the preparations for a Miss Venezuela *casting*.

Making a Spectacle of One's Self

How does it feel to make a spectacle of one's self? Each of us experiences this in very different ways, but in order to successfully make a spectacle of one's self (intentionally), we must also project a certain form; we must accomplish legibility. These forms of spectacular legibility are varied—let us not assume that all spectacles are feminine, or on a stage for that matter. Nor are all spectacles intentional, but there are many ways one can make a spectacle of one's self. Here I would like to consider what we might call *felicitous* spectacle—that is, a spectacle that accomplishes what it sets out to do—a spectacle where one feels in command, and where one receives the kind of attention one desires.[16] Felicitous spectacle requires some kind of display, and an audience—real or imaginary—that can provide the kind of recognition one seeks. Consider the small-scale spectacle of Rudy Cantú, who imagines the moment of reward: the rice (his audience) applauds his phantom performance, and he takes his bows. Or perhaps that of the young hockey player practicing in her driveway, narrating for herself: "she shoots, she scores!" And the crowd goes wild. Felicitous spectacle thus can be an element in the ways we dream ourselves into being.[17]

Of course, real crowds are not always as generous as imaginary crowds. If you are to manage an actual audience, then you run certain risks. The feeling of managing an audience proved difficult to articulate for many of the people I interviewed in the Miss Venezuela *casting*. However, one contestant, Lenora, had considered this question at length. What follows is a transcript of a video taken during the makeup sessions in one of the regional *casting* I visited in the preparations for Miss Venezuela in 2003. The transcript has been translated and edited for clarity, and I intersperse some discussion of the events as they unfold.

Lenora is a bit older than most of the contestants. While I do not ask contestants to disclose their ages, she had already completed her university studies in psychology and was working as a drug-treatment counselor at a local NGO. She would have been approximately twenty-two or twenty-three years old at the time. The setting is a galley-style makeup room. House and Spanish pop music pump out of a portable stereo. A tall mirror and makeup counter run the length of the front and back walls. The makeup artist Marco Antonio is in foreground doing makeup on a seated contestant. Lenora is in background, sitting up against the mirror, on the makeup counter along the back wall. She is tall, with long black hair, and she wears a black leotard, a *faja* around her waist, and six-inch black heels, which she occasionally removes after practicing her runway walk.[18] Gaston, my research assistant, and I are asking questions as Marco Antonio works on the seated contestant. Lenora stalks up and down the length of the room practicing her runway walk, adjusts her *faja*, and periodically does leg lifts on the counter. From the beginning, Marco Antonio has been teasing Lenora and pointing out her education as a psychologist:

MARCO ANTONIO: This one here, Lenora, she's worthy of study. Because how can a *psychologist* sign up for a beauty contest?
OCHOA: Oh yes, I did want to . . . [*Lenora looks up and smiles*]
MARCO ANTONIO: So how do you . . . apply it to yourself, how do you see it, putting yourself in a beauty contest for everyone else to judge you? You, as a psychologist, how do you see that?
LENORA: I'm not doing it to be judged.
MARCO ANTONIO: No, well, but there is a judgment.

In contesting Marco Antonio's claim, Lenora invokes a common trope in the discourse of beauty pageants—that they are more about internal beauty than they are about physical beauty.

LENORA: But beauty has other faces. I mean, it's not just about physical beauty, but also about the beauty you have inside, and intelligence is fundamental. You can't get anywhere if you have a peanut for a brain. These things complement each other.
OCHOA: . . . So what does it feel like, not just physically, but emotionally, getting on that runway?

Marco Antonio interjects and continues the ribbing, taking the opportunity to sexualize the contestants—a process that produces a *mujerona* (stage persona).

MARCO ANTONIO: No, well, they come.

OCHOA: Huh?

MARCO ANTONIO: They *come*!

Marco Antonio means that the beauty pageant contestants orgasm when they are walking runway. I turn beet red. Lenora maintains a poker face during Marco Antonio's interjection.

MARCO ANTONIO: Of course. *Of course*! . . . Because I think that a person who gets up on a runway, and then she feels just so — *divina* (divine) — it's like a kind of illness, isn't it?[19] I think so. Or no? You, as a psychologist . . .

LENORA: Not necessarily. That's a very narcissistic impression of all of us.

MARCO ANTONIO: Ah, yes, there is narcissism.

LENORA: Narcissistic.

MARCO ANTONIO: Narcissism. Of course. *Of course*!

Lenora's demeanor changes as she speaks. She holds her body more upright, shoulders squared, and begins to bob her head with attitude. Making direct eye contact as she speaks, Lenora weaves her head to one side and gives a challenging look.

LENORA: So it will be a look, I will be more omnipotent than anyone and I am getting up right here [on this runway]. I mean, look at me.

MARCO ANTONIO: Of course.

She holds our attention for a moment, and then the makeup session dissolves into chitchat. In a short while, we return to the topic of runway:

OCHOA: I'm trying to understand what is going on. What does the runway accomplish for someone in terms of projecting one's self?

LENORA: For me?

OCHOA: Aha.

LENORA: It's beauty . . . integral beauty. That's what runway walking means to me. An integral beauty. Because I already have the other kind. Beyond the physical. Internal beauty. My peace within myself, and my performance and the goals I have accomplished as a professional. For now. And this is a complement, a hobby, another facet of my life. That some people [in my life] are beginning to get to know. . . . And to see if it can be done, I mean, why not?

Lenora returns to the discourse of the beauty within, but she emphasizes the affective dimension of the performance—that is, in order to do well on stage, she has to feel right within herself, and that confidence radiates from within. To Lenora, this is what makes for a successful runway walk: the interior feeling produces the performative affect required for a successful runway performance. I make the rookie mistake of going on for too long about what I think. Marco Antonio interrupts me with a probing question for Lenora, again intended to scandalize us: "So, Lenora, what do you think about a delicious *cachapa*?" Cachapas are a kind of sweet corn pancake in Venezuela, and indeed very delicious. That is not what Marco Antonio means though. *Cachapa* also means (simultaneously) women's genitals and an unspecified lesbian sex act.[20] Everyone cracks up. I get very flustered and try to recoup: "Well, I mean how you hold your body, the way you walk with a certain projection and presence. I want people to talk to me about that. But for a lot of people, well, runway walk is runway walk; they don't think about it much . . ." Here Marco Antonio interjects again, this time with his expertise, reflecting another common trope about beauty contests in Venezuela, the distinction between a beauty queen's runway and a model's:

MARCO ANTONIO: Yes but the difference between a *miss* runway walk and that of a model—they have nothing to do with each other. Models are like a clothes hook, they are a clothes hanger and they exhibit a rag. They don't exhibit themselves. But the *misses* are exhibiting themselves. They are selling *themselves.* That's where the illness of the whole thing comes about. Understand? Because a model walks by and she is a hanger, a hook, understand, that goes by and exhibits a rag and that's it. But they don't. What they exhibit is themselves, or rather, "here I am," understand?

LENORA [*Trying to get a word in edgewise*]: Well, my intention, what I can . . .

MARCO ANTONIO: No, not yours, generalize.

OCHOA: No, I want to know what she intends.

MARCO ANTONIO: Oh, okay.

LENORA: Is to impose myself. And that they look at me. Here *I* am.

GASTON: Of course.

OCHOA: And with that look you can control [the scene]?

LENORA: With my, yes, I think I reflect [*unintelligible*] and I control.

She holds everyone's attention for the moment of her intervention but is constantly undermined by both Marco Antonio and Gaston:

LENORA: How do I do it? Looking each one of them in the eyes.

MARCO ANTONIO: You had to interview this one because she's crazy.

GASTON: *Divina*, yes you are crazy.

Lenora smiles, lies back on the counter, and starts doing leg lifts. Marco Antonio says, "No, it's a divine insanity [*es una locura divina*], understand? I mean, completely. You have to, you have to have all kinds. Not everyone can be wound properly."[21]

Lenora starts talking about another contestant, whom she indicates is totally crazy. Marco Antonio agrees. I ask again about what it means to impose oneself as a woman:

LENORA: Well that's precisely it. I have developed my masculine side.

OCHOA: Ah, you see it as developing your . . . tell me more about that.

MARCO ANTONIO: This one is divine because . . . no but I love it. Welcome.

LENORA: My masculine side because it's not the one of pleasing people, of saying, "ay, I give you everything." No. It's "look at me, here *I* am . . ."

MARCO ANTONIO: Welcome to the combo.[22]

Marco Antonio begins a side conversation with himself, insinuating that Lenora has just proved herself to be a lesbian; he is welcoming her to the queer club.

LENORA: ... and ... [she screws up her face to emphasize her point]: *I'm* in charge. [*Smiles*]
MARCO ANTONIO: Spectacularly beautiful.

Marco Antonio remarks on Lenora's beauty and craziness alongside his insinuations of her lesbianism. This all serves to undermine the point that Lenora is making about how she holds attention, but she pays him no mind. Having made her point, she goes back to her leg lifts. Marco Antonio continues his conversation with himself under his breath, greatly amused. I continue to speculate about subjectivity, much to everyone's disinterest. Lenora reenters the conversation, addressing Gaston and me and ignoring Marco Antonio: "It couldn't be any other way, because . . . you break [yourself]. No, you need that masculine side. . . . Between the masculine and the feminine. Of course, look the feminine because it's like deference; you have to display, you have to . . . [say], "see me." But then . . ." Lenora makes an interesting distinction here between *looking* and *seeing*. Previously, she had used the word *mírame* (look at me), particularly when she described using her masculine side. Now she uses the word *véame* (see me) to describe the feminine side of the runway, reminiscent of John Berger's assertion that "men act and women appear" (1972, 47). However, in Lenora's gendered distinction between offering one's self up to be seen and commanding that one be looked at, the woman — in this case, her — appears to have some purchase in the act of representation, at least to decide how she will project herself within the conventions of the runway. So you have to employ that feminine side, according to Lenora, but also the masculine. To demonstrate this, she begins to mime the runway walk in place, moving her shoulders in cadence, then she suddenly stops on a dime, elbows bent, hands on her hips in the classic beauty queen pose. She nods her head definitively and says, "Here *I* am." She throws out a show smile that lasts for a fraction of a second and proclaims, "The fiercest one" (*la más arrecha*).[23] Lenora sweeps her hand as if to indicate the audience or judges, then relaxes her pose and brings her hand to her lap.

There are many things going on simultaneously in this scene. I have kept the interactions as intact as possible because the context is important to the ways Lenora develops her theory about what it takes to walk runway successfully. This example serves to more fully illustrate that relationship between the stylist and the contestant that is essential in producing the stage persona, what is often called a *mujerona*, as described in chapter 3.

It also clearly shows three important ways that stylists intervene in the relationship with *misses*: through expertise, sexualization, and humor. I focus more on Lenora. Lenora's ability to articulate how it feels to command a runway and her gendered analysis of spectacularity are central to the ways I have developed the concept of spectacular femininities.

What we have in this scene is the negotiation of two ideas about how it feels to make a spectacle of one's self. Both Marco Antonio and Lenora refer to the kind of internal state one must have in order to successfully walk a runway. For Lenora, this is an inner peace, confidence in one's accomplishments, omnipotence, and a "masculine side" that commands attention. Marco Antonio's reading of successful runway is quite different. He, albeit with tongue firmly in cheek, insists on the insanity and delusion required. First he implicates the sexuality of beauty queens as being tied up in their spectacularity by asserting that they orgasm on the runway. Then he appropriates Lenora's term, *narcissism*, ignoring her critique of his first interpretation. He suggests that since *misses* are selling themselves rather than the clothes they are wearing, there is a kind of mental illness in selling one's self, and that this makes that person insane. When Lenora describes her use of her masculine side, Marco Antonio takes this to be a sign of her lesbianism, and he tries to interpellate her into his, and our, queerness.

The two interpretations, Marco Antonio's and Lenora's, could not be more different. Lenora's is based on a sense of her own agency and ability to work the gendered expectations of her audience and judges. With Lenora's sense of interiority, it almost does not matter how the judges or audience members react—her inner peace and confidence are paramount. Marco Antonio describes a neurotic, hypersexual, narcissistic, and, ultimately, queer interiority. The difference might be summed up in the different ways they use the phrase *here I am* (*aquí estoy yo*). Lenora consistently emphasizes the *I* in the phrase, while Marco Antonio places the phrase in the context of exhibiting, deemphasizing, the *I*. This and Marco Antonio's insistence on his expertise and the ways contestants are required to submit to it are key points of contention in the conversation. Later on in the session, we talk some more about the limits of submission. I ask Lenora about how she will use the experience of being a Miss Venezuela contestant. She replies:

> You know what is interesting to me? I'm interested in this world,
> of course. But more than that, what we go through here. And how

I, I mean, having the experience, for me it's easier to relate to this group, and to get through that way. With whatever message. Help, motivation, whatever. Because I've been through it. And what we go through here is not at all easy. It's not out-of-this-world either, but it has its moments. There are key moments. I think in those mo—. . . there are moments in which each one of these candidates needs . . . someone to help her.

Marco Antonio agrees: "No, no, and it requires a huge sacrifice, understand? I mean, you have to leave behind a part of yourself to please others." Lenora tries to say something to the contrary, but Marco Antonio cuts her off.

MARCO ANTONIO: Because you have to have the face that I feel like you should have.

LENORA: Mmmhmm.

MARCO ANTONIO: So, if you're too stubborn [and say,] "no, no, no, I'm going with my face, who does he think he is . . ." Understand? So, it's a big conflict. You have to put on what I think looks good on you.

Unable to interject during Marco Antonio's tirade, Lenora instead signals with her hand, first to herself, then waves her finger "no" and mouths, "not me." Marco Antonio continues, ". . . because you will look beautiful that way." Lenora smiles in disagreement. Marco Antonio carries on, "To put it one way."

Gaston takes up the theme of expertise.

GASTON: Well I think that all the, or rather the vision . . . of the specialist, because in the moment that you submit yourself to all of these . . . influences . . .

MARCO ANTONIO: All of these bad influences.

GASTON: Well, good ones, bad ones, what is certain is that there are influences, in other words some stranger who doesn't know you, and who in one look says to you, "Eh, you need to have green eyes, and your nose has to go . . . on the back of your head," or rather, supposedly there are specialists.

LENORA: In some cases, in some cases, but it's not that way for all.

GASTON: Of course. It depends. For example if I go to you as a patient and you prescribe me a regimen, or establish a discipline for me, I should comply with that regimen or discipline.

LENORA: Of course.

GASTON: Independent of whether or not I think it's . . . convenient or not, because you have some training, some preparation in life that is . . . guiding me toward something. So under that same principle you could, in reality, accept all the suggestions that Marco Antonio makes, for example. Understand?

LENORA: I understand. But what I don't understand is the why. I'm going about my life, in me, my way. If they tell me, "your hair should be like this, I don't know," perfect. They're the professionals.

GASTON: Well, see . . .

LENORA: But beyond that, that they tell me "you need green eyes," well, no, man, they're black, understand?

GASTON: Of course.

LENORA: Or, "your hair will be red," well no.

Lenora brushes her long raven hair with her hand. I jump in with my own analogy, as we have discussed Lenora's work with HIV patients:

OCHOA: Well and also that absolute power of the professional isn't always the case. Because what happens is, for example, a doctor gives you a treatment, that doctor has to — and they've worked on this a lot in the world of HIV, no? — the doctor has to pay attention to the effect of the treatment on your body, on your schedule, your life, your quality of life, and that negotiation between the professional and the patient . . .

LENORA: That is accomplishing treatment adherence.[24] . . .

GASTON: Of course it's totally different values because when you talk about your health, it's your *health*, which is not your beauty. So the values are totally different. For that reason, you can reject someone who says, "make your eyes blue, or purple, or, red like a rabbit, or pink." Understand? So you will say, "what a *look* you've given me!"[25]

LENORA: Well, because of that it's, well, for example, my values are my health. Not beauty. You know? Or rather, not, "dang, I can't eat," because . . . I know I needed to drop weight but I went to see a specialist. Because I didn't want to . . . because it meant submitting myself to something absurd. I mean, in *my* case. With a regimen, with a specialist, who will tell me how it should go.

Lenora was unique among most of the women I talked to in asserting her health as a primary value in the competition. By asserting this value, Lenora is able to place the stylists' expertise in a different category from the medical expertise that Gaston was using for comparison. Lenora contests Marco Antonio and Gaston's claims about the nature of being a beauty queen. Lenora shows us how, by enacting the dimension of spectacle, a *miss* can negotiate power and project her idea of herself onto a public. Lenora *shows* us what it takes to get up on the runway and keep your sense of yourself. She, like the *transformistas* on that early evening on Avenida Libertador, tells us what it means to make a spectacle of one's self.

Conclusion

I have linked the forms of femininity accomplished by *transformistas* and *misses* to spectacularity. I have discussed three approaches to the idea of spectacle, two of which specifically address the question of relationships between gender and spectacle. Examples derived from in situ video recording during my fieldwork at two different sites describe the elements of spectacular femininities, or femininities that employ the conventions of spectacularity in their production. Following a characterization of the performed speech act as described by Butler, I have described spectacular femininities as involving three elements: staged, presented before an audience, and subject to interpretation. I have identified these elements as (respectively), the production of spectacle, the mode of address, and self-consciousness about reception.

I described how a group of *transformistas* on Avenida Libertador employed mode-of-address conventions and self-consciousness about reception to produce highly legible forms of femininity and to call attention to the contradictions surrounding their presence on the avenida. Backstage at a Miss Venezuela *casting*, I described how the process of the production of spectacle and the mode of address provide opportunities for a participant to articulate her understandings of what is required to accomplish a successful runway presence. Both examples reveal the rich contexts in which *misses* and *transformistas* produce their femininities with respect to the conventions of spectacle.

The chapters in this part, "On the Body," have shown the ways discourses materialize in the body at the level of carnality and self-presentation. Both of these chapters consider how *misses* and *transformistas* mediate national, transnational, racial, and gender ideologies through their bodies. These mediations are not unique to *misses* or *transformistas*, of course, but they do take specific forms based on conventions of representation and social legibility specific to the contexts in which they emerge. I have tried to show the Venezuelan context in a way that honors its complexity. At the end of the video session on Avenida Libertador, I play the role of photographer through the video camera, of a photo that is posed for but never taken. The streetwise Andrea, never one to linger on unnecessary interactions on the Avenida, reminds me how perfunctory this all is for her: "Aha, and the photo? Did you take it? Are you done yet?"

Epilogue

Democracy and Melodrama

FRIVOLITY, *FRACASO*, AND
POLITICAL VIOLENCE IN VENEZUELA

Venezuelans are living a collective hypnosis bordering on hysteria. It's really very unhealthy. But we have to understand that we are in the eye of the hurricane and that in the
future normality will return to our lives. Politics, the way it's seen now, as an exclusive
topic of interest, seems to me as pathological as the disinterest that we have had for it in
the past. We have moved from frivolity to hysteria: this is the path we Venezuelans have
taken in the last years. — RAFAEL ARRÁIZ LUCCA, in Rubén Wisotzki, "Rafael Arráiz
Lucca ve un país 'de pobreza política escandaloza' "; my translation

"We have moved from frivolity to hysteria," the Venezuelan poet and political commentator Rafael Arráiz Lucca said in a January 13, 2003, interview for *El Nacional*, the Venezuelan newspaper of record as the days of
the *paro petrolero* (petroleum strike) that started in December 2002 wane.[1]
The last thing people were worried about in Venezuela when I got there
was my research topic: beauty pageants and *transformistas*. The year that I
was in Caracas for fieldwork was one filled with regular interruptions, political tension, economic uncertainty, street protest, and terrible anxiety —
what Arráiz Lucca calls hysteria — a mounting fear that violence would
erupt, that looting would break out. What is most striking about Arráiz
Lucca's assessment of the situation is how thoroughly *feminized* Venezuelan political culture is for him. Frivolity and hysteria: two decidedly
feminized forms of affect that narrate the impossibility of Venezuelan participation in rational political culture. A kind of civilization and *barbarie*
argument, in a gendered guise.

As I conclude this wide-ranging meditation on femininity in Venezuela, I want to take up the frivolity that Arráiz Lucca accuses Venezuelans of having. The many years of "pathological disinterest" that lead to the crisis moment from which he speaks appear to be the fault of a Venezuelan citizenry that is constantly failing to meet the requirements for modern democracy, first because of its disinterest in the political and then because of its irrational emotional response to crisis. But this idea of *fracaso* (failure) is quite familiar in Venezuela—it is a narration of the failure to be modern. This *fracaso* of modernity is something that has come up in various forms in this book—through the conflation of Caracas and death and the imagined history of the word *coroto* in chapter 2, the magical state and its impulse to bring order to the disorderly city in chapter 3, the specter of excess in plastic surgery of chapter 5; the anxiety and sense of inevitability that Venezuelans will fail to be modern recurs constantly. Political science reinscribes this failure of modernity, characterizing Venezuela as a land of "fragile democracy" (Canache 2002), a site of "unraveling democracy" (McCoy and Myers 2004), a case that reaches "the limits of democracy" (Arroyo Talavera 1983), or, more optimistically, a country constantly engaged in "the search for order, the dream of progress" (Lombardi 1982). At the same time, Venezuelans can revel in both their accomplishment of modernity and their decided rejection of its aesthetics. This is one of the things that has always enchanted me about Venezuela: that it can simultaneously love, reject, covet, subvert, and manipulate the aesthetics of modernity in so many ways.

But the political crisis of 2002 and the ensuing years of conflict seem to have made everyone want to get a bit more "serious." The Bolivarian Revolution, the process of social transformation proposed by Hugo Chávez, has also focused a very different kind of attention on Venezuela and changed its identity and recognition on the global stage. Venezuela is now invoked as either an example for the Left of revolution that is working or a cautionary tale for the Right about the spread of communism. Neither appropriation is accurate, nor are these interesting ways to approach and understand what Venezuela is. What is interesting, to me, about Venezuela is the way the people of this country have found to struggle with the legacy of the modern colonial world system, the cultural forms that have emerged in response to this long process and the many attempts to contain the bodies and minds of people that emerge through these encounters. Frivolity is one of the cultural forms that we could argue has emerged in this way—

certainly it is not the only one, but it has been an important form for the *transformistas, maricos,* and *misses* I worked with.

If we think of frivolity as a form of disidentification with seriousness — a particularly masculine form of seriousness that inhabits politicized discourse — then frivolity becomes a space of possibility and engagement for people who are excluded from the Venezuelan political imaginary. It is also a manifestation of centuries of disenfranchisement through patriarchy, homophobia, and transphobia. I think of my own initial engagement with Venezuela as ensconced in this kind of disenfranchisement; my travel to the country was initially a queer and diasporic tracing of my own conditions of possibility. My first trip to Venezuela, where I encountered that memorable flight attendant, was a frustrated attempt to take the bus across the border with a cousin who didn't have the proper papers because she had been born in Venezuela of undocumented Colombian parents. This landed me square on the border between Colombia and Venezuela trying to figure out how to continue my journey as I got my cousin back home — a kind of subnational travel. I was barely aware of the presidential elections going on at the time, and I dimly remember the military man who was on his way to winning. I have clearer memories of the *transformistas* I met on the beach on Isla Margarita, a moment of mutual recognition that I hadn't experienced much around my family. I didn't go to Venezuela to learn about the Bolivarian Revolution; I went to understand how queer and trans people survive and invent their lives in this region.[2] In some ways, I went to Venezuela to learn more about the conditions of possibility for my own existence. This is what I mean when I say this is a queer diasporic ethnography.

Of course, I quickly learned about Venezuela's new president after I started graduate school and saw the excitement of gay and lesbian groups in Caracas as they discussed the 1999 constitutional reforms when I first visited in the summer of 2000. From that moment of optimism and enthusiasm, I saw over the ensuing years an increased polarization, anxiety, and fear in Venezuelan political culture, and this process reverberated in the communities I was most connected with. Support or opposition to Chávez divided the LGBT movement. During this time the same kinds of violence and discrimination as always visited the lives of *transformistas,* who were still excluded from practically all formal aspects of Venezuelan society. Though there were sympathetic actors in the Chávez administration, in the early days there was not a lot of openness to tracking human rights violations or addressing the conditions of *transformista* life in Venezuela. From 2000 to 2009, Chavista LGBT activists pushed the boundaries of the Movimiento Quinta República (MVR, Fifth Republic Movement) and the recent (2008) Partido Socialista Unido Venezolano (PSUV, United Socialist Party of Venezuela), Chavez's political parties, as well as the government to address LGBT issues, meeting with both frustrations and successes.[3]

In 2007, one of the *transformistas* who worked on Avenida Libertador sought help from Misión Negra Hipólita (see chapter 1), a Bolivarian mission that addresses the needs of urban street people throughout Venezuela. When she and her boyfriend were turned away, she went to the Ministerio del Poder Popular para la Participación y Protección Social (Ministry of Popular Power for Social Participation and Protection) to denounce their exclusion and succeeded in getting into a treatment center in Petare, on the far-east side of Caracas. There she found a receptive psychologist and drug-treatment counselor, and she brought about twelve of her *transformista* friends and their boyfriends to the center. The group had hopes of establishing a housing program, but the last I heard, the house that had been promised was not released and the group had disbanded, frustrated by their multiple attempts to navigate the government bureaucracy. This example best illustrates what the Bolivarian Revolution means in Venezuela: unprecedented institutional opening for the most marginalized Venezuelans, enticing possibilities to imagine and realize solutions, and frustrating centralized bureaucratic implementation. The Bolivarian Revolution has made things happen in Venezuela that I had never even dreamed could happen—such as the idea of a *transformista* thinking that she had the right to insist on support from her government and following the channels necessary to hold the government to providing that support. That was completely unthinkable before this administration. At the same time, the revolution replicates much of the affective forms of social control and access that previous administrations have employed. To think of the Chávez administration as much different from previous forms of managing power in Venezuela is to ignore the strong continuities that have marked Venezuelan governmentality for at least the last century. What Chávez did change is political *discourse* in Venezuela: he opened up the imaginary of citizenship and the sense of entitlement to protection and benefit from the state to people who have historically been disenfranchised. Though other populist efforts back to the nineteenth century have also purported to change politics in Venezuela, Chávez succeeded in addressing actors, like the *transformistas* of Misión Negra Hipólita, who had previously not seen the state as a possible advocate or protector.

During my time in Venezuela, I began to realize that I too, though for different reasons, had not included the state as a possible site of intervention in my political imaginary. For those queers and people of color who came of age in the United States of Ronald Reagan and AIDS, the state was simply not interested in our continued survival. Appeals to the state seemed pointless, and our relations to the state were dampened by the growing nonprofit sector that, particularly in the case of HIV, developed as the interface between communities and the state funds that were available to address the AIDS epidemic. So the state was not at all the object of the kinds of queer third-world survival I worked to create in the United States. When I went to Venezuela, I was startled to see LGBT groups talking about the constitution, as well as copies of the new constitution and existing laws governing commerce, children, and adolescents; telecommunications; and myriad other topics for sale on sidewalks and street corners, all laid out, vendor after vendor. The state had always been so tedious to me, not at all a site of possibility.

But one thing I have learned in Venezuela is that where we encounter sites of impossibility, we begin to imagine other kinds of possibility. Laura Pérez says it more directly: we "hallucinate" (1999, 39). We invent other ways to be active participants in our worlds. Renato Rosaldo calls this *cultural citizenship*: "The right to be different and to belong in a participatory democratic sense" (1994, 402). I want to suggest that Venezuelan frivolity is exactly this kind of hallucination—a productive form of belonging in a system of modern democracy that relies on an Enlightenment subject of rights as its primary actor. While frivolity might also be seen as a kind of distraction from politics, I have argued throughout this book that frivolous things such as glamour are politics in and of themselves. Frivolity, as a position, is an important structure of feeling in Venezuela, particularly for *transformistas* and *maricos*.

In proposing frivolity as a kind of possibility, I risk both trivializing the struggles of the *transformistas* I am trying to honor here and collapsing the frivolous into a way to seduce people into doing "real" politics. What I seek to transform, instead, is the imaginary of political possibility itself, informed by how *transformistas* have developed to negotiate the landscape of power in which they find themselves in Venezuela.

At the same time as it can be a political possibility, frivolity can indeed also reinscribe hegemonic forms of order. In fact, frivolity can simultaneously reinscribe *and* subvert power. This is what makes the frivolous interesting to me. One clear example of the way frivolity can reinscribe hegemonic power is in what I call *miss*-ing race (see chapter 1). *Miss*-ing race is the way the figure of the *miss* in Venezuela reinscribes Eurocentric aesthetics by "disappearing" the discourse of race into the hybrid terrain of *criollismo* (Creoleness), part of what Winthrop White calls the "myth of racial democracy" (1999, 12). But the *misses*, and the apparatus that produces them, *miss* race by sublimating any mention or appearance of marked racialized categories into the larger project of competing on a global level. By simply ignoring and redirecting, the *miss* disappears what is not convenient. This is a technique of frivolity—what Venezuelans call *haciéndose la loca* (acting like you don't know)—that effaces any kind of criticism and lets it slip away. *Miss*-ing, ultimately, is the effacement of that which is considered ugly, conflictive, or inconvenient for the fabulous (national or individual) fiction of the beautiful. It is a move that simply shifts the terms of discussion to the privileged category with a wave of the hair. Let me be clear: I am not proposing frivolity as a redemptive political tactic; I am showing how it becomes a site for the negotiation of power.

Perhaps Arráiz Lucca's characterization of Venezuela's "laughable" political culture is best exemplified by the inclusion of a *miss* in the presidential elections of 1998: "I laugh when people say Venezuela has a political culture. Imagine, a country that chooses Hugo Chávez over the possibility of electing [the former Miss Universe] Irene Sáez. Who can deny that such a country suffers from a scandalous political poverty?" (Wisotzki 2003, A12).

At one point in the 1998 presidential campaign, Sáez had more than 60 percent of the popular vote (McCoy 2004, 276). Sáez, one of the most recognized figures of Venezuela's golden age of beauty, won the Miss Universe title in 1981. After finishing her studies, she began her political career in the early 1990s and successfully campaigned to serve as mayor of the wealthy Chacao district of Caracas. She prioritized the "beautification" of Chacao, including moving "vagrants" out of Chacao's public spaces, making aesthetic improvements to sidewalks and plazas, and outfitting the Chacao police with pith helmets and khaki shorts. Indeed, Sáez "*miss*-ed" Chacao by beautifying it and moving street people over to the neighboring Libertador district. Her mayoral administration received much praise, and her campaign for the presidency was initially well received. She finished the election a distant third, however, after accepting support from the Comité de Organización Política Electoral Independiente (COPEI, Committee of Independent Electoral Political Organization), the Christian democratic party of previous administrations. Still, Sáez was a viable candidate for the presidency of Venezuela in the 1998 elections, and this is what Arráiz Lucca sees as laughable and frivolous. The choice between Sáez and Chávez seems ridiculous to Arráiz Lucca because neither "acts" presidential. This is a charge that was often leveled against Chávez by the Opposition. Arráiz Lucca's critique is an attempt to discipline a people who do not react like good, modern citizens to events unfolding in the public sphere. It is of particular interest to me that the way he tries to discipline political culture is by shaming Venezuelans. This is done, specifically, by feminizing them as political subjects. And so the choice between Sáez and Chávez is already figured as a laughable failure, and the people who would choose between them as ridiculous subjects, evidence of a "scandalous political poverty."

Democracy and Melodrama

By the time of Arráiz Lucca's interview, I was wondering what indeed I was doing in Venezuela. Even the Organización Miss Venezuela debated whether or not to hold a pageant in 2003. I went to Venezuela to study frivolous things: beauty and femininity. Venezuela had made a name for itself on the global stage through its beauty pageant industry, and I had actively avoided the realm of democratic politics precisely because this discourse alienated and excluded the queer and trans people I care about by requiring them to be so-called serious political subjects. Because of this, some colleagues saw the questions in my study as not political or even frivolous. However, the study was intended to get at something very serious: how people imagine the possibilities for their survival, particularly when they are in socially marginalized positions.

As president, Chávez very skillfully created symbolic and political recognition for people previously marginalized in Venezuelan society and its politics — thus expertly attending to the affective needs of a large constituency. At the same time, the privately owned media in Venezuela, in particular the national press and television broadcasters, exploited a "tragic structure of feeling" (Ang 1985, 46), using their ability to circulate messages as a tool to polarize public discourse and mobilize masses; this is not because Venezuelans were being brainwashed by their president or their private media, but rather because the stories told by the president and the media resonate with Venezuelans' own struggles. Instead of perpetuating this polarized system, those who want to effect social transformation in Venezuela must find sites and opportunities within the current conjuncture and outside its binary logic, and they must acknowledge the affective dimension of politics. In this observation, I follow the approach of Latin American and British cultural studies in paying attention to the frivolous space of melodrama.

In a book titled *Cine, democracia y melodrama* (2001), Alfonso Molina writes about the relationship over the last forty years between the trajectory of Venezuelan politics and the cinematic melodrama of the campy revolutionary Venezuelan filmmaker Román Chalbaud. In Molina's book I was looking for the sort of conflation of narrative strategy and political history that I had sensed in my encounters with Venezuelan public culture, but the melodrama I found was another one. Molina *recited* the melodrama of Venezuelan politics in the twentieth century: dictatorship, resistance, democracy, excess, readjustment, and violence. Fernando Coronil reframes the usual story of Venezuelan political history by "placing regional developments within global transformations," accounting for these representations of the failure of modernity in Venezuela (Coronil 1997, 15). Luis Duno-Goldberg's (2004) work on media constructions of the masses from 2000 to 2003 also remarks on the dichotomy of civilization and barbarie in Venezuelan political culture—this clean-cut conflict is one of the basic ingredients in melodrama. The representations of Chavistas and Opositores (members of the Opposition) in broadcast and print news during this time period show very clearly a divide between a whiter, more "civilized" Opposition and a darker, more "barbaric" Chavismo. While these distinctions are not necessarily so clear in actual political practice, the ways Venezuelan political culture is aestheticized through this dichotomy belie the deep social anxiety of *fracaso*, or failure to accomplish modernity, that haunts Venezuela. So we have a well-defined conflict and an underlying tension—all we need now are some good characters and scandal to have our melodrama. On the day I returned to Caracas under the Opposition general strike of 2003, I realized how profoundly the struggle between civilization and barbarie, and a deep anxiety about *fracaso*, affected not just political culture but also the ways people related to each other and the stories they used to narrate these relations. It all started with a small white poodle named Popcorn.

January 4, 2003

I return to Caracas after visiting family in the United States over the holidays. The *paro petrolero* has dragged on for thirty-three days at this point. The dollar is nearly twice what it was the same time the previous year, and headed skyward. Flights to and from Caracas have been rescheduled and canceled. American Airlines will not keep its planes at Simon Bolívar International Airport overnight, I'm told. A friend meets me at the airport and we take a bus back to my apartment in the Sabana Grande district of Caracas. On the entire trip back, I have sensed a tension in the air, much uncertainty, many people wondering why I decided to come back to Caracas. At gate E11 in the Miami International Airport, I had seen a family reading a newspaper. The headline: "Estamos listos para la guerra" (We are ready for war). After I unpack I decide to spend the night with some friends, fearing more the loneliness of being back in Caracas than any kind of risk to my safety.

At the foot of my apartment building, I hail a cab — not everyone is on strike, apparently. We pass by a huge, angry crowd near the funeral parlors by my building. Down the street is the hot Chavista encampment in front of Petróleos de Venezuela in La Campiña. My friends' neighborhood is eerily quiet. Security is tight — extra guards stand at the entry gate and scrutinize me and the cab driver. When I arrive at my friends' apartment, I can see that Eliot and Raisa[4] have worked very hard to counter the tense mood outside. The lights are dim; lounge music is on the stereo. Eliot greets me at the door and shoves a tumbler full of eighteen-year-old rum into my hands. For a moment in my return to a troubled Caracas, I feel comfortable and safe in this queer group of upper-middle-class NGO workers.

At eight in the evening, the clanking sounds of the evening's *cacerolazo* (pot banging) fill the subdivision. After a few minutes, Raisa decides to turn on the news to see what is going on. They have been telling me about the Opposition protests in Los Ilustres the day before, which were met with rocks and gunfire from an unruly crowd. The Globovisión newscast shows blurry images panning across a field of lanky, dark-skinned men who have covered their faces with T-shirts (*encapuchados*) mythical figures of *caraqueño* protest.[5] In slow motion, they throw rocks and aim guns. Despite these representations, reports later come out that tear gas canisters had been fired into the crowds of Chavista protesters, who were trying to block the progress of an Opposition march to Los Próceres, and confirm that both sides were throwing rocks.[6] Two young men, both government supporters, were killed in the four-hour standoff. The crowds in front of the funeral parlors near my apartment were mourning their deaths.

Also in slow motion is footage of breaking news. Another young, lanky man in a red T-shirt (the trademark of Chavista protesters) pulls out a gun, fires (presumably in the direction of the Policía Metropolitana), puts the gun back into his waist pack, and disappears into a crowd. This is in front of the funeral parlor, moments after I passed it on the way to Eliot and Raisa's. The news drones on with its circular narration, telling and retelling the events of the hour before, representing a violent Chavista mob packing heat. Dramatic music and the reporter's tone swell. Raisa turns the volume up. Eliot yells "¡Ya! ¡Apágalo!" (Enough! Turn it off!) and smacks the power button. "I can't keep hearing the same thing over and over," he says. Our friend Gaston breaks a mischievous smile and says, sarcastically, "Cálmense" (Calm down). We sit down to dinner.

As we are about to eat dessert, a commotion breaks out on the usually quiet street below. A girl shrieks, in the most grievous scream I have ever heard, "¡Maaaaamiiii!" At this point Raisa is sure that Chavistas have invaded the apartment complex and are killing children. Dogs bark and yelp crazily. The girl is still screaming. Neighbors have clamored up to the windows and are yelling down: "¡Asesino!" (Killer!) and "¡El coño de tu madre, no joda!" The shrieking and crying continues. I go to the window and see a woman leading away a German shepherd. A young girl sits on the steps of the apartment building, inconsolable. Two women run to her. At first I think she has been bitten, but then I look through another window and see a small white poodle lying on the sidewalk. Cotufas is its name: Popcorn. People hurl insults at the owner of the German shepherd, who is trying to get back into her house: "¡Perro asesino! ¡Puta! ¡Ramera! ¡Bruta!" (Killer dog! Whore! Worse kind of whore! Brute!) She manages to get in. An angry crowd gathers at the foot of the building. I worry that the neighbors will turn on the dog's owner, who has come out again to defend the German shepherd. Eliot and I decide to go out and investigate. The German shepherd's owner is indignant; insults and harsh words are exchanged. We decide to go back upstairs after agreeing with a couple of old men on the outskirts of the crowd that the German shepherd should be put down. People in the crowd say the poodle was a hero. The German shepherd had always been aggressive, and this was bound to happen. For a moment everyone forgets about the shootings in La Florida.

The Melodramatic Imagination

This incident involved several elements that I encountered throughout the rest of my time in Venezuela: private media coverage of street protests and violence, the violent potential of certain people and places, the conversion of angry people in the street into crowds or mobs, the public that people created by yelling or banging pots out of their windows, and the posterior interpretation of violence as fitting within a narrative structure of predictability: this was bound to happen, it's in a dog's nature to kill; the poodle sacrificed itself.

It is this last element that invoked the relationship to melodrama: I saw that even in this attack, in which the dogs had no (stated) political position; the public of the attack, which included me and my friends, had a story that we could overlay on events as they unfolded. Participants neatly fit into preexisting roles. A mechanism of recognition—recognition of genre—allowed us to make associations between the players and an imaginary script that we all knew too well. Chavistas were invading. Brutality (the German shepherd) attacked and destroyed delicate beauty (the poodle), who sacrificed itself to spare the most precious participant, innocence (the girl). Always a gendered, raced, and classed story.

Ien Ang, in her study of melodrama *Watching* Dallas: *Soap Opera and the Melodramatic Imagination*, asserts that a melodramatic metaphor (like heroism, or in her example, alcoholism) "derives itself from a *lack* of originality and uniqueness: precisely because it constantly recurs in all sorts of popular narratives, it takes on for viewers a direct comprehensibility and recognizability" (1985, 65; emphasis in original). Some of the elements of the melodramatic genre, as understood by Ang, are: its episodic character, its endlessness, the coexistence of narratives in a wide universe of characters, and the fragmentation of themes in order to ignore "too concrete social or cultural references" and privilege the emotional universe of "personal life" (1985, 59). In my experience of Venezuelan public culture throughout this time, I saw each one of these elements surface except one: the coexistence of narratives and characters.

To invoke melodrama is not to minimize the emotional force of living in a time where it feels as if the world has been turned upside down (a phrase the Venezuelan folklorist Yolanda Salas used in our conversations about the situation). The Bolivarian Revolution represents a profound change in the administration of government in Venezuela, and in the ways power and resources are distributed. As tensions mounted in Caracas and my friends saw either their Bolivarian hopes or Opposition dreams frustrated, I began to perceive Venezuelan politics as embedded within an affective structure. I am trying to get at a more fundamental issues: the structures that evoke our emotional responses to social transformation; the articles of faith that, when profoundly shaken, leave us thinking in terms of a zero-sum game; and the forms to which we have been acculturated over a long historical process to consider legible, safe, comfortable, even pleasurable. Whether these are faith in political or religious doctrine or faith in the modern world system, they are part of the tragic structure of feeling of melodrama: "The notion that in life emotions are always being stirred up, i.e. that life is characterized by an endless fluctuation between happiness and unhappiness, that life is a question of falling down and getting back up again. This structure of feeling can be called the *tragic* structure of feeling: tragic because of the idea that happiness can never last forever but, quite the contrary, is precarious. In the tragic structure of feeling emotional ups and downs occupy a central place" (Ang 1985, 46; emphasis in original).

Through structures of feeling we become familiar with certain forms and stories, which come to define the legibility of other stories we encounter. And we insert our own terms of familiarity, the classed and gendered narratives we have used to understand what is safe and what is threatening for us. The tragic structure of feeling in Venezuela rests in the anxiety about accomplishing modernity that has haunted this land since its inception as a vice royalty. This struggle about modernity manifests itself not just in democracy and revolution but also in the discourses of beauty, development, petroleum, and medicine.

Articles of Faith in Modernity

It is perhaps too easy to ask people to have faith in revolution. Wait until your university can't cut you a paycheck for six months and tell me how much faith you have in redistribution. Wait until the power goes out for three days or your food-transportation system is paralyzed. When the socially enfranchised participants of Venezuela's Opposition sense a threat to their worldview, they react with the tools available to them. These articles of faith in modernity—that the truth is knowable, that the truth is relevant to self-determination, that life is impossible or at least undesirable without order, that progress is the goal of existence—are foundational myths that need to be addressed, and not in a cynical or operationalist mode, before social transformation can occur.

Throughout my time in Venezuela, I moved further away from my affinity for *revolution*, which I came to see as a reversal of a teleological process stuck within the same linear vision of time, and more toward *transformation*—not only because that is what the *transformistas* were doing with their gender but because I returned to Antonio Gramsci's distinction between a war of position and a war of movement (1999, 222). Transformation of hegemony requires a "long process of enculturation" (Martín-Barbero 1993, 88) because hegemony works by normalizing the dominant. Those who would counter hegemony must do so poetically, attending to *el feeling* of social transformation. In "Publics and Counterpublics," Michael Warner explains that a dominant public can take its lifeworld for granted, "misrecognizing the indefinite scope of [its] expansive address as universality or normalcy," while a counterpublic must poetically establish its lifeworld as it strives to transform rather than replicate (2002, 88).

As the years have passed and my companions in Venezuela have weathered hopes and disappointments, gradual change and *fracasos*, institutional apertures and bureaucracy, material decay, new possibilities, moral outrage, and resignation, I have worked in the United States as its own political perversions and illusions have played themselves out. My focus is always on the frivolous: those people most excluded from political possibility because of how ridiculous the idea is that they have any politics. It is in the lives of *transformistas*, of translatina immigrants to the United States, making their survival out of impossibilities, that I have found the core of political possibility. It's not pretty though, and there are a lot of moments when it feels as if my heart is falling out of my chest: *despechos*.

As *Queen for a Day* went to press, Venezuelans experienced the *despecho* of losing the charismatic leader of the Bolivarian Revolution, Hugo Chávez, in March 2013 after a long struggle with cancer. Many mourned, some rejoiced with rancor, and the Bolivarian Revolution marches on, for better or for worse. I spoke to friends in the wake of the funeral who talked about the deep transformations they had seen in the time since Chávez took power. Of this I am quite sure: Chávez transformed Venezuelan political culture and the political imaginary of the most marginalized Venezuelan subjects. He hailed people into citizenship who had previously not considered themselves the agents of claims on the state. This resulted in a profound aperture in the government for LGBT projects, assuming, of course, their legibility as Bolivarian projects. This is consistent with other kinds of transformations in the shape of the state in Venezuela. At the same time, the government continues to reinforce a juridical and political climate that rejects mechanisms of identity and family recognition, and political culture still openly relies on homophobic slurs as a form of discrediting candidates on all sides. A lot more imagination and world making needs to take place to create a progressive environment for what is called *sexual diversity* in Venezuela.

In this book I have shown the ways *transformistas* invent the very possibility of their own survival, and the ways this survival reflects the realities of Venezuela as a product of modernity in the Americas. It is my hope that this book helps us pay attention to frivolity, glamour, imagination, impossibility, and melodrama as we struggle against the forces that marginalize us in the world, as we struggle to make our lives. In Venezuelan political culture, melodrama mediates not only the power relations between elites and masses but also *fear*: of dreams not fulfilled, of trust repaid with corruption and theft, of disorder and economic ruin, of disenfranchisement and starvation. It is in this sense that melodrama is a serious matter. It is one of the tools that Venezuelans use to understand the events they are encountering. It is also a structure of feeling into which they will retreat when they feel threatened, thus providing a realm of political possibility or manipulation. Certainly it is more comforting to some people to know how the story is going to turn out than to make it up as you go along.

Notes

Introducing . . . The Queen

1 The term *cisgender* is a newer term that describes "nontransgender" people. The term comes from the Latin prefix *cis*, which is the opposite of *trans* and means "on the same side." The cis-trans opposition is used in chemistry, molecular biology, and genetics and was appropriated from this usage to name people whose gender identities are aligned with the sexes they are assigned at birth in order to avoid imposing a sense of normativity on nontransgender people. Susan Stryker (2008, 22) provides a more detailed explanation of this and other relevant terms in *Transgender History*.

2 Juana María Rodríguez defines queer *latinidad* in her book of the same title (2003). By *latinidad*, I invoke the cultural forms that have emerged in the Iberian (Spanish and Portuguese) colonization of the Americas (sometimes including the Philippines) and the subsequent national and imperial formations that have shaped, displaced, and otherwise affected the diverse people and cultures entangled in this encounter. *Latinidad* names a set of cultural and linguistic similarities that index Latinas and Latinos in the United States as much as Latin Americans, and is used as a term of hemispheric analysis that acknowledges the colonial and imperial history and present of the Americas. Note that some non-English words and uses of English words in non-English speech are italicized throughout this text.

3 *Travestista* is actually the Colombian word used to describe transvestites or cross-dressers. Other places use words like *travestí*.

4 In this book I will use the acronym LGBT, short for "lesbian, gay, bisexual, and transgender" to describe the terms of political currency for sexually diverse communities in international organizing and civil society. As I argued in an article titled "Perverse Citizenship" in 2008, these civil society categories are often not inclusive of many forms of gender and sexuality in Venezuela, and in Latin America more broadly. Amnesty uses these categories "because they are the English terms most commonly used in the international human rights discourse" (Amnesty International USA 2001, vii). I use LGBT when I refer specifically to advocacy efforts within the realm of civil society and international social movements. I avoid using these terms to identify communities or individuals unless they adopt these terms themselves. Instead, I use the categories of gen-

der and sexuality that the communities and individuals to which I am referring employ.

5 It bears mentioning that *transformista* is not the only word used to describe the women I have described in this definition, although it is a generally understood word. Still, it can be a very ambiguous word that does not have a fixed meaning. Several of the *transformistas* I talked to, despite their usage of the word, also said they used *chica de apariencia* (a girl who looks like a girl). I encountered this usage most in the classified ads for sex work in local dailies. There, *transformista* was almost never used, but there are many ads for *chicas de apariencia* in the back pages of *El Universal*.

6 The term *achievement of sex-status* is proposed by Harold Garfinkel in his book *Studies in Ethnomethodology* (1967), in which he considers the extended case study of "Agnes," a white transsexual woman from the U.S. Midwest whom he counsels after she approaches Robert Stoller's UCLA Gender Reassignment Clinic for a sex change. Garfinkel uses the term to describe how Agnes "passes" as a woman. I use the term to consider the fundamental performative acts necessary for social legibility, as Garfinkel often did in ethnomethodology. Accomplishment is a key element of Garfinkel's framework, which Don H. Zimmerman and Candace West used to propose sociological inquiry into the "accomplishment of gender" (1987, 131). See note 5 in chapter 5. In this sense, accomplishment applies both to women who are cisgender and women who are transgender. I employ this framework specifically to examine the *accomplishment of femininity*.

7 In saying this, I want to be careful not to reify the notions of center and margin; instead I want to recognize that power operates in a variegated way in Venezuela, and that people position themselves strategically with respect to the power invested in the state, capital, and mass media. This is not to say that *misses* in Venezuela are marginalized, but rather that all Venezuelans must negotiate the ways that power is trafficked and margin is produced. *Misses* and *transformistas* employ similar tools in these negotiations.

8 In the category of "woman" I am placing all cisgender women (sexed female at birth and live as girls or women) as well as all people, regardless of birth sex, who live as girls or women.

9 The word *miss* is taken from the English word used in the name of the pageant but is used in Venezuelan Spanish to refer to beauty queens. The *i* in *miss* is pronounced in the Spanish as a long *e* (the *e* of *cheese*).

10 Venevisión's branding campaign changed in 2010 to "Venevisión Es Como Tú" (Venevisión is like you). The campaign purported to convey "closeness and identification with its viewers," a change from the more direct affiliation with the beauty queens of earlier in the decade. See Venevisión, "Venevisión Es Como Tú," press release, January 7, 2010, accessed March 15, 2010, available at: https://web.archive.org/web/20100611211916/http://www.venevision.net/enterate/enterate.asp?id_noticia=/enterate/actualidad/252/informacion.htm; my translation.

11 Miss Venezuela has won international beauty pageant titles in the three major international beauty pageants (Miss Universe, Miss World, and Miss International) in 1955, 1979, 1981, 1984, 1985, 1986, 1991, 1995, 1997, 2000, 2003, 2006, 2008, 2009, and 2013.

12 In his study of Latin American melodrama, *Communication, Culture and Hegemony: From the Media to Mediations* (1993), Martín-Barbero demonstrates that power and marginality are negotiated—at both the national and individual scale—through the *mediations* of modernity in Latin America. Mediation is a set of behaviors that produces a relationship between what is considered "fantasy" and what is considered "real life": "If a mythology 'functions,' it is because it responds to the questions and unexplained mysteries, the collective wonderings, the fears and hopes which neither rationalism at the level of knowledge nor progress at the level of action has managed to abolish or satisfy. The political impotence and social anonymity in which the great majority of people live makes them yearn for a larger ration of daily fantasy as a kind of supplement-complement to their everyday existence. This, according to [Edgar] Morin [in his 1962 work *L'esprit du temps*], is the real mediation, the function of a medium, which mass culture fulfils day by day: the communication between the real and the imaginary" (56).

13 According to Martín-Barbero, "Mediations refer especially to the articulations between communication practices and social movements and the articulation of different tempos of development with the plurality of cultural matrices" (1993, 187).

14 Martín-Barbero connects the consumerization of the masses to the project of development and the cultural logic of consumption: "If we are able to consume the same things that developed peoples consume, then, clearly, we have finally achieved development" (1993, 180). He cites the importation of the "North American *model* of television" as the most influential factor in this shift—not simply privatization of networks, or importation of content, but rather "the tendency to constitute, through television, a single public" (181; emphasis in original). Hence, the content of media messages is not as determining as the ritual constitution of audience-member subject positions.

Martín-Barbero, García Canclini, Daniel Mato, and others call for a nuanced and historicized approach to the analysis of power and signification in the project Estudios Culturales Latinoamericanos (Latin American Cultural Studies). This project directly distinguishes itself from the U.S.-based Latin American Cultural Studies project. See particularly García Canclini's introduction to *Consumidores y ciudadanos* (1995a), "El diálogo norte-sur en los estudios culturales," and Mato's book *Estudios y otras prácticas intelectuales latinoamericanas en cultura y poder* (2002). The differences between U.S., British, Estudios Culturales Latinoamericanos, and Latin American Cultural Studies have been a source of much discussion and debate. Latin American scholarship on culture and power has a very different genealogy than that of Britain or the United States, rooted in the public and political role of the *letrado* (lawyer), and in engagements with popular culture that have their roots in nineteenth-century nation-building movements. Estudios Culturales Latinoamericanos in particular, but also Latin American Cultural Studies, emphasizes the coloniality of power in the region through a genealogy that delves into the colonial period in Ibero-America to understand contemporary relations of power. Specifically, scholars working in Estudios Culturales Latinoamericanos actively resist the presumption that cultural studies models have been imported into Latin America, and assert that estudios culturales were going on well before the introduction of British or U.S. cultural studies (see Martín-Barbero 1997).

15 See Ann Cvetkovich (2003), David Eng (2010), Eng and Alice Hom (1998), Gayatri Gopinath (2005), Lawrence La Fountain-Stokes (2009), Martin Manalansan (2003), and Benigno Sánchez Eppler and Cindy Patton (2000) for further discussion of this literature. Tom Boellstorff (2007) also briefly discusses some of this literature as it relates to cultural anthropology.

16 For example, Sánchez Eppler and Patton, in their introduction to the volume *Queer Diasporas*, invoke the following categories: "gay, homosexual, lesbian, joto, internacional, tortillera, like that, battyman, bakla, katoi, butch, et cetera" (2000, 3). This usage suspends the visibility and particularity of each of these terms in a move to resignify (re-resignify?) the word *queer* to include these categories. Time will tell if the U.S.-based vernacular usage of *queer* in popular culture will eclipse this attempt and leave us with the *queer* of *Queer Eye for the Straight Guy*. For now, it still seems worth trying to keep the category "queer" open and inclusive.

17 La Fountain-Stokes cites Manolo Guzmán's term *sexile* and makes note of the focus on queer migration in his discussion of Puerto Rican queer diasporas, invoking three important anthologies, Brad Epps, Keja Valens, and Bill Johnson González's *Passing Lines* (2005); Arnaldo Cruz-Malavé and Manalansan's *Queer Globalizations* (2002); and Eithne Luibhéid and Lionel Cantú Jr.'s *Queer Migrations* (2002). See La Fountain-Stokes (2009, xix).

18 In his introduction to *Queer Ricans*, La Fountain-Stokes summarizes the different dynamics of first-generation, second- and third-generation, and 1.5-generation migrants (2009, xxi). *First generation* refers to people who migrate as adults; second and third generation are the descendants of first-generation migrants, typically born in the host country. Members of the 1.5 generation are "immigrants who leave their home country and go to their host country as children[,] . . . and as such, have intimate connections to both places during their formative years" (176n48).

19 See Gopinath (2005, 6–15) for an excellent discussion.

20 In her definition of diaspora space, Avtar Brah conflates "the Native" and "indigenous," an unfortunate move that is even more complicated when considered in a Latin American context: "Diaspora space as a conceptual category is 'inhabited' not only by those who have migrated and their descendants but equally by those who are constructed and represented as indigenous" (2003, 615). This formulation, while intended to problematize a static notion of origin,

eclipses the possibility that, of course, not all indigenous people stay put, and that one can be both simultaneously indigenous *and* diasporic. The elision of these power dynamics in spaces of intimacy such as "home" misses the opportunity to render multiple forms of resistance and negotiation visible. While non-heteronormative subjects don't often articulate their experiences in these terms, a queer diasporic critique is attentive to these intersections and points of conjuncture.

21 See Blackwell (2006) for an excellent articulation of the politics of scale among indigenous feminists across borders.

22 Homi Bhabha famously employs Freud's idea of the *unheimlich* (uncanny) in his formulation of "unhomeliness," which Bhabha defines as "the condition of extra-territorial and cross-cultural initiations" to describe the affective characteristics of an "interstitial perspective" (1994, 9). In trying to name this Otherness, he invokes the metallic taste of "everything that ought to have remained . . . secret and hidden but has come to light" (10).

23 Manalansan's ethnography *Global Divas* (2003) has been a source of inspiration for my concept of queer diasporic ethnography. Manalansan's subtitle reveals that *Global Divas* is an ethnography *of* diasporic subjects: *Filipino Gay Men in the Diaspora*. But it is not the object of study alone that makes his book a queer diasporic ethnography—it is the kind of questions that Manalansan produces in his own transits and literacies through these diasporic spaces. This distinguishes Manalansan's approach from the ethnographies of other anthropologists of sexuality who travel for ethnographic work but who do not situate themselves within diaspora. In articulating a queer diasporic ethnography, I am not arguing for the exclusive privileging of diasporic ethnographers. Rather, I am delineating the underpinnings of a specific form of inquiry that works through a queer diasporic critique.

Another work that I would place within the notion of queer diasporic ethnography is Gayatri Reddy's *With Respect to Sex* (2005). Reddy's study of *hijra* and *koti* negotiations of sex and gender and power and marginality in Hyderabad and Secunderabad performs an important corrective to previous ethnographic work on hijra, which has often presented non-Western gender formations as encapsulated curiosities for Western consumption. Instead, Reddy insists on understanding hijras' lives "within the domain of sexuality as well as its articulation within the broader contexts of everyday life in South Asia" (2). Reddy is even more reticent to discuss her own positionality than Manalansan, and she doesn't claim any kind of queer diasporic approach. She begins the ethnography with a hijra's speculation on her gender presentation: " 'She has the body and face of a woman, she is wearing female clothing, but she has such short hair. Maybe she is a young boy of thirteen or fourteen.' That is the reason I spoke to you initially, you know" (1). At the very end, Reddy describes herself as one of the "Cast of Main Characters": "Living in America; born in Hyderabad; thirty years old; upper-middle-class; thin, frail-looking; convinced she would get malaria in the field but never did; short-haired; looks younger than her age;

bespectacled; soft-spoken, sometimes naïve, open to new experiences, constantly asking silly questions; photographer, inveterate note-taker" (234). It is
Reddy's diasporic relationship to Hyderabad and the United States and her nonheteronormative gender presentation that mark her position with respect to her
hijra and koti informants. Reddy's ethnography is not one *on* queer diasporic
subjects, nor necessarily *by* a queer-identified subject, but her approach is one I
would characterize as fitting within queer diasporic ethnography because of its
location within diaspora and sexual alterity.

24 El Interior is part of a social mapping used in Venezuela, which figures El
Exterior as the world outside of Venezuela, and El Interior as the Venezuela outside of Caracas. I would translate this concept as "the provinces."

1. *Belleza Venezolana*

1 Diego Montaldo Pérez, Un siglo de misses, series published as an insert in the
Caracas newspaper *Últimas Noticias*, September to December 1999, available at
Hemeroteca Nacional de Venezuela, call no. 791.620987U54; my translation.

2 This phrase was repeated often during fieldwork with the Miss Venezuela organization and its casting system. It is also, I later learned, the name of the website
of the missólogo Julio Rodríguez, who has an excellent archive of news of Miss
Venezuela and other beauty pageants in Venezuela: http://www.bellezavenezo
lana.net/.

3 I am employing *form* here to mean both bodily form and performance genre.

4 Both Montaldo Pérez (1999) and the Museo Jacobo Borges (2000) attribute this
information to *Élite*, October 26, 1957. Unfortunately, I was unable to find this
issue to cite directly.

5 For a few examples: "Las reinas del Volante," *Élite*, September 3, 1927; "Muchachas bonitas," *Élite*, November 19, 1927; and "Damas honorables," *Élite*, December 3, 1927.

6 This feature ran from 1925 through 1930; an example can be found in *Élite* 82.

7 See *Élite*, June 1, 1929.

8 "Ultimo concurso internacional de belleza de Galveston: 'Miss Universo,' timida
y extraña al 'flaperismo,' es una gentil reina de la gracia femenina," *El Universal*,
July 11, 1929, 1, 4. This story provides an earlier chronology for the Miss Universe title than that provided by Sarah Banet-Weiser (1999) and the Miss Universe organization itself, both of whom date the first Miss Universe competition
to 1952, after Catalina Swimwear's departure from the Miss America pageant in
1951. The *El Universal* coverage suggests that a Miss Universe contest was being
held far earlier, with thirty-four U.S. contestants, eight Europeans, and two
South Americans (Cuba and Brazil). The *Galveston Daily News* reported that the
International Pageant of Pulchritude was held in Galveston, Texas, from 1920 to
1932 (Cempa 2009). This is the same pageant reported in *El Universal*. The Galveston pageant is thought to be the first organized on an international scale. See
McClymer (2005) for additional context.

9 "Venezuela en el Concurso de Bellezas Interamericanas," Nuestra página column, *Élite*, June 1, 1929 (there were no authors or page numbers in the magazine at this time); my translation.

10 Indeed, pageantry actually increased in importance later on in the twentieth century with the introduction of the Cuban expatriates Osmel Sousa and Joaquín Riviera. Riviera was the choreographer and director of the legendary spectacles at the Tropicana Club in Havana, and the team has been heralded for the enormity of the spectacles produced for the contest, particularly during the 1980s and 1990s.

11 "La Elección de la 'Señorita Caracas,'" Nuestra página column, *Élite*, January 25, 1930; my translation.

12 This appropriation is quite standard in Venezuelan Spanish, and in many cases dates back to this time period, when representatives of North American and English petroleum interests mixed socially with Venezuelan elites. Along with *miss*, there is the "venezolanization" *pana* (partner), as well as English words that pepper the pages of *Élite* of this time, such as *flirt* and *feeling*. These words are commonly used in contemporary Venezuelan Spanish. Note that the Miss Universo coverage from 1929 also incorporates the term *misses*.

13 "Venezuela, por la gracia de Dios, es un florido carmen de mujeres guapas," *El Universal*, May 27, 1929, front page; my translation.

14 Montaldo Pérez 1999, 9.

15 These are standard racial categories in Venezuela and in much of Latin America and the Caribbean. *Negra* means "Black," *india* means "indigenous," and *criolla* means "Creole." See chapter 2 for a complete discussion of Duijm's place as the prototypical Venezuelan beauty queen.

16 Of course, it's only symbolic fluidity—racialization and racism are very much in evidence in Venezuela, but they don't look anything like U.S. racial formations.

17 There were some interventions intended to reinforce the beauty of Afro-descendant Venezuelans during the time that Chávez was in office, but the aesthetic of the *misses* during this time period did not significantly changed.

18 The *casting* is an event held in various locations throughout Venezuela to choose contestants for the national pageant. *Casting* is the word used—an Anglicism in Venezuelan Spanish—rather than the more "democratic" form of local beauty pageants leading to state titles and then to the national pageant, as is practiced in many other countries, including the United States. *Casting* (no "s" in the Venezuelan plural) are conducted like beauty pageants, including several rounds of parading contestants before the judges and audience. They are billed as entertainment but have a contest form. The key difference is that the idea of *casting* leaves ultimate authority with the director—that is Sousa or a representative of the Miss Venezuela organization—to select the cast.

19 See also Alain Chartier (2000, 50–51) for his discussion of the Venezuelan beauty industry and its regard for Blackness.

20 By "Asian" he means smaller and more almond shaped than rounder "European"

eyes. And D.A. is actually referring to the "medium" to which you would cook a steak. The original Spanish quote is: "La muchacha blanca sin ser muy blanca, blanca bronceada de pelo preferiblemente muy liso, con ojos un poco achinados de color marron o claro sin ser azul ni verde. Es como un término medio: no llega ser la rubia ni la morena del barrio."

21 The original Spanish is: "Tienen nariz delgada y labios finos. Son más mezcladas y se parecen más a las blancas."

22 The original Spanish is: "En Venezuela no hay negras lindas, ya que sus narices son anchas y sus labios son demasiado gruesos."

23 I would argue, as Charles Briggs (2004) does, that the indigenous is simply, pur-posefully, invisible in Venezuelan national discourse.

24 Many thanks to an anonymous reviewer for pointing out this kind of pessimism in an earlier draft of my argument.

25 Thanks to Nancy Raquel Mirabal, who provided key insight into this under-standing of the mediations of race and nation.

26 Venezuela has twenty-six states.

27 Oddly enough, Delta Amacuro is often associated with indigenous populations in Venezuela, so this mapping of race onto the states doesn't necessarily reflect the distribution of the Venezuelan population.

28 David M. Guss's (2000) study on cultural performance in Venezuela provides an excellent analysis of the role of Fundación Bigott in the "business of popular culture" (101).

29 Meneses refers here to Carlos Andres Pérez, president of Venezuela from 1974 to 1979 and 1989 to 1993. These are also, incidentally, very close to the golden years of both *misses* and petroleum in Venezuela.

30 The pageant returned to its traditional venue, the government-run Poliedro de Caracas, in 2004.

31 Producto Online (organizational author), "Patria, PAN y Polar." Online feature published August 2000, marked as Issue 203. Accessed October 2007. Available at: http://web.archive.org/web/20070819025521/http://www.producto.com.ve /203/notas/polar.html.

32 I first heard of these advertisements in the seminar "Globalización, cultura, y transformaciones sociales," held in the social sciences faculty of the Universidad Central de Venezuela and led by Daniel Mato. Unfortunately, the videos are no longer online and details such as production and broadcast date have not been made available to the public.

33 The *negrita* in Venezuela and the mammy in the United States are analogous fig-ures, though they are not the same in that they represent very different colonial and racial regimes with distinct histories. However, the techniques of stereotype and representation make them very recognizable figures.

34 I originally found these videos on the Polar website as part of a multimedia feature on the history of the brand. The feature included videos that were also uploaded to YouTube. PAN Caracas is available at http://www.youtube.com /watch?v=pkf7kH8eszc. The other videos are no longer available online or in

archives, though I have a copy of the multimedia presentation and videos in my research materials. The transcriptions and translations of the videos are mine.

35 *Caracas: cómo has cambiado*
desde aquella fundación
Pero el tiempo te ha dejado
un caudal de tradición

Cuatro siglos han pasado
y aunque muchos pasarán
las arepas han quedado
gracias a la Harina PAN.

36 *Como el harpa suena con su*
constante vibrar, así Harina pan
conserva su constante calidad.
. . .
Harina pan sí tiene lo que Ud.
busca: calidad. Calidad constante y
criolla.

37 See Anita Berrizbeitia (2004) for a study of his landscape design at Parque del Este.

38 *En las vacaciones comemos empanadas,*
hallacas, y arepitas de maíz.
Porqué no hay problemas pilando ni moliendo
Las hacemos con Harina pan
Vivan las vacaciones
Vivan las diversiones
Aquí todos somos felices
y todos vamos a cantar
PAN, PAN, PAN!

39 See Peggy Andersen (1989) and Kimberly Pace (1994) for documentation of Aunt Jemima's periodic transformations, in which the trappings of servitude are gradually removed but "her smiling face . . . is the same." M. M. Manring (1998) has a more historical treatment of Aunt Jemima's career.

40 See Yolanda Salas de Lecuna's *Bolívar y la historia en la conciencia popular* (1987) for an extended discussion of this genealogy.

41 Misión Negra Hipólita, "Expresión de amor en la revolución," February 5, 2010. Accessed July 14, 2010. Available at: http://web.archive.org/web/2010020600 5932/http://www.misionnegrahipolita.gob.ve/webfmnh/web/website.php /organizacion; my translation.

42 See the MNH's website, http://www.misionnegrahipolita.gob.ve/ (accessed November 8, 2013).

43 An example can be found at: http://www.misionnegrahipolita.gob.ve/web
/fmnh/web/uploads/galeria/35c9f8f6b290c92dc76e1b9e2c817835730eba01.jpg
(accessed November 8, 2013).

2. La Moda Nace en Paris y Muere en Caracas

1 *La Venezuela Saudita* refers to Venezuela's status as a country with what at the
time appeared to be limitless petroleum wealth. Terri Karl's (1997) work on
Venezuela as a "petro-state" is helpful in understanding the excesses and para-
doxes of this time period.

2 See chapter 1 for a more detailed discussion of sanitary citizenship (Briggs and
Mantini-Briggs 2003). See chapter 4 for more on modernity and the production
of space.

3 See Arturo Almandoz (1999) and (2000), as well as his 2004 book *La ciudad en
el imaginario Venezolano*, for detailed descriptions of this fascinating history.

4 This documentary is included in the collection of the Biblioteca Nacional de
Venezuela. Herrera and Manaure produced it sometime between 1978 and
1983, according to the catalogue, but the publication date for the film is 1981. It
is remarkable to many that such an early example of trans-specific film exists
in Venezuela, and certainly Herrera and Manaure were bold in producing this
representation. This is, however, in line with the Venezuelan tradition of avant-
garde art and film throughout the twentieth century and very reflective of the
aesthetics of Caracas of the late 1970s and 1980s, also known as La Venezuela
Saudita because of the influence of petrodollars. The film was a result of the
directors' work in the film department of Universidad de Los Andes and had
limited circulation, though its reach was broader than most thesis films. It is
very occasionally screened by the Cinemateca Nacional for events of LGBT
interest. Herrera was very helpful in understanding the history of the film
and its production and for this I thank him.

5 I have learned since first writing this that the dip may have also been inspired
by another dip in Rome's Trevi Fountain, which appeared in Federico Fellini's
La dolce vita (1960). Thanks to B. Ruby Rich for pointing this out and providing the reference I failed to recognize with my limited film knowledge. Given
that Venezuela, La Contessa, and many other *transformistas* of this era used
Milan as a reference point, it is more likely that the reference is to the Italian
film.

6 The Bolivarian government, through the Petróleos de Venezuela, S.A. (PDVSA),
the social and cultural arm of the national petroleum company, inaugurated the
fifth version of the fountain in 2009. See PDVSA, Gobierno Bolivariano de Venezuela, Ministerio del Poder Popular para la Energía y Petróleo, "PDVSA la estan-
cia: Lo nuevo," August 10, 2009, accessed July 9, 2010, http://web.archive.org
/web/20090830005209/http://laestancia.pdvsa.com/index.php/nuevo/nuevo
_most/157; and Radio Nacional de Venezuela, "Concluyó segunda fase de con-
strucción de fuente de Plaza Venezuela," transcript, April 23, 2009, accessed July

19, 2010, http://www.rnv.gov.ve/noticias/index.php?s=130ae2782d010b42072e04
e8e6211306&act=ST&f=28&t=95748&st=0&.

7 This national law, declared unconstitutional in 1997, was used to persecute sex
workers and homosexuals throughout much of the twentieth century. See Immigration and Refugee Board of Canada (1998) for a discussion of its impact on
human rights for gay men and transgender women in Venezuela.

8 I invoke the idea of perversion in multiple senses—the celebratory queer senses
as much as those that horrify, those senses that describe atrocity. Without simultaneously considering both senses of perversion, an accounting of queer lifeworlds falls short; it risks isolating queer and transgender people from their full
social, economic, and historical contexts.

9 Note here that I make this claim specifically for *transformistas* and not for other
kinds of trans people in Venezuela. See the introduction for a more detailed
parsing of this term.

10 See chapter 1 for one example of this kind of inclusion.

11 These perversions included Roger Casement's own sodomitical tendencies
(Taussig 1987, 13–14).

12 The spatialization of power into a core-periphery model is a hallmark of world-
systems theory (Wallerstein 1974) and dependency theory, but precedes this
work by twenty years. Peter Worsley (1990) provides a good overview of this
process, one that Arif Dirlik (2004, 131) calls "a product of Eurocentric map-
pings of the world to deal with the postcolonial situation that emerged after
World War II." Another useful review of the concept as it has been used in
archaeology and ethnography is Michael Rowlands (1987).

13 In this, Michel Foucault's notion of productive power has been especially helpful (1977, 194).

14 The Chilean artist Juan Dávila has famously painted portraits of Simón Bolívar
as a "transvestite," often seminude with exposed breasts and vulva, flipping off
the viewer with his middle finger (see Brett, Benjamin, and Dávila 2006). These
paintings, the source of much consternation in Venezuela, Chile, and other
countries after they were originally displayed in 1994, represent a queer "pollution" of the idea of Bolívar and the artist's response to Bolivarian patriotism
(well before the Bolivarian Revolution). While my mention of "Bolívar in Napoleon drag" has the effect of invoking these images, I am specifically referring to
the fact that Bolívar, like many revolutionary leaders of his day, including Tous-
saint Louverture, dressed in a Napoleonic uniform and participated in a political
and cultural circuit informed by the European Enlightenment and the French
Revolution. It is transcultural drag all by itself, no twentieth-century queer
resignification required.

15 See Jun Ishibashi (2003), who lists the following "types" he encountered in his
survey of Venezuelan ad agencies: "*nórdico, europeo, rubio, latino, venezolano
(o criollo), moreno, trigüeño, negro, indio, oriental (asiático)*" (Nordic, European,
blonde, Latino, Venezuelan or Creole, brown, dark-skinned, Black, indigenous,
oriental or Asian) (43).

16 See chapter 1 for more on these oil tankers.

17 Eduardo Planchart Licea also reports this in his history of the pageant in a supplement created for the *Miss Venezuela* exhibition at the Museo Jacobo Borges in 2000. See Planchart Licea 2000 and Montaldo Pérez 1999.

18 While there are many ways of contesting and reshaping marginality—resistance, revolution, opposition, acculturation, and syncretism, to name a few controversial ones—I want to focus specifically on glamour as a technology of intimacy, which has marked my experience with Latin American gay men and transgender women, and with Venezuela as a place.

19 Carol Dyhouse (2010) presents a cultural history of glamour as it relates to femininity, primarily in the United States and England. She focuses more on presenting examples of glamorous people and things than on accounting for the emergence and functions of glamour. She seems to follow Gundle on the origins of glamour but suggests that glamour gives women access to a form of agency.

20 An early example of the emergence of this class is the great tulip crash of 1637, the first stock exchange collapse in recorded history. Tulips originated from the Ottoman Empire. See Egon Friedell and Allan Janik (2009) and Anne Goldgar (2007) for more on tulip mania.

21 In the Spanish colonization of the Americas, these were the *hidalgos*, a form of colonialist masculinity that I discuss in a chapter on Catalina de Erauso, the Lieutenant Nun (Ochoa 2007).

3. *La Reina de la Noche*

1 Note here that the term *marico* equates to the word *fag* in English—it is a word that is used as an insult to refer to a gay man. At the same time, like *transformista*, *marico* is a word used by in-group members to describe and name themselves. My use of the term here and later in this part attempts to honor the way Venezuelan gay men use this word, while at the same time recognizing that the word is used to describe a kind of abject male femininity that is employed in the process of producing beauty. To replace *marico* with the North American term *gay* would be to erase this economy of gender and signification.

2 Though these events are called *casting* (in Venezuelan Spanish), they are not run like a casting for actors. Rather, they are produced as large events with sponsors, judges, and an audience and take the form of beauty pageants.

    To honor the confidentiality of research participants, I have changed the location of the *casting* pageant as well as the names of the participants, except when public figures are involved.

3 For those unfamiliar with twenty-first-century Venezuelan politics, there has been a long period of political polarization in Venezuela since the 1998 presidential election of Hugo Rafael Chávez Frías. One key moment in this polarization was an attempted coup on April 11, 2002, led by a group of elite politicians and military that called itself the Oposición (Opposition). The coup attempt hap-

pened in the wake of three days of protest and a general strike called by Fede-cámaras (the Venezuelan federation of chambers of commerce) and escalated by shootings on Puente Llaguno in Caracas. The president of Fedecámaras at the time, Pedro Carmona Estanga, declared himself president of Venezuela. This resulted in massive political mobilizations in the street and the breakout of more politically motivated acts of violence among protesters. Chávez was reinstated to power on April 14. For more on the coup and the political climate in Venezuela during this time, see Steve Ellner and Miguel Tinker Salas (2007), Eva Golinger (2006), and Thomas Ponniah and Jonathan Eastwood (2011).

4 See Jesus Antonio Aguilera (1973) and David M. Guss (2000) for documenta-tion of the international folklore site designation in this time period in Vene-zuela.

5 For a more detailed history of Carúpano, see Ricardo Alberto Mata (2001).

6 I use this construction to highlight the Atlantic and Caribbean nature of place making in Carúpano, conscious of Anna Tsing's (2001) excellent critique of the language of flows in globalization discourse.

7 The Centro Italo-Venezolano is a society of Italian-descended Venezuelans who form social clubs in many cities and larger towns. These clubs are roughly com-parable to Colombo clubs in the United States for Italian Americans. The clubs provide space for social gatherings and celebrations. Incidentally, the Miss Sucre pageant in 2005, a regional casting for Miss Venezuela, was held at this same location. It is one of the bigger venues in Carúpano.

8 See Guss (2000) for another example of the commercialization of folk celebra-tions such as Carnaval in Venezuela.

9 Mark Johnson (1996) describes a similar practice in *bakla* (a category of trans-femininity) beauty pageants in the southern Philippines; contestants use this as an opportunity to create a feminine persona and to critically comment on the personae created in the national beauty pageant. Contestants provide names, measurements, hobbies, and career aspirations, which are read by the emcee to the audience as the contestant sashays down the catwalk.

10 I did hear of some makeup artists and hairstylists who participated in gay beauty pageants and went on from there to work at higher levels in that industry, all the way up to the Miss Venezuela pageant.

11 More recently, the televisual beauty pageants both in Venezuela and inter-nationally have incorporated other mechanisms for spectator participation, such as text messaging and Internet voting.

12 Here Sandy uses the feminine form: "Una piensa de una forma, la otra de la otra."

13 TúTV is the local channel that broadcasts the pageant.

14 Shakira is a *transformista* performer who lip-synched to the Colombian pop singer in the show but did not compete for the crown. She has breast implants and takes hormones.

15 I use the concepts of center and periphery very consciously here; see chapter 2

for an extended discussion of this idea. A common geopolitical formation in Venezuela is a distinction between Caracas and *el interior* (the rest of the country outside the Caracas metropolitan area). In this formation, caraqueños have imposed the mistaken idea that they are the brokers for information about *el exterior* (the rest of the world), clearly replicating the discourse of center and periphery.

16 The location of this *casting* and the names of the participants have been changed, except for that of Sousa, the actual president of OMV, because of his position as a public figure.

17 The election of Miss Caracas of 1936 presented a similar moment of crisis for beauty pageant democracy: the winner, Olga Salvatti Vizcarrondo, was recruited by the pageant organizer at the last minute. He pronounced her the winner shortly upon her arrival at the pageant. The other candidates, "fúricas e indignadas" (furious and indignant), stormed out of the pageant before the bathing suit competition. This kind of impromptu scene stealing became quite normal in the Miss Venezuela pageant of later years. It was almost structured into the regional *casting* I observed: the OMV representative — often Sousa himself — would frequently interrupt the pageant at the crowning moment and select several contestants to take with him to prepare for the national pageant in Caracas. See Montaldo Pérez 1999, my translation.

18 This idea of participation has also been expanded to the national audience through the recent addition of text messaging, *American Idol* style, so that consumers can register their "vote" through a text message during or immediately after a broadcast. Osmel still has the last word though.

19 Plastic surgery and beauty statistics are available on the International Society of Aesthetic Plastic Surgery (ISAPS) website (which keeps track of world statistics on cosmetic surgery and nonsurgical aesthetic procedures). Available at: http://www.isaps.org/isaps-global-statistics.html, accessed November 9, 2013. The problem with these numbers is that they are essentially the numbers of the five Venezuelan plastic surgeons who are members of this organization, all in Altamira or Las Mercedes in Caracas. Among these surgeons, they did fourteen hundred procedures in 2003. There is no way to know how many procedures actually took place in Venezuela in that or any year, even by accredited plastic surgeons. See also Sander L. Gilman (1998, 1999).

20 Any man who is actively involved in the production of *misses* has his sexuality called into question, and is often presumed to be homosexual. This does not necessarily mean that all men who work with the pageant are gay — quite the contrary. However, among this particular specialization, makeup, men were often quite open about their homosexuality, but they did not exteriorize these details of their lives to larger publics, who by and large ignored the makeup artists anyway.

4. *Pasarelas y Perolones*

1 Please note that not all *transformistas* do sex work, but this chapter specifically refers to those who do on Avenida Libertador. Also, not everyone identifies as a *transformista*. There are transgender women in Venezuela who are not *transformistas*, as well as transsexual men and women.

2 Another bridge in Caracas became famous worldwide during the attempted coup of April 11, 2002: Puente Llaguno. This bridge, which is at the intersection of Avenidas Baralt and Urdaneta, is closer to the center of Caracas and is not the kind of *pasarela* I am describing here, though it certainly did become a kind of global stage.

3 Thanks to Charles Briggs for pointing this out.

4 During my time on the Avenida I never saw a client approach a *transformista* on foot.

5 Solano is differently positioned with respect to traffic than is Libertador. Foot traffic is heavier, and automobiles go in one direction only, toward Plaza Venezuela. The road is wide enough, at four lanes, for clients to pull over when contracting an escort and let other cars pass. A car can pick up a sex worker, pull into a nearby alley, complete the transaction, and get back on the road fairly quickly. Traffic moves slower on Solano, so drivers can look longer at sex workers without drawing too much attention. Cars on Libertador would sometimes slow down in swift traffic to catch a glimpse of the *transformistas*, an action that often resulted in irate honking from the cars behind. This made the act of viewing *transformistas* far more noticeable than that of viewing the men and women who worked on Solano. To my knowledge, sex work did not generally go on in public view on the Búlevard de Sabana Grande. One block south, on Avenida Casanova, cisgender women sex workers worked both in brothels and on the street, further west in Chacaíto. Casanova is similar to Solano in that traffic flows in one direction only (east), across four lanes. There is heavier foot traffic, with various eating establishments and shopping malls close by. The sidewalks are narrower, and there is more street lighting than on either Libertador or Solano. Several unmarked establishments on Casanova serve as brothels. Clients walk in and must park cars, if they have them, elsewhere. Further east, lone women stand on sidewalks waiting for clients. Only twice did I see *transformistas* working on Casanova, and this was because a few of them had stopped working on Libertador over a turf dispute. They worked very close to one of the bars on the Búlevard de Sabana Grande that served as a refuge for *transformistas*. Given that this bar was so conveniently located, I do wonder why *transformistas* didn't work Casanova more frequently, and my sense of it is that because of the heavier foot traffic, they were more vulnerable to violence and less visible on the street.

6 Here I am recalling Dipesh Chakrabarty's excellent chapter "On Garbage, Modernity, and the Citizen's Gaze" in *Habitations of Modernity* (2002), which considers the rhetoric of rubbish, order, and citizenship. See also the discussion of pollution in chapter 2.

7 Thanks again to Charles Briggs for this insight.

8 Fernando Coronil and Julie Skurski (1991) discuss the semantics of representation in the wake of El Caracazo. Also see Luis Duno-Gottberg (2004) for an excellent analysis of race, class, and the representation of looting mobs in post-Caracazo Venezuela.

9 One of these caught fire in October 2004 — an incident taken up by the news media as an indictment of Chávez's poor administration, but really it was a problem that had been many years in the making.

10 Note that this is not strictly limited to Caracas elites, nor does it imply specific living conditions. Many people live in these kinds of buildings, which are themselves in various states of repair, but all are characterized by strong security systems and uniform access to infrastructure such as electricity, water, and sewer.

11 Although I could not pin down dates, contemporaries of the Avenida Libertador project have told me that the *transformistas* have always been there, well before the 1980s. Sadly, I found no *transformistas* of that time period whom I could interview. Many, even those who were in their late teens or early twenties in the film *Las TRANS de Caracas* had already died by the time I arrived in Caracas. I do have an informant who told me that when he was growing up near Plaza Los Cedros on Avenida Libertador in the mid- to late 1970s, he would talk to the "señoras *transformistas*" he met on the corner. Another informant, who was part of Entendido, a gay-liberation organization in the 1970s, told me he remembers the *transformistas* on Libertador from 1978 to 1979.

12 The Venezuelan architect Gaston Torres Marquez graciously assisted me with initial research into my question about the beginnings of Avenida Libertador, and the librarians at the Colegio de Ingenieros de Venezuela patiently helped me sift through these dusty materials. My thanks to them for their assistance.

13 This is a problem that recurs in the volumes of *Memoria y cuenta*, with large expenditures to compensate landowners for displacement, and the Pérez Jiménez administration funded the Banco Obrero for eradication of "vivienda insalubre" (unhealthy housing). The Banco Obrero became a very different entity with the advent of the democratically elected administrations, and eventually became responsible for developing massive housing projects throughout Caracas and other Venezuelan urban areas.

14 Avenida Libertador is not one of these main highways. It is, rather, a secondary expressway with a local level.

15 Here I am drawing from Anna Tsing's (1993) concept of the signification of modernity.

16 There are *transformistas* who work in El Centro, mostly along Avenida Baralt and in brothels. There are also *transformistas* who work from their neighborhoods, often as hairdressers who will occasionally take on clients for sex work. There is some slippage here between paying clients and those men who are considered somewhat boyfriends, who bring gifts and help out when needed. There are also many *transformistas* who work using classified advertising and cell phones and

pagers. This work is seen as more upscale because it involves the acquisition of a cell phone and placing an ad in the paper. It also affords another modicum of safety, in which the *transformista* can make arrangements to meet the client at a hotel, where she is on familiar terrain and protected. Some of the *transformistas* who were on Avenida Libertador also worked with cell phones. The sex-worker advocate Nury Pernia, of the organization AMBAR (Asociación Civil de Mujeres por el Bienestar y Asistencia Recíproca, or Women's Civil Association for Wellness and Mutual Aid), pointed out to me that this kind of sex work was not actually policed in Caracas, nor was it illegal under the Venezuelan penal code. What is illegal in the penal code is offering sexual services in the *vía pública* (thoroughfare) (from the Ordenanza de Convivencia Ciudadana [Citizenship Coexistence Ordenance] in Caracas) and profiting from the sex work of another (*proxeneta*).

17 Daniella Gandolfo's (2009) ethnography of Lima, Peru, describes the public nudity of activist women, who also bared their breasts in public, though *transformista* nudity does not appear to work in the same ways Gandolfo describes.

18 I have documented the kinds of abuses and violations faced by *transformistas* in Venezuela in chapter 2 of this book, and in Ochoa (2008). See also Carrasco and Ochoa (2003).

5. Sacar el Cuerpo

1 The names of all interviewees cited in this chapter have been changed. The interviews were all conducted in Spanish and the translations are mine.

2 *Loca* is the feminine version of "crazy." It is also used throughout the Spanish-speaking world to refer to gay men and transgender women.

3 An anonymous reviewer pointed out similarities between this description of *transformistas'* living quarters and the introduction to Don Kulick's ethnography *Travestí* (1998). In his introduction, Kulick takes more time to describe the way Banana prepares herself for an evening of sex work in Salvador, Bahía, Brazil. Though living situations for *transformistas* in Caracas are sometimes similar to those Kulick describes, my focus in this passage is on Norkeli's nonchalance in answering my question.

4 In *The Empire of Love*, Povinelli articulates the concept of carnality as against a notion of "corporeality" to mark "flesh as the physical mattering forth of [juridical and political] maneuvers" (2006, 7). In this way she traces the fate of the flesh in disciplinary regimes.

5 Garfinkel calls this the "achievement of sex-status" in *Ethnomethodology*, where he describes the "endless, ongoing, contingent accomplishment" of everyday practices as one of the core elements of his approach. Candace West and Don H. Zimmerman use Garfinkel's study of Agnes to coin the phrase "accomplishment of gender" (1987, 131) and apply Garfinkel's notion of managed achievement to cases beyond Agnes. West has employed this framework with another author

to propose a way of "accounting for cosmetic surgery" (Dull and West 1991). I specify the gender being accomplished in my usage, thus *the accomplishment of femininity*.

6 Hausman (1995) discusses this issue at length, employing Barthesian semiotics to ground her inquiry in "the body."

7 As Garfinkel put it: "This news turned the article into a feature of the same circumstances it reported, *i.e.*, into a situated report. Indeed, if the reader will re-read the article in light of these disclosures, he will find that the reading provides an exhibit of several prevailing phenomena of ethnomethodological study" (1967, 288).

8 Kulick (1998) has documented silicone-injection practices in his work on *travestís* (transvestites) in Salvador, Bahía. The *transformistas* I talked to did not mention silicone, though I know it is possible to get silicone injections in Venezuela. This didn't seem to be a common practice among *transformistas* during the time I was in Caracas. While Kulick describes many practices of transformation, he does not connect these ideas to a wider sense of medical governmentality in Brazil, as does, for example, Alexander Edmonds (2010). This chapter will focus on these logics of the body as they manifest themselves in the lives of *transformistas* and *misses*.

9 See chapter 2 for an extended discussion of the space of death as it relates to *transformista* existence.

10 Wahng asserts that this terminology of *Korean sex slaves* is more accurate in describing the relations of power between Korean women and the Japanese Army during the Second World War than is the more widely used term *comfort women*. See also Wahng (2009). Based on his description of the research, I believe that Wahng's use of the term *Korean sex slaves* privileges the political project of naming over the feelings of the subjects he is describing. Recognizing that both projects are important, I choose to use the generally understood term *transformista*, which can sometimes be taken as an insult, over the more diplomatic *chica de aparencia* (feminine-looking girl), to reflect the negotiation that these women have with the social stigma that the name *transformista* can imply.

11 By *trans subjects* here I am including transgender, transvestite, transsexual, and intersex subjects as they have been addressed in the Anglophone literature.

12 For a discussion of queer theory in anthropological inquiry, see Tom Boellstorff (2007).

13 Susan Stryker, "cfp: Transsomatechnics," Trans-Academics.org, September 17, 2007, accessed September 13, 2013, http://www.trans-academics.org/cfp%3A_transsomatechnics.

14 Hausman uses cosmetic and plastic surgery virtually interchangeably in this argument, with the primary distinction being that cosmetic surgery is a subspecialty of plastic surgery.

15 *Protocols for Hormonal Reassignment of Gender* (San Francisco: Tom Waddell Health Center), July 24, 2001, accessed November 9, 2013. Available at: http://

web.archive.org/web/20070315211232/http://www.dph.sf.ca.us/chn/HlthCtrs
/HlthCtrDocs/TransGendprotocols.pdf. An updated (2013) version of the
protocols is available at http://www.sfdph.org/dph/comupg/oservices/med
Svs/hlthCtrs/TransGendprotocols122006.pdf (accessed November 9, 2013).

16 The WPATH has issued the "Identity Recognition Statement," which condemns
the requirement of sex-reassignment surgery in order to recognize an individual's gender identity. See wpath, press release, June 16, 2010, accessed August
11, 2010. Available at: http://www.wpath.org/uploaded_files/140/files/Identity
%20Recognition%20Statement%206-6-10%20on%20letterhead.pdf.

17 Anne Balsamo's work on cosmetic surgery in her book *Technologies of the Gendered Body* (1996) seeks to embed cosmetic surgery in the technological production of gendered bodies. For Balsamo, the bodies produced through cosmetic
surgery become available for reading the forms of personal surveillance, confes-
sion, and inscription of "the dominant cultural meanings that the female body
is to have in postmodernity" (78). Using Balsamo's approach, we can read not
just gender but also race, class, and nation on the modified bodies of *misses* and
transformistas.

18 Both Sander L. Gilman (1999) and Alexander Edmonds (2010) discuss the syn-
thesis of art and science in plastic surgery and provide a critique of Frances's
idea of "harmony." Edmonds provides an excellent portrait of another "modern
Pygmalion," the famed Brazilian plastic surgeon Ivo Pitanguy (2010, 47).

19 Dull and West (1991) also document self-esteem as an important legitimating
strategy for aesthetic surgery.

6. Spectacular Femininities

1 In defining *spectacular femininities*, I offer two caveats. First, the example of Rudy
Cantú reminds us that spectacular acts can occur in everyday contexts. Second,
it is important to note that spectacularity can be but one dimension of femininities produced on multiple registers and through various forms of discourse.

2 These examples were developed through the use of video cameras in the two
contexts. I used the cameras as part of the research to assist in recording interactions, but once we had begun working with the cameras, I noted how both
transformistas and *misses* addressed the camera as a way to access an imaginary
audience. The use of conventions of address persisted despite the understanding
that the video would be used exclusively for research and would not be edited or
distributed. This initial observation led me to develop the concept of spectacularity that I articulate in this chapter.

3 A complete review of this literature is not the goal of this chapter. For one such
review, consult Douglas Kellner (2003). Beeman (1993) provides a useful overview of the category of "spectacle" in anthropology.

4 In the case discussed here, Baudrillard is publishing in the Parisian newspaper
Libération in 1987.

5 Doane's masquerade is certainly an important way to describe this "mascu-

line gaze," but while Doane treats the masquerade as artifice, hiding the "real" woman, I ask: what does this particular way of accomplishing femininity *do* for its practitioners? The masquerade might hint at some of the limits of spectacular femininity, but its exclusive focus on gender signifiers and ideology ignores the role of media *practices* in these forms of femininity, as well as the ways these are put to use by women.

6 See Jesús Martín-Barbero (1992) for a map of these conventions as they relate to melodrama in Latin America.

7 Warner's definition of a "public" is relevant in terms of thinking about the first two elements, theatricality and audience.

8 I have used pseudonyms throughout this chapter for my interviewees. All interviews were conducted in Spanish and the translations are mine.

9 As I have discussed previously, *marico* translates roughly to "faggot," here it is used as a slur among *transformistas* to indicate the person is acting like a man, and a gay man at that, by hogging the camera.

10 Shaidé uses the term *elaboramos*, which means "work" in the sense of a production process. For example, in a chair factory, you would say "elaboramos sillas" (we make chairs), or you could say "elaboramos aquí en la fabrica" (we work here in the factory). The sense is more industrial or occupational than the more informal word *trabajar*, and this reflects a difference in Shaidé's voice as she addresses the camera.

11 The term *transfor* is shorthand for "*transformistas*" and is used with a masculine article, *los*, rather than a feminine article.

12 As discussed in chapter 3, these are the ideal measurements (in centimeters) for a beauty queen. They roughly translate to 36-24-36 in U.S. units.

13 This phrase, *estoy para servirle*, is a commonly used courtesy when finishing a semiformal exchange. Karla uses the most humble and polite language of all of the girls in presenting herself.

14 Elizabeth Povinelli's notion of carnality is quite useful in harmonizing what tends to be treated as the two distinct and bounded fields of "the body" and "the social." Carnality, as Povinelli defines it, is "flesh as the physical mattering forth of [juridical and political] maneuvers" (2006, 7). It is precisely carnality that is unlinked in Butler's distinction between "performed" and "linguistic" dimensions of the speech act. See chapter 5 for a more extended discussion of this concept.

15 See "Corporate History," Miss Universe, accessed May 6, 2010, http://www .missuniverse.com/info/corporateinfo.

16 Slipping on a runway while modeling, as the Miss USA winners from 2007 and 2008 did in their respective Miss Universe competitions, is an example of an infelicitous spectacle.

17 It is also important to note how spectacle works at the level of the body — felicitous and infelicitous spectacles *feel* quite different.

18 A *faja* is a neoprene or Lycra corset used to compress the abdomen and hips. The word for "runway walk" is *pasarela*, which I discuss at length in chap-

ter 4. It is also the word for "runway," the actual platform where one walks. At times in this chapter, I will use *runway* and *runway walk* interchangeably in keeping with this usage in Spanish.

19 *Divina* means "divine," but is gendered feminine and is used quite a bit as an adjective among *maricos*. I have left it untranslated in order to communicate the gendered dimension of the word as it is used by both Marco Antonio and Gaston.

20 *Cachapera* is one word for "lesbian" in Venezuela. *Haciendo cachapas* (or making cachapas) is how many of the gay men I met in Venezuela referred to lesbian sex. This usage was understood and sometimes used among the lesbians I know in Venezuela, but to my understanding the terminology is not used among lesbians to talk about what we actually do when we have sex. For the record, when Marco Antonio asked Lenora directly if she was interested in being with another woman, she said that she did not have anything against lesbians, but that she herself was quite comfortable in her heterosexuality.

21 The phrase Marco Antonio used is *ser cuerda*, which means "to be wound like a watch."

22 *Bienvenida al combo* means something akin to "welcome to the band."

23 *Arrecha/o* is slang in Venezuela for "sexiness," "ferocity," or "demonstrating one's excellence at something." It can also mean to be quite angry or frustrated. When used in other countries, *arrecha/o* has sexual overtones, and can mean "sexually excited," this usage is less common in Venezuela.

24 Lenora employs a clinical term from her psychology practice here.

25 Here the word *look* is italicized to reflect its usage in Venezuelan Spanish.

Epilogue. Democracy and Melodrama

1 The *paro petrolero*—initially a walkout of white-collar workers at Petróleos de Venezuela and then generalized to sympathetic businesses—was called by the Confederación de Trabajadores de Venezuela (CTV, Venezuelan Worker's Confederation) and Fedecámaras (Venezuelan Federation of Chambers of Commerce), who were leaders in the Opposition coalition that had previously attempted to oust Chávez earlier that year (Ellner 2007, 87). Indeed, it was the president of Fedecámaras, Pedro Carmona Estanga, who assumed power as president of Venezuela in the April 2002 coup attempt. The strike petered out in February 2003. Fernando Coronil's chapter "State Reflections: The 2002 Coup against Hugo Chávez" in Ponniah and Eastwood (2011) provides a historical interpretation of these events.

2 Of course, queer and transgender Venezuelans still survive and invent their lives both inside and outside the Bolivarian Revolution, as they have with every other administration.

3 See Cathy A. Rakowski and Gioconda Espina's chapter "Advancing Women's Rights from Inside and Outside the Bolivarian Revolution, 1998–2010" in Ponniah and Eastwood (2011) for a detailed and balanced discussion of feminist

advocacy and the Bolivarian Revolution. They include attention to the LGBT, or more recently *sexodivers@* efforts to dialogue with the Revolution.

4 These names are pseudonyms.

5 Luis Duno-Gottberg's (2004) examination of the representation of the violent mob (*turba*) in caraqueño social protest provides good context for understanding the figure of the encapuchado, though Duno-Gottberg does not explore this figure directly. The term *encapuchado* refers to the way protesters use T-shirts, ski masks, or hoods to cover their faces in order to protect their identities or avoid inhalation of tear gas.

6 *El Nacional*, January 4, 2003, A6.

References

Aguilera, Jesús Antonio. 1973. *Noticias de Carúpano*. Caracas: Graficas Continente.

Ahlbäck, Anna, and Pia Engholm. 1997. "Miss Venezuela vs. Miss Sweden, or Diamonds Are a Girl's Best Friend." MA thesis, Stockholm School of Economics.

Almandoz, Arturo. 1999. "Longing for Paris: the Europeanized Dream of Caracas Urbanism, 1870–1940." *Planning Perspectives* 14: 225–48.

——. 2000. "The Shaping of Venezuelan Urbanism in the Hygiene Debate of Caracas, 1880–1910." *Urban Studies* 37 (11): 2073–89.

——. 2004. *La ciudad en el imaginaro venezolano: De 1936 a Los Pequeños Seres*. Caracas: Fundación para la Cultura Urbana.

Amnesty International USA. 2001. *Crimes of Hate, Conspiracy of Silence: Torture and Ill-Treatment Based on Sexual Identity*. New York: Amnesty International USA.

Andersen, Peggy. 1989. "Aunt Jemima Getting a Make Over—New Hairstyle, Same Smile." Associated Press, April 27. Accessed July 14, 2010. Available at: http://www.lexisnexis.com/lnacui2api/api/version1/getDocCui?lni=3SJF-GPG0-002S-Y18N&csi=304478&hl=t&hv=t&hnsd=f&hns=t&hgn=t&oc=00240&perma=true.

Anderson, Benedict. 1991. *Imagined Communities: Reflections on the Origin and Spread of Nationalism*. London: Verso.

Andrade, Oswald de. 1999. "The Cannibalist Manifesto." Translated by Stephen Berg. *Third Text* 13 (46): 92–96.

Ang, Ien. 1985. *Watching Dallas: Soap Opera and the Melodramatic Imagination*. London: Methuen.

Appiah, Kwame Anthony. 2006. *Cosmopolitanism: Ethics in a World of Strangers*. New York: W. W. Norton.

Arroyo Talavera, Eduardo. 1983. "Elections and Negotiation: The Limits of Democracy in Venezuela." Dissertation, London School of Economics and Political Science.

Bailey, Cameron. 1988. "Nigger/Lover: The Thin Sheen of Race in 'Something Wild.'" *Screen* 29 (4): 28–43.

Balsamo, Anne Marie. 1996. *Technologies of the Gendered Body: Reading Cyborg Women*. Durham: Duke University Press.

Banet-Weiser, Sarah. 1999. *The Most Beautiful Girl in the World: Beauty Pageants and National Identity*. Berkeley: University of California Press.

Baudrillard, Jean. 1994. *Simulacra and Simulation*. Ann Arbor: University of Michigan Press.

——. 2002. *Screened Out*. Translation by Chris Turner. London: Verso.

Beeman, William O. 1993. "The Anthropology of Theater and Spectacle." *Annual Review of Anthropology* 22: 369–93.

Benavides, O. Hugo. 2006. *The Politics of Sentiment: Imagining and Remembering Guayaquil.* Austin: University of Texas Press.

Berger, John. 1972. *Ways of Seeing.* London: British Broadcasting Corporation, Penguin Books.

Berlant, Lauren. 1991. *The Anatomy of National Fantasy: Hawthorne, Utopia, and Everyday Life.* Chicago: University of Chicago Press.

———. 1997. *The Queen of America Goes to Washington City: Essays on Sex and Citizenship.* Durham: Duke University Press.

———. 2008. *The Female Complaint: The Unfinished Business of Sentimentality in American Culture.* Durham: Duke University Press.

Berrizbeitia, Anita. 2004. *Roberto Burle Marx in Caracas Parque del Este, 1956–1961.* Philadelphia: University of Pennsylvania Press.

Bhabha, Homi K. 1994. *The Location of Culture.* London: Routledge.

Bisbal, Marcelino. 2007. "Los Medios en Venezuela. ¿Dónde estamos?" *Espacio Abierto* 16: 643–68.

Blackwell, Maylei. 2006. "Weaving in the Spaces: Indigenous Women's Organizing and the Politics of Scale in Mexico." In *Dissident Women: Gender and Cultural Politics in Chiapas,* ed. Sharon Speed, R. Aída Hernández de Castillo, and Lynn Stephen. Austin: University of Texas Press.

Boellstorff, Tom. 2007. "Queer Studies in the House of Anthropology." *Annual Review of Anthropology* 36: 17–35.

Borges, Ezequiel. 2000. "Osmel Sousa: La Miss Venezuela no tiene prototipo." In *Miss Venezuela.* Catalogue #27. Caracas: Museo Jacobo Borges.

Brah, Avtar. 2003. "Diaspora, Border and Transnational Identities." In *Feminist Postcolonial Theory: A Reader,* ed. Reina Lewis and Sarah Mills, 613–34. New York: Routledge.

Brett, Guy, Roger Benjamin, and Juan Dávila. 2006. *Juan Dávila.* Sydney: Miegunyah Press, Museum of Contemporary Art.

Briggs, Charles. 2004. "Theorizing Modernity Conspiratorially: Science, Scale, and the Political Economy of Public Discourse in Explanations of a Cholera Epidemic." *American Ethnologist* 31 (2): 164–87.

Briggs, Charles, with Clara Mantini-Briggs. 2003. *Stories in the Time of Cholera: Racial Profiling during a Medical Nightmare.* Berkeley: University of California Press.

Butler, Judith. 1993. *Bodies That Matter: On the Discursive Limits of "Sex."* New York: Routledge.

———. 1999. *Gender Trouble: Feminism and the Subversion of Identity.* New York: Routledge.

———. 2004. *Undoing Gender.* New York: Routledge.

Butler, Judith, and Sara Salih. 2004. *The Judith Butler Reader.* Malden, MA: Wiley-Blackwell.

Canache, Damarys. 2002. *Venezuela: Public Opinion and Protest in a Fragile Democracy.* Coral Gables, FL: North-South Center Press.

Carrasco, Edgar, and Marcia Ochoa. 2003. *Informe sobre impunidad: Venezuela.* Proyecto ILGALAC-OASIS-Unión Europea. Caracas: Acción Ciudadana Contra el SIDA.

Cempa, Joe. 2009. "Group Bringing Back 1920s Beauty Pageant." *Galveston County Daily News,* April 24. Available at: http://web.archive.org/web/20110928061014/http://galveston dailynews.com/story.lasso?ewcd=d1afdd366b6ac934.

Chakrabarty, Dipesh. 2002. *Habitations of Modernity: Essays in the Wake of Subaltern Studies.* Chicago: University of Chicago Press.

Charier, Alain. 2000. *Le Mouvement Noir au Venezuela: Revendication identitaire et modernité.* Paris: L'Harmattan.

Cisneros, Sandra. 1991. "Remember the Alamo." In *Woman Hollering Creek, and Other Stories,* 63–67. New York: Random House.

Cohen, Colleen Ballerino, Richard Wilk, and Beverly Stoeltje. 1996. *Beauty Queens on the Global Stage: Gender, Contests, and Power.* New York: Routledge.

Cohen, Lawrence. 1995. "The Pleasures of Castration: The Postoperative Status of Hijras, Jankhas, and Academics." In *Sexual Nature/Sexual Culture,* ed. Paul R. Abramson and Steven D. Pinkerton, 276–304. Chicago: University of Chicago Press.

Colegio de Ingenieros de Venezuela. 1966. "Una Gran Avenida Para Una Gran Capital." *Boletín* 72 (January), 22–25.

———. 1971. "Unidad Residencial en la Avda. Libertador: Descripción del proyecto." *Boletín* 127 (February), 48–49.

Coronil, Fernando. 1997. *The Magical State: Nature, Money, and Modernity in Venezuela.* Chicago: University of Chicago Press.

Coronil, Fernando, and Julie Skurski. 1991. "Dismembering and Remembering the Nation: The Semantics of Political Violence in Venezuela." *Comparative Studies in Society and History* 33 (2): 288–337.

Cruz-Malavé, Arnaldo, and Martin Manalansan, eds. 2002. *Queer Globalizations: Citizenship and the Afterlife of Colonialism.* New York: New York University Press.

Cvetkovich, Ann. 2003. *An Archive of Feeling: Trauma, Sexuality, and Lesbian Public Cultures.* Durham: Duke University Press.

Das, Veena. 2009. *Life and Words: Violence and the Descent into the Ordinary.* Berkeley: University of California Press.

Davies, Vanessa. 2004a. "Derechos de las travestis son violados cada noche en la avenida Libertador." *El Nacional* (Caracas), September 6, B12.

———. 2004b. "Los 'trans' salen a conquistar su puesto en la sociedad venezolana." *El Nacional* (Caracas), September 5, B17.

Debord, Guy. 1983 [1967]. *Society of the Spectacle.* Translated by Ken Knabb. London: Rebel Press.

———. 2002. *Comments on the Society of the Spectacle.* London: Verso.

Dirlik, Arif. 2004. "Spectres of the Third World: Global Modernity and the End of the Three Worlds." *Third World Quarterly* 25 (1): 131–48.

Doane, Mary Ann. 1982. "Film and the Masquerade: Theorizing the Female Spectator." *Screen* 23 (34): 74–87.

Douglas, Mary. 1966. *Purity and Danger: An Analysis of Concepts of Pollution and Taboo.* New York: Praeger.

Dull, Diana, and Candace West. 1991. "Accounting for Cosmetic Surgery: The Accomplishment of Gender." *Social Problems* 38 (1): 54–70.

Duno-Goldberg, Luis. 2004. "Mob Outrages: Reflections on the Media Construction of the Masses in Venezuela (April 2000–January 2003)." *Journal of Latin American Cultural Studies* 13 (1): 115–35.

Dyer, Richard. 1986. *Heavenly Bodies: Film Stars and Society.* New York: St. Martin's Press.

Dyhouse, Carol. 2010. *Glamour: Women, History, Feminism.* London: Zed Books.

Edmonds, Alexander. 2010. *Pretty Modern: Beauty, Sex, and Plastic Surgery in Brazil.* Durham: Duke University Press.

Ellner, Steve. 2007. "Trade Union Autonomy and the Emergence of a New Labor Movement in Venezuela." In *Venezuela: Hugo Chávez and the Decline of an "Exceptional Democracy",* ed. Steve Ellner and Miguel Tinker Salas. Lanham, MD: Rowman and Littlefield.

Eng, David L., 2010. *The Feeling of Kinship: Queer Liberalism and the Racialization of Intimacy.* Durham: Duke University Press.

Eng, David L., and Alice Hom. 1998. *Q & A: Queer in Asian America.* Philadelphia: Temple University Press.

Enright, Michael J., Antonio Francés, and Edith Scott Saavedra. 1994. *Venezuela: El reto de la competitividad.* Caracas: Ediciones IESA.

Epps, Brad, Keja Valens, and Bill Johnson González, eds. 2005. *Passing Lines: Sexuality and Immigration.* Cambridge, MA: David Rockefeller Center for Latin American Studies and Harvard University Press.

Fausto-Sterling, Anne. 2000. *Sexing the Body: Gender Politics and the Construction of Sexuality.* New York: Basic Books.

Fiol-Matta, Licia. 2002. *Queer Mother for the Nation: The State and Gabriela Mistral.* Minneapolis: University of Minnesota Press.

Foucault, Michel. 1977. *Discipline and Punish: The Birth of the Prison.* Trans. Alan Sheridan. New York: Pantheon Books.

Gandolfo, Daniella. 2009. *The City at Its Limits: Taboo, Transgression, and Urban Renewal in Lima.* Chicago: University of Chicago Press.

Garber, Marjorie. 1992. *Vested Interests: Cross-Dressing and Cultural Anxiety.* London: Routledge.

García Canclini, Nestor. 1995a. *Consumidores y ciudadanos: Conflictos multiculturales de la globalización.* Mexico City: Editorial Grijalbo.

———. 1995b. *Hybrid Cultures: Strategies for Entering and Leaving Modernity.* Minneapolis: University of Minnesota Press.

García Díaz, Luis. 1996. *Breve historia de Carúpano: Los hechos de ayer, hoy en sus manos.* Caracas: Editorial Kinesis.

Garfinkel, Harold. 1967. *Studies in Ethnomethodology.* Edgewood Cliffs, NJ: Prentice Hall.

Gilman, Sander L. 1998. *Creating Beauty to Cure the Soul: Race and Psychology in the Shaping of Aesthetic Surgery.* Durham: Duke University Press.

———. 1999. *Making the Body Beautiful: A Cultural History of Aesthetic Surgery.* Princeton, NJ: Princeton University Press.

Goldgar, Anne. 2007. *Tulipmania: Money, Honor, and Knowledge in the Dutch Golden Age.* Chicago: University of Chicago Press.

Golinger, Eva. 2006. *The Chavez Code: Cracking U.S. Intervention in Venezuela.* Northampton, MA: Olive Branch Press.

Gopinath, Gayatri. 2005. *Impossible Desires: Queer Diasporas and South Asian Public Cultures.* Durham: Duke University Press.

Gramsci, Antonio. 2000. *The Gramsci Reader: Selected Writings 1916–1935.* New York: New York University Press.

Grosz, Elizabeth. 1994. *Volatile Bodies: Toward a Corporeal Feminism.* Bloomington: Indiana University Press.

Güerere, Abdel. 1994. "Producción de telenovelas." Working paper no. 10, Proyecto Venezuela Competitiva. Caracas: Ediciones IESA.

Gundle, Stephen. 2008. *Glamour: A History.* Oxford: Oxford University Press.

Guss, David M. 2000. *The Festive State: Race, Ethnicity, and Nationalism as Cultural Performance.* Berkeley: University of California Press.

Halberstam, Judith. 1998. *Female Masculinity.* Durham: Duke University Press.

Hall, Stuart. 1997. *Representation: Cultural Representations and Signifying Practices.* Thousand Oaks, CA: Sage.

Hannerz, Ulf. 1990. "Cosmopolitans and Locals in World Culture." *Theory Culture Society* 7: 237–51.

Hausman, Bernice L. 1995. *Changing Sex: Transsexualism, Technology, and the Idea of Gender.* Durham: Duke University Press.

Holland, Sharon Patricia. 2000. *Raising the Dead: Readings of Death and (Black) Subjectivity.* Durham: Duke University Press.

Immigration and Refugee Board of Canada. 1998. *Venezuela: Information Regarding the Situation of Homosexuals: Interview with the Director of Acción Ciudadanía Contra El SIDA (ACCSI),* January 1. Accessed November 9, 2013. Available at: http://www.refworld.org/docid/3ae6ad 8d30.html.

Ishibashi, Jun. 2003. "Hacia una apertura del debate sobre el racismo en Venezuela: Exclusión e inclusión estereotipada de personas 'negras' en los medios de comunicación." In *Políticas de identidades y diferencias sociales en tiempos de globalización,* ed. Daniel Mato, 33–61. Caracas: FACES-UCV.

Izaguirre, Boris. 2000. *Morir de glamour.* Madrid: Espasa Calpe.

Jagose, Annamarie, and Don Kulick. 2004. "The GLQ Forum: Thinking Sex/Thinking Gender." *GLQ: A Journal of Lesbian and Gay Studies* 10 (2).

Johnson, Mark. 1997. *Beauty and Power: Transgendering and Cultural Transformation in the Southern Philippines.* Oxford: Berg.

Karl, Terry Lynn. 1997. *The Paradox of Plenty: Oil Booms and Petro-States.* Berkeley: University of California Press.

Kellner, Douglas. 2003. *Media Spectacle.* London: Routledge.

Kofman, Jeffrey. 2009. "In Venezuela, Beauty Is Born . . . and Made." ABC News, October 8. Accessed April 25, 2011. Available at: http://abcnews.go.com/Nightline/miss-venezuela -beauty-pageant/story?id=8780813&singlePage=true.

Kulick, Don. 1998. *Travesti: Sex, Gender, and Culture among Brazilian Transgendered Prostitutes.* Chicago: University of Chicago Press.

Kulick, Don, and Charles Klein. 2009. "Scandalous Acts: The Politics of Shame among Brazilian Travesti Prostitutes." In *Gay Shame,* ed. David M. Halperin and Valerie Traub, 312–38. Chicago: University of Chicago Press.

La Fountain-Stokes, Lawrence. 2009. *Queer Ricans: Cultures and Sexualities in the Diaspora.* Minneapolis: University of Minnesota Press.

Lavenda, Robert. 1996. "'It's Not a Beauty Pageant!': Hybrid Ideology in Minnesota Community Queen Pageants." In *Beauty Queens on the Global Stage: Gender, Contests and Power,* ed. Colleen Ballerino Cohen, Richard Wilk, and Beverly Stoeltje. New York: Routledge, 31–46.

Livingston, Jennie. 1992. *Paris Is Burning.* Videorecording. Academy Entertainment/Image Entertainment.

Lombardi, John V. 1982. *Venezuela: The Search for Order, the Dream of Progress.* New York: Oxford University Press.

Luibhéid, Eithne, and Lionel Cantú Jr., eds. 2002. *Queer Migrations: Sexuality, U.S. Citizenship, and Border Crossings.* Minneapolis: University of Minnesota Press.

Mahmood, Saba. 2005. *The Politics of Piety: The Islamic Revival and the Feminist Subject.* Princeton, NJ: Princeton University Press.

Manalansan, Martin. 2003. *Global Divas: Filipino Gay Men in the Diaspora.* Durham: Duke University Press.

Manring, M. M. 1998. *Slave in a Box: The Strange Career of Aunt Jemima.* Charlottesville: University of Virginia Press.

Márquez, Patricia. 1999. *The Street Is My Home: Youth and Violence in Caracas.* Stanford, CA: Stanford University Press.

Martín-Barbero, Jesús. 1992. *Televisión y melodrama: Géneros y lecturas de la telenovela en Colombia.* Ed. Jesús Martín-Barbero and Sonia Muñoz. Bogotá: Tercer Mundo Editores.

———. 1993. *Communication, Culture and Hegemony: From the Media to Mediations.* Trans. Elizabeth Fox and Robert A. White. London: Sage Publications.

———. 1997. "Nosotros habíamos hecho estudios culturales mucho antes que esta etiqueta apareciera: Una entrevista con Jesús Martín-Barbero." *Dissens* 3: 47–53. Cali, Colombia: Universidad Javeriana. http://www.javeriana.edu.co/pensar/Rev33.html.

Mata, Ricardo Alberto. 2001. *Carúpano: De pujante urbe a ciudad decadente (visión antropológica).* Caracas: Fondo Editorial Tropykos.

Mato, Daniel. 1994. *Teoría y política de la construcción de identidades y diferencias en América Latina y el Caribe.* Caracas: UNESCO, Editorial Nueva Sociedad.

———. 2002. *Estudios y otras prácticas intelectuales latinoamericanas en cultura y poder.* Caracas: CLACSO.

McClymer, John F. 2005. *The Birth of Modern America.* Maplecrest, NY: Brandywine Press.

McCoy, Jennifer. 2004. "From Representative to Participatory Democracy?: Regime Transformation in Venezuela." In *The Unraveling of Representative Democracy in Venezuela,* ed. Jennifer McCoy and David J. Myers, 263–96. Baltimore, MD: Johns Hopkins University Press.

Ministerio de Obras Públicas. 1960–64. *Memoria y cuenta.* Caracas: República de Venezuela.

Molina, Alfonso. 2001. *Cine, democracia y melodrama: El país de Román Chalbaud.* Caracas: Editorial Planeta.

Montaldo Pérez, Diego. 1999. "Un Siglo de Misses." Published in series, inserted in the Caracas newspaper *Últimas Noticias,* beginning in September 1999. Caracas: Cadena Capriles. [Available at Hemeroteca Nacional de Venezuela, call no. 791.620987U54]

Montero, Maritza. 1998. "Identidad, belleza y cultura popular." In *Venezuela: Tradición en la modernidad; Primer simposio sobre la cultura popular,* ed. Fundación Bigott, 109–25. Caracas: Equinoccio, Ediciones de la USB.

Montes Giraldo, José Joaquín. 1979. "Para la Etimología de 'Corotos.'" In *Thesaurus: Boletín del Instituto Caro y Cuervo* 34 (1–3). Bogotá, Colombia: Instituto Caro y Cuervo. Accessed September 10, 2013. http://cvc.cervantes.es/lengua/thesaurus/pdf/34/TH_34_123_197_0.pdf.

Moraga, Cherríe. 1986. *Giving up the Ghost: Teatro in Two Acts.* Los Angeles: West End Press.

Muñoz, José Esteban. 1999. *Disidentifications: Queers of Color and the Performance of Politics.* Minneapolis: University of Minnesota Press.

Museo Jacobo Borges. 2000. *Miss Venezuela.* Catalogue no. 27, coord. Ana María Carrano. Caracas: Museo Jacobo Borges.

———. 2000. *90-60-90.* Publication no. 50, coord. Ana María Carrano. Caracas: Museo Jacobo Borges.

Nanda, Serena. 1990. *Neither Man nor Woman: The Hijras of India.* Belmont, CA: Wadsworth.

Nelson, Diane M. 1999. *A Finger in the Wound: Body Politics in Quincentennial Guatemala.* Berkeley: University of California Press.

Newton, Esther. 1970. *Mother Camp: Female Impersonators in America.* Chicago: University of Chicago Press.

Ochoa, Marcia. 2007. "Becoming a Man in Yndias: The Mediations of Catalina de Erauso, the Lieutenant Nun." In *Technofuturos: Critical Interventions in Latina/o Studies,* ed. Nancy Raquel Mirabal and Augustin Laó Montes, 53–76. Lanham, MD: Rowman and Littlefield.

————. 2008. "Perverse Citizenship: Divas, Marginality and Participation in 'Loca-lization.'" *WSQ* 36 (3–4): 146–69.

Ong, Aiwha. 1999. *Flexible Citizenship: Cultural Logics of Transnationality*. Durham: Duke University Press.

Ortíz, Fernando. 1995. *Cuban Counterpoint: Tobacco and Sugar*. Durham: Duke University Press.

Pace, Kimberly A. 1994. "The Washington Redskins Case and the Doctrine of Disparagement: How Politically Correct Must a Trademark Be?" *Pepperdine Law Review* 22 (December): 7–55. Available at: http://www.lexisnexis.com/lnacui2api/api/version1/getDocCui?lni=3S3T-B450-00CV-74Y3&csi=142673&hl=t&hv=t&hnsd=f&hns=t&hgn=t&oc=00240&perma=true.

Pérez, Laura. 1999. "El Desorden, Nationalism, and Chicana/o Aesthetics." In *Between Woman and Nation: Nationalisms, Transnational Feminisms, and the State*, ed. Caren Kaplan, Norma Alarcón, and Minoo Moallem, 19–39. Durham: Duke University Press.

Planchart Licea, Eduardo. 2000. "El Miss Venezuela: Un Fenómeno Cultural." In *Miss Venezuela*, ed. Museo Jacobo Borges. Catalogue 27. Caracas: Museo Jacobo Borges.

Pollak-Etz, Angelina. 1991. *La Negritud en Venezuela*. Cuadernos Lagoven. Caracas: Editorial Arte.

Ponce Z., María Gabriela. 2005. "Condiciones diferenciales de vida en la ciudad de Caracas." *Temas De Coyuntura* 52 (December): 33–66.

Ponniah, Thomas, and Jonathan Eastwood, eds. 2011. *The Revolution in Venezuela: Social and Political Change under Chávez*. Cambridge, MA: Harvard University David Rockefeller Center for Latin American Studies.

Porter, Michael E. 1990. *The Competitive Advantage of Nations*. New York: Free Press.

Povinelli, Elizabeth. 2006. *The Empire of Love: Toward a Theory of Intimacy, Genealogy, and Carnality*. Durham: Duke University Press.

Pratt, Mary Louise. 1992. *Imperial Eyes: Travel Writing and Transculturation*. London: Routledge.

Prieur, Annick. 1998. *Mema's House: Mexico City: On Transvestites, Queens, and Machos*. Chicago: University of Chicago Press.

Rama, Ángel. 1996. *The Lettered City*. Durham: Duke University Press.

Reddy, Gayatri. 2005. *With Respect to Sex: Negotiating Hijra Identity in South India*. Chicago: University of Chicago Press.

Ríos, Alicia. 2004. "Forerunners." In *The Latin American Cultural Studies Reader*, ed. Ana Del Sarto, Alicia Ríos, and Abril Trigo. Durham: Duke University Press.

Robbins, Bruce. 2007. "Cosmopolitanism: New and Newer." *boundary 2* 34 (3): 47–60.

Rodríguez, Juana María. 2003. *Queer Latinidad: Identity Practices, Discursive Spaces*. New York: New York University Press.

Rosaldo, Renato. 1994. "Cultural Citizenship and Educational Democracy." *Cultural Anthropology* 9 (3): 402–11.

Roscoe, Will. 1991. *The Zuni Man-Woman*. Albuquerque: University of New Mexico Press.

Rosenblatt, Angel. 1987. *Estudios sobre el habla de Venezuela: Buenas y malas palabras*. Caracas: Monte Avila Editores.

Rowlands, Michael. 1987. *Centre and Periphery in the Ancient World*. Cambridge: Cambridge University Press.

Salas de Lecuna, Yolanda, with Norma Gonzalez Viloria and Ronny Velasquez. 1987. *Bolívar y la historia en la conciencia popular*. Caracas: Universidad Simón Bolívar, Instituto de Altos Estudios de America Latina.

Sánchez-Eppler, Benigno, and Cindy Patton, eds. 2000. *Queer Diasporas*. Durham: Duke University Press.

Sandoval, Chela. 2000. *Methodology of the Oppressed*. Minneapolis: University of Minnesota Press.

Schein, Louisa. 1997. "The Consumption of Color and the Politics of White Skin in Post-Mao China." In *The Gender/Sexuality Reader: Culture, History, Political Economy*, ed. R. N. Lancaster and M. di Leonardo. New York: Routledge.

Scheper-Hughes, Nancy. 1992. *Death without Weeping: The Violence of Everyday Life in Brazil*. Berkeley: University of California Press.

Schifter, Jacobo. 1999. *From Toads to Queens: Transvestism in a Latin American Setting*. New York: Harrington Park Press.

Sedgwick, Eve Kosofsky. 1990. *Epistemology of the Closet*. Berkeley: University of California Press.

Spade, Dean. 2011. *Normal Life: Administrative Violence, Critical Trans Politics, and the Limits of Law*. Boston: South End Press.

Spade, Dean, and Sel Wahng. 2004. "Transecting the Academy." GLQ 10 (2): 240–54.

Stoltje, Beverly. 1996. "The Snake Charmer Queen: Ritual, Competition, and Signification in American Festival." In *Beauty Queens on the Global Stage: Gender, Contests, and Power*, ed. Colleen Ballerino Cohen, Richard Wilk, and Beverly Stoeltje. New York: Routledge.

Stone, Sandy. 1991. "The *Empire* Strikes Back: A Posttranssexual Manifesto." In *Body Guards: The Cultural Politics of Gender Ambiguity*, ed. Julia Epstein and Kristina Straub, 280–304. London: Routledge.

Stryker, Susan. 2008. *Transgender History*. Berkeley, CA: Seal Press, 2008.

Sullivan, Nikki. 2009. "Transsomatechnics and the Matter of 'Genital Modifications.'" *Australian Feminist Studies* 24 (60): 275–86.

Taussig, Michael. 1987. *Shamanism, Colonialism, and the Wild Man: A Study in Terror and Healing*. Chicago: University of Chicago Press.

Tejera, María Josefina. 1983. *Diccionario de venezolanismos*. Vol. 1, *A–I*. Caracas: Academia Venezolana de la Lengua, Universidad Central de Venezuela, Facultad de Humanidades y Educación, Instituto de Filología "Andrés Bello."

Trexler, Richard C. 1995. *Sex and Conquest: Gendered Violence, Political Order, and the European Conquest of the Americas*. Cambridge: Polity Press.

Troconis de Veracochea, Ermila. 1993. *Caracas*. Caracas: Grijalbo.

Tsing, Anna. 1993. *In the Realm of the Diamond Queen*. Princeton, NJ: Princeton University Press.

———. 2001. "Conclusion: The Global Situation." In *The Anthropology of Globalization: A Reader*, ed. Jonathan Xavier Inda and Renato I. Rosaldo, 453–87. London: Blackwell.

Valentine, David. 2004. "The Categories Themselves." GLQ 10 (2): 215–20.

———. 2007. *Imagining Transgender: An Ethnography of a Category*. Durham: Duke University Press.

Wahng, Sel. 2009. "Vaccination, Quarantine, and Hygiene: Korean Sex Slaves and No. 606 Injections during the Pacific War of World War II." *Substance Use and Misuse* (44): 1768–802.

Wallerstein, Immanuel. 1974. *The Modern World System: Capitalist Agriculture and the Origins of the European World Economy in the Sixteenth Century*. New York: Academic Press.

Warner, Michael. 2002. "Publics and Counterpublics." *Public Culture* 14 (1): 49–90.

West, Candace, and Don H. Zimmerman. 1987. "Doing Gender." *Gender and Society* 1 (2): 125–51.

Wisotzki, Rubén. 2003. "Rafael Arráiz Lucca ve un país 'de pobreza política escandaloza.'" *El Nacional* (Caracas), January 13, A12.

Worsley, Peter. 1990. *The Three Worlds: Culture and World Development*. Chicago: University of Chicago Press.

Wright, Winthrop. 1990. *Café con Leche: Race, Class, and National Image in Venezuela*. Austin: University of Texas Press.

Index

accomplishment: of femininity, 5, 9, 17; of gender, 5, 159–61, 248n6, 263n5; of modernity, 142–46, 234; of sanitary citizenship, 49

Acquired Immune Deficiency Syndrome (AIDS), 70, 237

altercentrismo, 37

audience, 109, 209, 218–21, 249n14

Avenida Libertador, 65, 73, 128–29; and activism, 151–52; construction, 139–42; description of, 129–32; and glamour, 139; and modernity, 142–46; and *pasarelas*, 148–50; and social geography, 132–38; *transformista* occupation of, 148–49, 152; and *transformista* tactics, 146–48

Baudrillard, Jean, 205–8

beauty, 2, 6, 22, 38, 73, 81, 89, 120, 150, 188, 199, 227, 258n1; contest, 24; and Eurocentrism, 34, 37–38, 56, 60–61, 67, 71; and hunger, 77; and hygiene, 9, 39; internal, 189, 223–25; and labor, 83–84; and migration, 13; Miss Venezuela pageant, 6–8; and modernity, 9, 23, 244; and nation, 25, 32, 40–41, 45; and national fantasy, 23; and performance, 97, 114, 224–25; and petroleum, 84; and plastic surgery, 189, 196, 260n19; and politics, 83, 243; and President Chávez, 43; and race, 32–38, 54–55, 85, 135, 253n17, 253n19; and sacrifice, 157; and sanitary citizenship, 39–40; Venezuelan, 22, 90–92. *See also* beauty pageant; beauty queens; *belleza venezolana*

beauty pageant, 24, 97, 253n10; and democracy, 99, 110–13, 119; and gay men, 102; and mass-mediation, 108; and modernity, 109; and nation, 24; and representativity, 117; as ritual form, 98–99, 105–6; and *transformistas*, 100, 107–10

beauty queens, 7; comportment, 113–14, 116. *See also misses*

Blackness, 32, 34–36, 40, 50, 53–56, 69–70, 75, 135, 253n17

body, logics of, 155–58, 161–62, 175; and carnality, 157–58; and modernity, 157–58, 199; modification, 172–73; *sacar el cuerpo*, 161–62

Bolívar, Simón, 15–16, 53, 81–83, 139, 164, 257n14

Bolivarian Revolution, 54–66, 68, 234–37, 244–45, 267n3

breast implants, 115, 162, 170, 174, 180–85

Butler, Judith, 167–68, 208–11, 219–21

cachapa, 225, 267n20

Cannibalist Manifesto, 75, 88

Caracas, 18, 26–27, 29, 40, 50–52, 60–61, 67, 72–73, 128, 139–41, 142–46, 152, 238, 252n24, 254n34, 255n35, 260n15; social geography of, 73, 132–38

Caracas Mortal, 59–61, 73

Caracazo, El, 137, 262n8

carnality, 72, 156–58, 160–61, 169, 263n4, 266n14

Carúpano, 99–102

casting, 99, 116–21, 253n18

center/periphery, 71–72, 248n6, 257n12

Chávez Frías, Hugo Rafael, 43, 54, 236–37, 239, 246

Chicana feminism, 12

cisgender, 2, 247n1

citation, 210

citizenship, 15, 236–37
civilization and barbarie, 243
colony/metropole, 61
consumption, 74; and Creole self-fashioning, 80–81
Coronil, Fernando, 71–72, 83, 142, 240
corporeality, 72, 169
cosmopolitanism, 74; cannibalist, 74–75; imagined, 10, 74
criollo (Creole), 32, 37, 75–76, 79–81, 83, 101, 143

death, 59, 61, 67, 74, 104, 201; and Blackness, 69–70; cultural logic of, 60; and modernity, 234; slow, 156, 169; space of, 64–65, 68–71; and *transformistas*, 164
Debord, Guy, 203–4
democracy: and Avenida Libertador, 139–42; and beauty pageants, 99, 110–13, 119
despechos, 245–46
diaspora space, 12, 250n20
distribution of life chances (Spade), 39, 157
Doane, Mary Ann, 205–6
Douglas, Mary, 65–66
Duijm, Susana, 33, 54, 81–88

embodiment, 158, 173, 175, 208
ethnography: feminist, 166–69; of media, 8; queer diasporic, 3, 11, 235, 251n23
ethnomethodology (Garfinkel), 158–61, 248n6
extralocal authority, 89, 104

femininity, 2, 6, 14; accomplishment of, 5, 248n6, 264n5; and beauty contests, 21, 108; and Blackness, 54; and the body, 158; and citation, 210; conventions of, 209; and ethnomethodology, 159; and frivolity, 235, 239; and gaze, 208; and glamour, 258n19; and *maricos*, 258n1; and masquerade, 205; and mediations, 9; and *pasarela*, 150; and performance, 212–17; and sex reassignment surgery, 179; and spectacle, 222, 266n5; spectacular, 2, 202–3, 208–9; and technology, 159, 172
flight attendant, 1–3, 75, 88, 235
fracaso (failure), 62, 234, 245
frivolity, 233, 235, 237–39, 245

Garfinkel, Harold, 158–61, 248n6, 263n5
gaze, 208
gender, 2, 10; accomplishment of, 159–61, 248n6, 263n5; and beauty pageants, 108; and *belleza venezolana*, 22; and carnality, 160; and citation, 209–10; and embodiment, 158; and empire, 165; as empirical question, 158, 164–66; and ethnomethodology, 159–61; and feminist ethnography, 166–69; and glamour, 6; and media, 203–8, 210; and modernity, 176; and nation, 10; nonconformity, 13; performativity of, 158, 202, 219; and plastic surgery, 170–73; policing of, 4; reassignment, 177; and representation of trans subjects, 164–65; and sanitary citizenship, 170, 176–78; signifiers, 266n5; and somatechnics, 173–76; and space of death, 164; and spectacle, 202–3; and speech acts, 219–20; technologies of, 265n17; and transformation, 161, 245; and *transformistas*, 5
gender identity disorder, 177
glamour, 76, 88–92, 104, 258n19, 139; and gender, 6
globalization, 11, 105

Harina PAN, 47–53
Harry Benjamin Society (WPATH) Standards of Care, 177, 265n16
Hausman, Bernice, 174–75
hegemony, 245
Holland, Sharon, 69–70
hormones, 162–64, 173
hygiene, 61, 143–44, 176
hyperfemininity, 208
hysteria, 233

Juraxis, Sandy, 102–4

La Contessa, 13, 64–65, 76–79
La Gran Colombia, 13
Las TRANS de Caracas (1981), 62–63, 256n4
Ley de Vagos y Maleantes, 65, 257n7
loca, 155, 238, 263n1

mammy figure (*negrita*), 48–56
marginality, 71, 93
maricos, 98, 100, 111–12; and *mujeronas*, 124

Martín-Barbero, Jesús, 9, 17, 81, 249nn12–14. *See also* mediations

masquerade (Doane), 205–6

materiality, 167

media, 5, 8–10, 24, 39, 116; and beauty pageant form, 108; and economics, 43–46, 194–97; ethnography of, 8; and gender, 203–8, 210; and nation, 22–23, 25, 30; and performance, 214–18; and plastic surgery, 174, 190; and politics, 240, 243–44; and racism, 35–38; reception, 9; and spectacle, 2; studies, 9, 203–8. *See also* mediations

mediations, 9, 169, 249nn12–14; and Avenida Libertador, 152; and beauty pageants, 98; of gender, 10, 169; of modernity, 9, 164; and scale (mass-mediation), 221–22

melodrama, 239–41, 243–44

micropolitics, 8

Ministerio de Obras Públicas (MOP), 140–42

Misión Negra Hipólita, 53–56, 236, 255nn41–42

misses, 5, 248n9; defined, 6; difference between *misses* and models, 225; as mediations of racial ideology, 33, 36; production of, 121–24

Miss Venezuela, 6–8; economic analysis of, 33, 43–45; international beauty titles won, 7, 249n11

modernity: articles of faith in, 244–45; Avenida Libertador, 142–46; in beauty contest, 24; and body, 157–58; and Harina PAN, 49; and media, 9; in *miss* body, 39, 46; and perversion, 14; and race, 85. See also *fracaso*

mujerona, 123–24, 227

nation, 13; and belonging, 64–66; and modern beauty contest, 24, 30

national brand (Berlant), 22, 49

nature, 15, 164, 188

oil tankers, 54–55

Organización Miss Venezuela, 5, 7, 21, 84, 98, 171, 185, 239

Oriente, 98

pasarela, as runway walk, 121–23, 149–50; and Avenida Libertador, 129; comparison of

miss and fashion model styles, 123, 225; description of, 227

performance, 2, 108; and beauty contest, 23–24, 98–99; and ethnomethodology, 159–60, 248n6; and gender, 212–17; and nation, 22, 39, 41, 254n28; and *pasarela*, 150, 224; and publics, 218–19; and race, 83; and spectacle, 202, 208–11, 222

performativity, 5, 158, 167, 202–3, 208–11; and citation, 209–11

periphery: negotiation of, 8

perversion, 14. *See also* modernity

petroleum, 84

plastic surgery, 170–74, 180–88; and aesthetics, 187–88; and commercialism, 186–88; and excess, 197–99; management of, 189–91; and nature, 188; and self-esteem, 191–94; and social mobility, 194–97; and third-party influence, 194–97

Policía Metropolitana (Caracas), 65, 147–49

politics of scale, 14, 16–18, 67, 72, 251n21

pollution, 62, 65–66, 136

Proyecto ContraSIDA Por Vida, 11

publics (Warner), 202, 211, 218–20, 245

queer, 11, 14, 67, 69–70, 75, 165, 210, 219, 228, 237, 250n16, 257n8

queer diasporic ethnography, 3, 11–14, 235, 251n23; defined, 13

queer *latinidad*, 11, 247n2

race, *miss-ing*, 23, 33, 36, 46, 238; beauty and nation, 32–34

racial democracy, 32

reception theory, 209

ritual form, 23–24, 29, 98–99, 108–9, 120, 125, 167, 249n1

Sáez, Irene, 238–39

Salas, Yolanda, 244, 255n40

sanitary citizenship, 39–40, 60, 157, 170, 176–78, 197–99. *See also* hygiene

scandal, 66–67, 110–13

self-medication, 163–64, 176, 198

Señorita Venezuela (1905), 25

sex change, 78, 174–76, 178–82

sex work, 76; and Avenida Libertador, 18, 128–29, 147–51